Big Data

Intellectual Technologies Set

coordinated by
Jean-Max Noyer and Maryse Carmès

Volume 7

Big Data

An Art of Decision Making

Églantine Schmitt

iSTE

WILEY

Introduction

Our philosophical literature is full of intricate accounts of causal theories of perception, yet they have curiously little do with real life. We have fantastical descriptions of aberrant causal chains which, Gettier-style, call in question this or that conceptual analysis. But the modem microscopist has far more amazing tricks than the most imaginative of armchair students of perception. What we require in philosophy is better awareness of the truths that are stranger than fictions. We ought to have some understanding of those astounding physical systems "by whose augmenting power we now see more/than all the world has ever done before".

Ian Hacking, "Est-ce qu'on voit à travers un microscope?" (1981)

Every innovation in knowledge technologies disrupts our relationship with reality, increasing our perception, memory and reasoning abilities. Scientific measuring instruments dedicated to observation reveal new aspects of reality, while tools dedicated to manipulation give us the ability to intervene in what is no longer immaculate nature, but a system made up of what we have found and what we have brought to it. The telescope has given us access to what is at a distance, the microscope to infinitely small particles and the X-ray has given access to the inner side of the material. Closer to home, the advent of digital technology has reinvented the way we record and share our knowledge. It is a new material for action and knowledge, as well as a new tool for manipulating and constituting this knowledge. The multiplication of the traces that we leave of ourselves on these digital materials now gives us a new access to our own culture.

Each innovation in knowledge technologies calls for a new epistemology, a new reasoned look at the objects we wish to learn about. While already relying on knowledge, these technologies augment our knowledge-producing thinking and our capacity for memory, learning and manipulation. Technology not only equips the scientific mind, but also pushes it beyond its limits, toward new theories of reality and new methods to apprehend it. These new approaches, hesitant and shaky, nevertheless build bridges between what we can see and manipulate, and our need for rationality. As Popper (1985) wrote: “Reason works by trial and error. We invent our myths and theories and we try them out: we try to see how far they take us”.

As such, the new approaches brought about by innovations in knowledge technologies are inevitably unsatisfactory, both in the light of our usual standards and because of their nascent character. They are always incomplete, insufficient and unacceptable. They will be criticized, amended, revisited and taken up at the root. Nevertheless, without the imperfection of these pioneering trials, there is nothing more to perfect than the deconstruction of what could have been done.

The multiplication of the traces we leave of ourselves on digital media is no exception to these observations. More or less indiscriminately referred to as big data, data sciences, algorithms or artificial intelligence, the reasoned and technically instrumented study of these traces emerges with its procession of “myths and theories”, as Popper says, that we formulate along the way. Similar to the dawn of Plato’s logos, the boundary between myth and science is still fragile, and it takes a sharp eye to distinguish between them. The myth tells a story that is more pleasant and easier to understand than the story of trial and error, full of technicalities, of the first achievements, thus spreading faster and further. The experimenter navigates by sight, as much from what they know as from what they would like to know, intertwining the two. They are the hero of the myth that is told to them, and that they tell themselves in order to find their way around. Although they draw inspiration from it, there is, as we shall see, nothing in the study of digital footprints that satisfies the criteria of contemporary sciences, whatever they may be, while having a fundamentally similar mode of emergence.

To understand what is at stake with the multiplication of digital footprints, we need to listen to the pleasant myth as well as to the technicalities, and take them both seriously. To account for these new knowledge technologies, we need to mobilize a benevolent philosophy of science, attentive to detail. We must opt for an attitude that is simultaneously descriptive and normative, because to describe things for the first time is to name them, that is to say, to lay down the terms in which they can be apprehended. Carrying out big data epistemology means building the theoretical apparatus and the conceptual position required to understand and study these large masses of data. It is about formulating an initial methodological paradigm, general enough to apply to any study project of this type, and specific enough to already guide the necessary adjustments to the actual situation of a project.

This simultaneously descriptive – almost historicizing – and normative approach – in the sense that its contribution is a method-prescribing paradigm – allows us to escape from another, less fruitful normativity: that of deconstruction. As we shall see, to brand a phenomenon a social construction is to lock it up and condemn it, as if it had nothing more to say beyond its status as a cultural artifact. To reduce it to a sociologizing object, a matter of power games between actors, is to boil it down to a pure exteriority. To avoid this pitfall, we choose to adopt a philosophical approach that integrates the object's internal and external properties, revealing the complexity of the belief system it constitutes, rather than bringing it back within the boundaries of a simple object, simple and straightforward, which only supports one aspect of analysis.

This stance mobilizes a certain conception of the philosophy of science. A certain conception of philosophy, first of all, conscious of the criticisms addressed to it and of its predilection for "intricate accounts of causal theories [with] curiously little to do with real life", according to the formulation of Ian Hacking, himself a philosopher, and quoted above in this introduction. The philosophy that we practice is constantly nourished by reality, through what the human and social sciences have to say about it, and by first-hand experience as to its purpose, which, as we shall see, benefits the author of these lines. It is a philosophy that wants to be defined by the object it gives itself and the developments it imposes on it, more than by a particular philosophical tradition, a specific school of thought. We will be obsessed with what has actually happened, with what is observable, with the material, practical and empirical conditions of the emergence of our object. We situate ourselves between science and technology as articulated by science and technology studies (STS). It will be as much a philosophy of science as it is a philosophy of technology, adopting a conceptual approach without being analytical, as well as a historicizing approach without being a history of science.

As a first step, we propose the hypothetical notion of computational cultural sciences to conceptualize rational practices of big data processing based on an epistemic continuity between the data, the tools and methods to manipulate it, and the conceptual and theoretical framework in which these processes take place. We thus propose the notions of trace and evidential paradigm (Chapter 1) to characterize the data studied and the ever-present breach they create on the object they are presumed to represent. The digital footprint makes it possible to produce nomological knowledge, relating to the general, as well as idiographic knowledge, highlighting what is particular. This production of knowledge requires epistemic continuity between data, methods and a conceptual framework in order for computational cultural sciences to emerge. This continuity is to date impossible to find in the historically attested cultural sciences that mobilize digital footprints (Chapter 2). Nevertheless, they propose several ways of fixing the data in a disciplinary approach, in particular based on the notion of corpus. Despite this notion, there is still an epistemological breach between the data and its analytical tools, now considered as separate components of our methodological paradigm. Data sciences provide these analytical tools (Chapter 3), but without articulating them with a specific theoretical framework: unlike computational approaches in the natural sciences, data sciences are not linked to a scientific theory through the notion of a model, but function as a theoretical toolbox, mobilized with an exploratory approach. Necessary but not sufficient to produce knowledge from digital footprints, they call for an additional component.

Once the specific role of tools and technical manipulation of data has been delimited, we examine the conditions of intelligibility and validity of knowledge produced from the calculation of data, through interpretation, narration and visualization. The required additional component is highlighted through a case study (Chapter 4) that re-mobilizes the digital footprint and data sciences, but also reveals specific forms of restitution, a multitude of epistemic cultures and interpretative know-how. Two forms of restitution are compatible with the computational sciences of culture (Chapter 5): the narrative, which gives reason for the investigation made on and with the digital footprints; and the system, which suggests various investigations in software form, and an additional figure, that of the user, capable of interacting with the system. In these two configurations, data visualization is both a heuristic tool for exploring traces, a language capable of making them intelligible, and evidential material of the knowledge produced (Chapter 6); in system configurations, design completes this visual language with possibilities of interaction and interpretation traces materialized in an interface.

Finally, whatever their form of restitution, the knowledge produced according to the methodological paradigm hereby constructed is part of an instrumentalist or pragmatist regime of validity, which makes actionability more than truth, the criterion for validating the results of digital footprint analysis (Chapter 7): these results, i.e. the knowledge thus produced, suggest and legitimize decisions, which in return confer on them a definitive epistemic value.

The dual descriptive and normative approach thus proposed allows us to construct a methodological paradigm for the analysis of digital footprints articulated around the notions of corpus, exploration, visualization and decision: this paradigm accounts for existing practices at work in a multitude of institutional contexts, while paving the way for future practices that will be able to adopt this framework.

Since we commit to a focus on the practical conditions under which knowledge emerges, we must now specify what were ours while writing this book: a dual activity as a PhD student at the University of Technology of Compiègne – a privileged place to observe the articulation between technology and knowledge – and as an employee of a software publisher specializing in big data called Proxem. In this company, action-research was undertaken that combined academic research with practical activity analyzing massive textual data governed by the need for effective intelligibility. Several tasks were entrusted to us, including carrying out studies based on the processing of big data in the fields of marketing and human resources, and analyzing and understanding the needs and uses of the software developed by the company. Through these different missions, and while immersed in the environment of this company, we were able not only to observe closely, but also to experience concretely, the emerging contemporary practices developed by the multiplication of the traces we leave of ourselves.

1

From Trace to Web Data: An Ontology of the Digital Footprint

The development of new masses of digital data is a reality that continues to give rise to a great deal of thought on the part of a multitude of actors and positions: researchers, engineers, journalists, business leaders, etc. Big data presents itself at first sight as a technological solution, brought about by digital companies and computer research laboratories to a problem that is not always clearly expressed. It takes the form of media and commercial discourses, rather prospective in nature, about what the abundance of digital data could change. One specificity of these discourses in relation to other technological and social changes is that they are *de facto* discourses on knowledge. They frequently adopt a system of enunciation and legitimation inspired by scientific research, and more specifically by the natural sciences, from which they take up the notions of data, model, hypothesis and method. In an article emblematic of the rhetoric of big data, and now refuted many times,[1] Chris Anderson (2008), then editor-in-chief of the trade magazine *Wired*, wrote:

> "There is now a better way. Petabytes allow us to say: 'Correlation is enough'. We can stop looking for models. We can analyze the data without hypotheses about what it might

1 For example by mathematicians Calude and Longo (2015), who conclude an article on artificial correlations in big data in the following terms: "Anderson's recipe for analysis lacks the scientific rigor required to find meaningful insights that can change our decision making for the better. Data will never speak for itself, we give numbers their meaning, the Volume, Variety or Velocity of data cannot change that".

tools that induce a specific configuration of players. In terms of the typology of players, the discourse on big data is more driven by the arguments of IT companies, which market big data processing solutions, than by players in natural science research. Relayed by the media, they are not so much aimed at researchers in the natural sciences as at the ecosystem of these software companies: customers, partners and candidates. They are particularly flattering for computer scientists (researchers, professionals or amateurs) who have to manipulate large amounts of data. Thus, whether they are developers or data scientists, they are presented and published, claims Pedro Domingos (2015), professor of computer science at the University of Washington, as gods who create universes:

> "A programmer – someone who creates algorithms and codes them up – is a minor god, creating universes at will. You could even say that the God of Genesis himself is a programmer: language, not manipulation, is his tool of creation. Words become worlds. Today, sitting on the couch with your laptop, you too can be a god. Imagine a universe and make it real. The laws of physics are optional".

In these terms, it is understandable that this type of player is quick to relay and take on board the big data rhetoric. If they are not necessarily the primary audience of the mythology of big data, those who must adhere to it, they are its heroes. This heroic status echoes a state of affairs where they are the population most capable of manipulating digital data. Thus, their technical skills make them *de facto* key players in big data, players whose practices are influenced by the corresponding rhetoric. Nevertheless, we will see in the following chapters that this configuration of players is incomplete. It is not enough to produce knowledge that emerges in a double technical and epistemic constitution.

Compared, for example, with a classical configuration in the natural sciences, where researchers, who possess the theoretical concepts and methodological knowledge of their disciplines, rely on other players who have the technical knowledge necessary to operate measuring instruments, the exploitation of big data by computer scientists alone is an incomplete configuration where technical skills are not complemented by theoretical knowledge relating to the object under study. There is no epistemic or methodological continuity between theory, models and tools, simply because there is, in this configuration, no theoretical framework. In terms of the classical functioning of science, this configuration is not a "new paradigm" as the rhetoric of big data would have it, but a problematic situation in which it is not possible to generate valid new knowledge.

From this perspective, the challenge of this book is to evaluate the role of these technical skills, but also to try to place them in a methodological continuity that integrates a theoretical framework, a conceptualization of data and knowledge validation standards. First, in the absence of standards for sampling and representativeness of inferential statistics, the question is how to assign an epistemic value to big data.

We can consider that the singularity of big data in relation to previous epistemic practices arises essentially from the data itself. In a first approach, they can indeed be considered as new data that do not come from scientific measuring instruments and are produced outside the framework of the natural sciences. In the typologies of "big data" outlined in the academic literature, astronomical or genomic data, for example, are absent or anecdotal. The analysis of 26 "types" of big data proposed by Kitchin and McArdle (2016) excludes these types of data. The sources listed are mobile communications, the web and social networks, sensors and cameras, transactions (such as scanning a barcode or making a payment with a credit card) and finally administrations. All these data have in common that they are produced by activities of human origin, and are therefore difficult to include in the field of natural sciences. It is not erroneous to consider that big data are very often new observables for the cultural sciences.

We will indeed rely on the distinction between the natural and cultural sciences, but we must now qualify it. Indeed, the study of life and health and data-intensive sciences are part of the natural sciences. The specificity of big data is therefore not their object but the status of their observables, from which will derive a completely different methodological framework than that of the Galilean sciences. The measurement of the objects of the world, directly analyzed in a theoretical continuity that ranges from the instrument to the publication, is replaced by an *a posteriori* exploitation of data that is always already secondary, almost always already materialized when one considers processing them. It is therefore a framework in which the influence of a certain conception of the cultural sciences dominates, but in which any object can be mobilized.

Based on this conception, which we will develop further, we will examine in the following chapters the conditions of possibility of the hypothetical computational sciences of culture. This is a formula that we propose to designate a set of epistemic practices combining a certain theoretical and methodological framework developed from the cultural sciences with the capacity to mobilize massive digital data and computational processing tools. In the mythology that we have analyzed, one element deserves to be taken into account for the obvious nature it has for practitioners: big data create a technical complexity that requires specific skills and does not allow the existing tools to be mobilized as they stand. The two essential components of these hypothetic sciences are as follows: (1) the epistemic culture of the cultural sciences (in the sense we are going to give them), with their capacity to conceptualize a relationship with reality, and (2) the technical culture of computer scientists capable of translating concepts and methods into concrete tools, compatible with the previously defined conceptual framework. We are going to show, on the one hand, that these components exist, but, on the other hand, that they almost never manage to articulate themselves, and that they therefore lack epistemic continuity between them.

On the one hand, the problematization of the status of data and its epistemic value is emerging in several research communities. Technically challenged by the new modes of access to the real world that might be available to them, because they do not have the skills available to computer scientists, these researchers are, on the other hand, sensitive to the epistemological problems they pose. While they do not necessarily try to solve them, they are at least theoretically convinced that a problem exists. If these players were able to acquire concrete technical means to process data, this could be done within a homogenous epistemic culture articulating research problems, data, tools and methods.

However, the same computer scientists have the practical skill to handle large volumes of heterogeneous data, or to develop the required objects, but do not, by definition, fit into the epistemology of the cultural sciences. Their intervention takes the form of manipulations governed not by an epistemic project relating to the human fact, but by the systematic exploration of the space of manipulability provided by computer science. We will come back and confirm this in detail in Chapter 3.

Before that, we will explain what status can be given to observables in the cultural sciences, and how these sciences construct a relationship with reality. In this perspective, we will thus see what conceptualization of digital data can be proposed in the field of cultural sciences, and what redefinition of the cultural sciences themselves is induced by the upsurge of these new observables.

1.1. The epistemology of the cultural sciences

Before developing what relationship with reality and what norms govern the computational sciences of culture, we need to clarify the origin and meaning of this term, particularly in relation to other disciplinary divisions. The notion of "cultural sciences" thus comes to us from the neo-Kantian school of Heidelberg, embodied in particular by Rickert and Windelband; the latter precedes the former historically and speaks rather of "spiritual sciences", but in a globally identical sense. In Windelband's work (2000), the sciences of the mind project suggests that there are several ways of approaching the question of culture philosophically: a normative approach, through a philosophy of culture that seeks to establish a universally valid norm for a future culture, and a descriptive approach, through a philosophy of cultural sciences, that reflects on how actual cultures can be studied empirically and how this empirical study can be founded in science. For a neo-Kantian like Windelband, this distinction between normative and descriptive refers to the Kantian separation between the ethics of the *Critique of Practical Reason* and the epistemology of the *Critique of Pure Reason*. In Kant's view, there is science only in terms of nature, whereas culture is seen from the point of view of values and pure subjectivity: culture is not a state of humanity but the process of cultivating oneself, a process seen as a human duty which is anthropologically constitutive of humanity itself (cultivating oneself is what makes us human).

One of the neo-Kantian projects is precisely to prolong (or dare we say, improve) the Kantian work by bringing about and legitimizing the cultural sciences project, that is to say of an objective, non-normative knowledge of culture. The philosophy of culture would no longer be just an internal philosophy of the subject, but also a transcendental philosophy of culture as an object. This philosophy, in the neo-Kantian outline, shows that the cultural sciences are characterized by both method and object. The natural sciences refer to both their method (the naturalization of phenomena and the search for laws) and their object (natural phenomena): to be absolutely rigorous, we should speak of the natural sciences of nature. Rickert (1997) prefers to speak of the historical sciences of culture, i.e. sciences whose method is historical and whose object is culture, and points out that "we lack a term, equivalent to 'nature', which would designate them as much in relation to their object as in relation to their method". This coupling between method and object is not systematic since the very distinction between natural and cultural sciences is rather a spectrum that serves to "present the two extremes between which almost all scientific work is situated" (Rickert 1997).

There is at least one natural science of the mind (psychology, according to Windelband). Moreover, the life sciences occupy a specific status vis-à-vis this spectrum: the study of life needs the concept of end to understand the role of an organ, a genetic trait, but this concept is only regulatory in that there is no purpose in life. Everything happens as if the study of life is part of a comprehensive regime envisaged as methodological fiction; it is also possible to naturalize the study of life by leaving the scale of the organism to head toward more specific objects such as the cell or organic matter. The example of life shows that the dichotomy between natural and cultural sciences is not mutually exclusive. Nevertheless, this distinction constitutes a key element of intelligibility to situate epistemologically works pertaining to what we today call humanities and social sciences, and particularly history.

The historical sciences of culture are concerned with cultural events, i.e. the results of human activities as humans aim toward an end. These forms of sciences are interested in the events in terms of peculiarity and individuality, in what makes them unique and singular in history; they are said to be individualizing or idiographic, i.e. they are based on the writing of the singular. There is nothing to stop us from imagining historical natural sciences that would highlight the singularity of a tree's leaf, a block of granite and a cluster of cells; there are, for example, historical approaches in biology tracing the historical evolution of an organism from one generation of individuals to the next. Medical practice, based on general biological knowledge, examines a patient in his or her singularity, before reducing identified symptoms to more general knowledge. Nevertheless, most natural sciences stick to the natural method, also known as generalizing or nomological, which attempts to identify laws, or at least general relationships between phenomena. Among our current disciplines, the cultural history sciences would more naturally correspond to general history (except serial history), history of art, history of religions, literary studies, and perhaps also anthropology as it targets a human group in its singularity.

Conversely, quantitative social sciences such as sociology or economics, non-existent in their present form during Windelband and Rickert's time, are more concerned with a nomothetic method applied to the study of cultural and social objects, with an epistemology of the extent to which observation and the collection of scientific data facilitate the emergence of statistical regularities and laws. Nevertheless, as will be seen below, they present a set of specificities linked to the singularity of their object, and in particular to the fact that the naturalization of human facts does not exhaust a human's capacity to see themselves as an end (Schurmans 2011). This capacity places the search for explanation and understanding in the quantitative social sciences within the realm of reasons (rather than causes) or condemns the researcher to remain on the phenomenological surface of human fact. Researchers give themselves as their object, making the distinction between subject and object artificial and purely methodological: whether they resemble or differ from the human groups that make up their object, they are the measure of everything that can be known in the space of the human fact, considered in the light of their irreducible subjectivity. From there, two main directions are possible for them: a search for scientificity through a phenomenological objectivism that neutralizes, or better integrates, the reflexivity that their object presents, or the maintenance of subjectivity in a pluralism of interpretations of the human fact, evaluated under other criteria than the scientificity proper to the nomothetic sciences of nature.

1.2. The footprint in evidential sciences

We will therefore consider computational cultural sciences as a certain form of the cultural sciences which, according to Rickert's conception, do not have a specific object, but instead are characterized by method: computational cultural sciences are defined as such because of their mode of access to reality and a certain way of approaching objects. This mode of access takes a classical form in the cultural historical sciences; however, it is also used in other contexts such as medical diagnosis or police investigation. This mode of access is the trace or footprint, which mobilizes an epistemological index paradigm. The footprint serves as a source for the historian for whom it attests to past facts which are, by definition, no longer accessible. Testimonies, remains and objects that have endured through time document what is no longer. For Paul Ricœur, the trace (or more precisely, the documentary trace, as opposed to the affective or corporeal trace) is to historical knowledge what direct or instrumental observation is to the natural sciences (Serres 2002), in other words, its empirical foundation. Several fundamental features distinguish the trace of measurement produced by scientific instruments. Its existence is not the consequence of the actions of the one who seeks to study it, so that it always has an origin that escapes its observer. It is also always part of a linguistic dimension (be it a summary symbolic language or a script) to which the concepts and methods of the cultural sciences, and particularly the language sciences, are naturally linked.

In the context of the web and social networks, the digital footprint is a historically attested notion, already loaded with meaning. It is in a way the counterpart of big data for researchers in the cultural sciences: a media concept, vague, axiologically charged, problematized from an ethical and political point of view because it is "most often reduced to an opposition between protection and exhibition of private life" (Merzeau 2013a) but also linked to epistemological traditions, including naturally that of the very short trace, which we will briefly retrace here.

It is easy to get lost in listing the nuances of the meaning of the word "trace", which can mean a clue, a mark or small quantity. The comparison between the footprints left in the snow and the historian's record makes it easier to understand but not to define. Conceptually, we will say that the trace is the material residue of an event that is always already in the past. It is what remains of the upsurge of a heterogeneous causality in an environment governed by its own causes: thus the step in the snow results, on the one hand, from the snow's physical system, from the way it falls, aggregates, deforms, maintains itself, and in this case is imprinted by a body; and, on the other hand, from the upsurge of another causal system, that of the walker's body or the animal that triggers the event, the step in the snow. The trace always has a materiality that allows it to persist and play the role of evidence. Although this meaning is, as we shall see, constitutive of the trace, there is an irreducible positivity of the trace that is not limited to the meaning that can be conferred upon it: it is always both a material form and a sign.

However, its epistemic mobilization does not focus on this materiality as such; it would otherwise be like studying the proverbial index when it points to the moon. As Serres (2002) rightly points out:

> "Like other general and complex terms (such as 'form'), trace is characterized by its intrinsic genitive, so to speak, i.e. its character of belonging, in the sense that the trace is always a trace of something; it does not define itself, it has no existence of its own, autonomous, at least ontologically, it exists only in relation to something else (an event, a being, any phenomenon), it is of the order of double, even of representation and only takes on its meaning under the gaze that will decipher it. Hence a certain difficulty, if not to define at least to characterize and especially to inventory the traces, since everything can become a trace of something."

Their use in an epistemic context is therefore better understood from their role than from their nature and materiality, which is the necessary but not sufficient condition for their "tracing". Traces are semiotic objects that can take any form as long as they represent something. From the perspective of the study of digital footprints, the focus is therefore not so much on understanding the material form that the trace can take, but rather on examining how it works and what makes it exploitable. In these terms, several conditions for the possibility of an epistemic use of traces based on their representational function emerge, and it will be seen that they are not to be taken as such for digital footprints.

On the one hand, the trace must come from an attested coupling with the event that it designates, to play its evidentiary role. Since a trace can often be falsified, it is only acceptable as evidence when its own traceability can be attested to, or at least reasonably assumed, for example with a high probability or confidence: the discourse accompanying epistemic mobilization of traces then serves to justify the confidence placed in the trace in question. It can only play the role of being evidence of something if it first proves its own authenticity. In the archival tradition, the document is seen as the material trace of the event, with which it has an organic, almost mechanical relationship. One effective way to make this coupling effective is to produce it voluntarily. As such, the notarized deed of sale is an iconic example of traceability. It is a document that the lawyer strives to make unforgeable because it must be almost performative of the actual sale: in the legal ideal, the "sale" event does not occur simultaneously with the legal deed but as a consequence of the legal deed, which is the necessary and sufficient condition for it. Making a trace is here an intentional act, of which the trace is the consequence, where the coupling between the trace and the event results from a particular effort, an intentionality made effective by a set of actions.

Nevertheless, this intentionality of the trace is not systematic. What systematically characterizes the trace, on the other hand, is to be the irreducible material residue of a past event. In fact, from the point of view not of the individual who produces the trace, but of the one who examines it, the meaning of the trace escapes at least in part from its author, a bit like the way the book escapes from its author and constructs its meaning through its readers: there is indeed an initial intentionality of action, but from which a displacement of intentionality occurs as soon as this trace is interpreted by a reader. Thus, in Krämer's (2012) case, the trace must be involuntary, left without the knowledge of the person or thing that produces it:

> "You don't make a trace, you leave it, without any intention. Likewise, erasing traces is like leaving a trail. And vice versa: as soon as a trace is consciously left and staged as such, it is no longer a trace. Only that which is unintentional, involuntary, uncontrolled, arbitrary, serious or draws these lines of division that can be interpreted as traces. Unlike the sign we create, the meaning of a trace exists beyond the intention of the person who generates it."

The fact that it is involuntary does not mean that it cannot be intentional. Thus, if I draw a mark in the ground with the intention of leaving a trace, the mark is not so much the trace of itself as the trace of my intention to leave a trace. From the observer's point of view, the trace is always interpreted at a level of intentionality other than that of the trace's author: the epistemology of the trace is an epistemology of the trace's reader.

Finally, a trace is such only if it has a meaning for an observer who is able to interpret it. It must not only be perceived (directly or indirectly, through an instrument or medium) but understood. It does not trace everything that is perceptible, but only that which is identified as such by a "selective perception of the environment" (Krämer 2012.). If all traces have a material positivity by which they are not purely constructed by selection, a trace is nonetheless the result of a selective process that singularizes (here in the sense of "detaching" rather than "making unique") an element in relation to its environment. For the tracker, the broken branch that signals the deer's passage is singled out not only from all the branches in the forest, but also by branches broken accidentally, by drying out, by the wind, or any other cause that is not the deer's passage. The latter is not singularized as such, but signaled by the singularized trace itself, differentiated from its environment. This singularization does not pre-exist the tracker, it results from his/her observation and interpretation talents. However, interpretation means the mobilization of a hermeneutic culture, of know-how linked to other knowledge mobilized in context, or in other words of a "habitus to target the trace as a trace, a tradition in which the interpretability of the trace is maintained" (Bachimont 2010a). The trace is therefore always a trace of something but also a trace of someone; everything can be a trace because the "tracing" of the trace proceeds from a coupling between a material remnant and its interpretative structure, between its material positivity and its intentional constitutive singularization.

So would the trace be to the human sciences what data are to the natural sciences? The interpretation on which it depends is not a science, but an art to which we recognize multiple practices, from the haruspex to the doctor to the intuitive understanding we use in our daily lives. There is no doubt that the natural sciences have a hermeneutic dimension, although the interpretation of the particle physicist may be more formally codified than that of the historian. It is therefore not the hermeneutic character of the trace that distinguishes it from the data of the natural sciences. When Ginzburg (1980) opposed Galilean science to the doctor's evidential paradigm, the detective or the art critic, he underlined the difference between their modes of understanding the object: on the one hand, the reproducible universal, and on the other hand, the singular individual. Natural sciences data are based on the repeatability of phenomena, their quantity and the criteria under which they can be considered similar. Hermeneutical disciplines are instead interested in the singularity of the phenomenon, in what characterizes this text, this person, this image – to which I point by designating it as so. Opting for an index epistemology of the trace is, in the terms of Heidelberg's neo-Kantism, to take an idiographic rather than a nomological perspective (Rickert 1997; Windelband 2000), seeking to understand the cultural significance of the trace in its singularity, rather than explain the causal mechanisms from which its existence derives.

We therefore propose to consider data as the plural of the trace. This passage in the plural is not a grammatical spin; it is made at the cost of the renunciation of qualitatively defining what makes the singularity of the trace and on the condition that we find what makes it possible to consider traces as a collective likely to present regularities. To substitute the trace generally is to mourn the inexhaustible richness of the singular event in order to record the commensurability of events and their reproducibility in time and space. From this reproduction emerges generality, not as a systematic feature, but quantitatively in the majority. From the general, singulars, deviations from the norm, can be reconstructed. Finally, whatever their apprehension system, the data considered as the plural of the trace are always initially deprived of their origin and of the knowledge of their conditions of emergence.

1.3. The log or activity history

If we now return to the digital environment, it is clear that digital footprints always appear in the plural (we do not say "one" but "several" digital footprints). Since digital technology is the ideal environment for repetition and formal commensurability, why is it still necessary to favor the term trace, which is linked to the notion of singularity?

The primary reason is historical and practical. Digital traces, or digital footprints, refer, in the first instance, to a computer device that allows a developer to diagnose their own work. By writing their program, they also defines how the different processes produce, while running, traces – the logs, thanks to which they will be able to debug their program, i.e. identify the source of the bugs or errors it produces. As Champin *et al.* wrote (2013):

> "Digital footprints have been used from the outset to facilitate the debugging of computer programs with the idea that a trained observer (the programmer in general), an analyst of the observation made, will be able to interpret the traces resulting from the execution of the program to understand its behavior and correct it if necessary."

Computer footprints[2] are therefore not aimed at knowledge as such, but at control (in the sense of verification and not "power over"); it is not a

2 Note the change from "digital footprint" to "computer footprint". The finding is that the formulation varies according to the speaker: in computing, we generally

question of understanding the user better, but of verifying that the program is working in the manner intended. Unlike the historian's mobilization of archives, they are not so much a scientific project as an engineering issue. They are, however, like the "analog" trace, a mode of access to the singularity of what produced them and will have to be interpreted to reconstruct and understand the event to which they bear witness. They are indeed upsurges of heterogeneous causality in an environment governed by its own causal norms. The environment is the event logging system governed by the program, and causality is what is captured by this system as an entry in the logs: a user interaction, a malfunction, the completion of a task, etc. The essential difference is that of the medium: the brushstroke, the fever and the fingerprint are material vestiges of the imprint of one object (or agent) on another, whereas the digital footprint is an informational fingerprint generated by a computational artifact. Thus, unlike the legal deed where the production of the trace is the result of an intentional process, the digital footprint is the result of a mechanical coupling between the logging system and the computer event.

In other words, in one case the footprint itself is interpreted as the result of an intention; in the other case, the coupling between the computer event and its "analog" cause (i.e. for simplicity, the program's user) is reconstructed by the reader when it exists.

Moreover, this passage from a material to an informational substrate has some consequences:

– any digital footprint can be timestamped;

– the trace must be discretized by a set of symbols (characters, pixels, etc.) and follow specific encoding;

– it is always already manipulable and calculable by nature (*ibid.*).

While the logs are primarily diagnostic tools of the program's behavior, they easily become tools for monitoring the user's behavior in front of the program. The program traces are then reinterpreted as traces of the program

speak of a computer trace, and in HSS of a digital footprint, with HSS researchers being more interested in the cultural significance of the object than in its technical modalities. However, the adjective "digital" generally refers to the cultural dimension of computing.

user. In this configuration, there is a detachment/distanciation/remote setting between the use situation and the monitoring situation. The machine on which the program is executed by the user is no longer necessarily the one on which the user's behavior is studied[3]. Concretely, three configurations can be presented according to the installation mode of the software:

– the user installs software on their own machine. The software runs autonomously on this machine. It may or may not produce logs that remain on the user's machine;

– the user installs the software on their own machine but the software sends information to the organization that provides it. Logs are generated on the user's machine but analyzed in the organization;

– the user does not install software, but uses an application directly online, typically in a web browser. Logs can be recorded on their machine, or directly on the server hosting the web application.

These different hardware configurations induce epistemic options that can be different: when access to the logs remains localized on the user's machine, consulting them is used to examine the use or operation of the software in its singularity, for example to identify a problem in the installation of the software related to the configuration of the machine. When, on the contrary, the logs are examined on another machine, typically the servers made available by the software publishers, this machine generally aggregates the logs of all users of the software around the world. As a result, it is no longer the singularity of one use that is examined, but the regularities and irregularities of all uses of the software. We thus move from the particular to the general, from the unique to the statistical, with digital footprints considered in the comparison mode, so as to identify, on the one hand, global measurements that will constitute standards and, on the other hand, more local measurements that will characterize divergences from the standard. The appearance of norms, comparisons and calculations marks the passage from the log considered as an idiographic trace of the user's

3 In terms of the division of labor within organizations, the design and monitoring functions are often separated: the developer who writes the program is not the analyst who studies the user behavior; the latter is often, in an industrial context, linked to marketing functions. They may be geographically separated, or even belong to different organizations and never exchange.

or program's behavior to the logs considered as data, that is to say nomological representations, or at least quasi-legal representations, of these behaviors.

This passage to logs considered in their plurality is also coupled with a sociological distinction; one must ask oneself who is speaking, which epistemic agent intervenes on the logs to determine what one is dealing with. Due to the division of labor between the engineering and marketing functions, for example, the same person rarely develops software and analyzes uses; when this happens, they take on distinct epistemic roles that are not always simultaneous, depending on the task they are working on at any given time. The computer scientist creates logs to assist them in verifying their program, while the analyst manipulates data to better understand the behavior of their users. Some are ultimately modalities for the constitution of a computational artifact, and others a mode of access to reality via a statistical representation. We thus find again the loss of the trace's constitutive origin, because the developer who created the system generating traces is not the one who analyzes and interprets them.

However, the distinction between program execution monitoring and user behavior analysis is far from being binary. Logging refers to a multiplicity of use cases with various epistemic projects, executed with varying degrees of success. The implementation of logs is the result of a multitude of decisions and is based on know-how gained from practice and the sharing of experience. Novice developers will tend to program few logs, which will produce information that is sometimes cryptic, not very contextualized, and will make it difficult or impossible to locate the problem. A more experienced developer will know how to project themselves in advance in the diagnostic situation to anticipate the contextualized information to be included in the logs: which action, which event, which process, which parameters, etc. In the operational phase (as opposed to the design phase where the developer can perform tests on his/her own machine), logs can be used to monitor a multitude of objects within an information system: programs and user actions, but also servers, information transfers, the operating system, programs, scheduled tasks, databases, etc. Thus, the idiographic/nomological distinction is not superimposed on the program/user opposition, as the analysis of the behavior of one or the other can be done under both terms of the distinction. As a result, log analysis cannot be reduced to the analysis of user behavior, which is generally the function attributed to the study of digital footprints: not all logs are digital footprints and, as we will see, not all digital footprints are logs.

Moreover, the analysis of user behavior by software publishers produces knowledge about the uses of a particular software, which is difficult to generalize to the relationship between IT and users in absolute terms, and is not, moreover, an end in itself. This review is an epistemic project for the marketing and commercial purpose of the company, which seeks to understand its users only in order to retain or attract them; while other motivations may exist, such as intellectual curiosity, it is at the individual level that they arise.

1.4. The digital footprint as a web log

The type of log analysis presented so far is a special case, nevertheless originating from the analysis of digital footprints. From the point of view of the knowledge they can produce, the question of digital footprints today has a scope that goes far beyond the examination of the uses of a software program by its publishers. Digital footprints are abundant in both quality and quantity: there are all kinds of them and they are produced on a massive scale. The digitization of a large number of economic sectors (commerce, banking, transport, etc.), the development of mass computing and the emergence of the web, among other factors, have made the recording of digital footprints a phenomenon massive enough to attract the interest of organizations other than software companies. The analysis of financial flows, purchasing behavior and instant conversations, to name just a few examples of activities that produce traces on computer media, has a scope that goes far beyond a company's study of its users. In fact, it is a whole universe of possibilities that opens up from the moment that one confers a certain value of generality, even universality, to the digital footprints. In particular:

– since computers are the very medium for some of these activities, recording them produces a full representation of them (at least from one point of view). For example, the totality of banks' financial transactions is now computerized; therefore, analyzing the traces of these transactions is equivalent to analyzing the totality of activity with regard to transactions;

– by their general increase, digital footprints become a mode of access to the study of cultural phenomena. In France, for example, since most individuals are equipped with a mobile phone[4], the analysis of their mobile usage traces becomes a source for the study of travel, communication habits, the structure of a person's social network, etc.;

– finally, by their systematic nature, they become for their authors a means of expression, re-appropriation, even self-construction.

The most notable case of this new abundance of traces is the web. In the literature on digital footprints, it is almost always about the web, even when this is not specified. The obviousness of the web, a major phenomenon known to all, makes it the example of a technical device producing digital footprints. The common use of the notion of digital footprint thus tends to exclude traces of the use of mobile phones, connected sensors and objects, programs connected to the Internet without going through the web and all private networks such as internal organizational devices. In contrast to other devices of the same kind, it has qualities that at least partly explain this evidential character:

– it relies on a global network used by nearly one in every two people on Earth, making it the largest communication network to ever exist;

– it benefits from a notoriety without equal;

– unlike the banks' information systems, it presents, for players other than the banks themselves, a certain level of openness that allows, with more or less technical complications, access to the traces left by its users;

– it is the medium of cultural uses and behaviors rich enough to make an exhaustive repertoire an impossible undertaking.

Due to the intensity of Internet use, it is technically possible to study a large number of traces: their digital materiality always already confers them with a technical manipulability and opens a domain of possibilities within which epistemologically desirable manipulations can emerge. With regard to web traces, several typologies have been proposed, depending on whether they are private or public, indexable by search engines, textual or relational, primitive or calculated and so on. Whether it is a question of the types of traces or of the typologies themselves, it is difficult to speak of traces of web

4. 92% of the population in 2015, according to CREDOC; see: http://www.arcep.fr/uploads/tx_gspublication/CREDOC-Report-enquort-enquete-diffusion-TIC-France CGE-ARCEP_nov2015.pdf [accessed November 16, 2017].

use without making lists more or less randomly, which only make it possible to account for their diversity without being able to measure their extent, but which nevertheless have the advantage of not suggesting any form of order or homogeneity of the phenomenon. The opposing trend is indeed toward a reduction in the extension of the trace's domain, notably through the prism of a specific notion that is of methodological interest. It is difficult to discern between a methodological simplification, i.e. a modeling of the phenomenon in the service of a research hypothesis and which makes it intelligible, and an ontological reduction that modifies the very definition of what a trace is according to the research hypothesis and leads to a circularity of reasoning on the object. These typologies are confronted with the problem of any classification of the world, necessarily reductive and simultaneously constitutive of our way of understanding it. In the literature on digital footprints, we find such simplifications whose epistemological status is not explained, and whose epistemological status is therefore unclear as to whether what is described designates the entire notion of trace or only a particular angle, open to a pluralism of varied approaches to the subject. Some of the work involved includes the following:

– Casilli (2012) proposes to approach digital footprints through the prism of their dimensionality, which can be unique (short text content), double (image, video, formatted text) or triple (3D visual immersion);

– Cardon (2013) finds representative traces of web use in those of social networks, notably Facebook, and search engines, essentially Google;

– George (2009) uses the notion of identity, as footprints can be representations of a declarative, active or calculated identity;

– Merzeau (2013b) classifies digital footprints as declarative, behavioral, or documentary according to a scale of intentionality in the constitution of the trace.

Although Louise Merzeau's classification seems reductive to us, we share her interest in the question of intentionality, which is one of the conceptual nodes of the notion of trace in general and of digital footprint in particular.

1.5. The intentionality of digital footprints

According to Krämer's conception mentioned above, a footprint can only be unintentional; the essence of a trace is that it is involuntarily produced and subject to the interpretation of the reader's trace. Yet Louise Merzeau rightly points out that much online content conceptualized as traces is, on the contrary, completely intentional, and even participates in a reflexive activity of self-construction. Consequently, the essence of the digital footprint is not strictly intentional or unintentional. The intentionality of our digital footprints exists by degree, in a self-manifest mode as well as in lapsus mode; the consciousness of being traced also exists by degree. Setting up a profile, or discussing on social networks are acts of communication that allow people to describe themselves autonomously or in reaction to others: these are perfectly intentional acts. At the same time, trace recording is always active, whether you like it or not:

> "Fully automated, this traceability is not a documentary layer that is annexed afterwards. It is the very condition of digital performativity. Just as we cannot avoid communicating, we cannot avoid leaving traces." (Merzeau 2013a)

Although the intentionality of digital footprints exists by degree, its inscription is always already preceded by a registration framework that is itself governed by a model of trace apprehension over which the user has little or no control. If I announce on Twitter that I am writing my thesis, my communicative intention is subsumed by the framework in which I express myself, and in which my announcement is a tweet, that is to say, content of a certain technical and conceptual format that can be apprehended and manipulated by Twitter or third parties who will interpret it and make it a clue to something else. In this sense, my tweet is for me a trace of my declaration (with which it has an organic relationship), and for these third parties a trace of a higher order, namely a trace of my intention to produce a trace of my declaration.

Moreover, the question of intentionality reflects a way of problematizing the digital footprint that is centered on human agents. When the operation of a program produces logs as discussed above, it is difficult to talk about the degree of intentionality or self-construction of the program. Operating systems and programs perform a multitude of planned or intended tasks that are not the direct result of a user's intervention; they are non-human agents in themselves that can produce traceable events. Philosophically, this does not mean that programs have intentions, and we would rather say that they are the result of the computer developer's intentionality who designed them in this way, but this question of program intentionality is relatively indifferent to our problem: it is enough to say that not all digital footprints are the result of the user's action. Although the literature favors traces produced by human users, by virtue of the anthropological considerations that they enable thematizing, nothing in the nature of the digital footprint imposes this limitation: whether it is a question of its technical materiality or its interpretability, its human origin does not appear to be a relevant or necessary distinction, nor moreover clearly discernible. Moreover, to assert that a trace is of human or non-human origin is in itself an interpretation. The complexity of technical systems is not an accident but a necessity for their operation, and is such that it is not always possible to discern the part played by one aspect or another. From a certain point of view, all digital footprints are of human origin insofar as they originate from man-made technical devices. From another point of view, the use of these devices is not purely intentional for humans, being an act of desire that would meet neither the obstacle nor constraint, but a technically instrumented gesture, and is thus conditioned by this instrumentation.

For example, Twitter is known for the 140-character limit it imposed (until November 2017) on posted messages; however, this is only one of the countless constraints I face when I want to write a tweet. The mere fact of accessing Twitter characterizes me culturally, socially and geographically: I'm likely to be quite young, male, urban, live in a developed country and have some knowledge and command of digital uses; I have a vested interest in knowing what a hashtag or a mention is. I must have a machine connected to the Internet, and I need to use the keyboard; if I want to use exotic characters that do not appear on its keys, I must know how to type them, or where to find them. Twitter may prevent me from using some of these characters, and may, *a priori*, block my access to its services, or *a posteriori*, delete one of my messages. If I use my cell phone to write my message, I may have some form of autocorrect writing assistance, which will automatically "correct" my message, offering me suggestions; I could decide to write my message only by systematically accepting the first word suggested by this feature. I can play and free myself to a certain extent from this 140 or 280 character limit by publishing an image of a text or a link to a longer text.

In any case, I have to deal with these constraints imposed directly by the tool (or more precisely, by the layers of hardware and software I use), or indirectly by the norms and habits formed with the use of the tool. Our ambition here is not to make a complete monograph of the predeterminations of the use of Twitter, but to show that as a user of a system producing traces, I am socioculturally and technically conditioned in the message I write, and that results from a play between my original intention of communication and the material form it will take (which is true, by the way, of any medium of expression including orality).

On the other hand, it may be difficult to find the source of the very intention behind a trace, and to continue to support its irreducibility in the computer system. Every computer generates logs when starting up that record the various processes that are executed for its startup: where is the intention in this case? Can we really reduce this recording to the action of the user turning on his/her computer, or to the work of the developer materialized in the program that produces logs? To take the example of Twitter, if I set up a bot that publishes tweets for me, then forget it exists and rediscover it sometime later, can we still talk about intentionality? Or if I were to configure this bot by using a creation tool that only asks me to set a certain number of elements, does my level of intentionality depend on the number of elements configured? If I finally have nothing left to do, except agreeing to provide my own tweets as a reference, from which new tweets will be automatically generated by recombination, can we still say that there is a human behind this account? Given that it is estimated that between 5% of accounts, or 24% of messages posted on Twitter come from social bots[5] and that some of them are sometimes indistinguishable from human users, is it really legitimate to consider an intentionality "direct" via the notion of an author, as an inherent characteristic of this social network?

As can be seen from these few examples, it is not certain that the culturally and theoretically charged notions of authorship or intentionality are relevant to characterize the production of digital footprints; at best, to save this notion, we can consider that intentionality is distributed among the different human agents that have contributed in one way or another to the tool used, and that a program that works automatically updates the intention of its designers *a posteriori*. In the end, we find that unintentionality is probably a more general modality, less likely to be subject to exceptions, applying to both human and non-human agents. On the other hand, rather than a binary separation between these two types of agents, it seems to us that in reality it is better to speak of agents entirely hybridized by humans

5. See https://www.ipsos-mori.com/researchpublications/publications/1760/The-road-to-representivity. aspx [accessed November 16, 2017].

and non-humans, according to degrees and modalities that are specific to them.

1.6. Data as theoretically-loaded footprints

This hybridization of humans and non-humans, which is not anecdotal, deprives a *priori* the digital footprints of their status as representations of human phenomena. On the one hand there are human facts that do not produce traces and on the other hand there are traces that do not point to human facts. In order to regain this status, it will be necessary to construct human fact data by selection and the theoretical construction of traces (for example, extracting tweets whose authors are reasonably certain to be human), or conversely, taking the modalities of this hybridization precisely as the object of investigation.

The trace is, so to speak, the data in their natural state, before it has been captured in an epistemologically constitutive gesture necessary for future operations. This gesture is a choice, a selection in "the given" of traces, oriented by a conceptualization or a theoretical viewpoint; thus, as with Duhem or Hanson in particular (Heidelberger 2003), the facts are theory-laden. The observation of facts is not the fact itself, it is already an interpretation motivated by a psychological, epistemic, but also technical, context. We can thus compare the digital footprints to the physical phenomena according to Duhem (1906):

> "An experiment in Physics is the precise observation of a group of phenomena, accompanied by the interpretation of these phenomena; this interpretation substitutes the concrete data actually collected by observation with abstract and symbolic representations that correspond to them by virtue of the theories that the observer admits."

Following our comparison, the constitution of data from digital footprints is an experiment (of an observational rather than interventional nature), which makes these data symbolic representations. The technical transaction (the collection and storage of data, which involves some computer data modeling) is accompanied by an epistemic transaction that gives them a certain intelligibility before they are manipulated, and is the condition for their subsequent intelligibility. Initial intelligibility is based on confidence in the validity of the data and a reconstitution *a posteriori* of its origin and conditions of emergence. Thus, this comparison confirms the well-known assertion that raw data never exist, and places any manipulation of data from digital footprints in a constructivism that invalidates any radically empirical approach. As we have seen, there are two main aspects to this constructivism:

– an epistemic aspect, as seen in Duhem's work, by which the data become symbolic representations;

– a technical aspect, to which we shall return in Chapter 3, by which they follow a formal representation established in advance, with a view to the manipulation that is planned to be carried out on them.

It also includes a psychological aspect, which traditionally consists of thinking that our perceptions of phenomena are also theory-ladden, or ladden with preconceptions and belief (Heidelberger 2003). Here, this allows us to maintain a constructivist position according to which the radically empirical position mentioned above is not so much an epistemological position as a psychological one, or at least an ethos suggesting behaviors and beliefs. In these terms, data are a preconstruction that must be deconstructed before it can be analyzed. In other words, this position is itself a belief that conditions the perception of digital footprints; although it is a problem for the epistemic construction of data, it is nonetheless a modality of data collection (by computer scientists in particular) that can only have consequences on the theoretical and technical choices that will precede this collection.

Moreover, in the epistemological gesture of data selection, the trace also becomes plural and momentarily loses its indexicality. It is no longer the index of a singularized fact in an environment but one element among others comparable and commensurable in a standardized set: a corpus, a set of data. As a result, several types of analyses are possible under different standards. On the one hand, one can analyze the traces that have become data in a quantitative way, by looking for measurable laws or quasi-laws, averages and statistical constants. Deviations from these laws are aberrations, statistical noise, similar to measurement error in the natural sciences. With this type of analysis, digital footprints make it possible to apprehend human phenomena nomologically, considered according to their statistical regularities, not necessarily mathematical as in the Galilean paradigm, but quantifiable, manipulable and calculable. Moreover, it is possible to reconstruct an indexicality of the trace, no longer at the individual level of the singular event, but precisely at the statistical level, by interpreting the deviations from the laws as supplements of meaning rather than as measurement errors. With this type of analysis, the nomological approach is also necessary but may only be transitory. It is an intermediate step in the constitution of meaning, which does not determine the type of knowledge produced. What determines it is not the type of treatment practiced, but what is done with it, how it is used and interpreted.

Through this plurality of approaches, the digital footprints place the computational sciences of culture in a third epistemological approach which is not that of the idiographic sciences, nor that of the natural sciences, and is based on new modes of access, particularly via the web, to empirical human phenomena of a certain kind. The epistemology of digital footprints is neither a Durkheim-style naturalism, which considers "social facts as things" (although it has similarities with Durkheimian quantitative social sciences), nor a "culturalism" based on the understanding of singular phenomena from the identification of additions of meaning in a norm. It is an epistemology that actually allows both approaches.

Naturalism, according to the definition proposed by Andler (2011), is "the philosophical theory according to which all sciences must and can aim to deal with their respective objects in the manner of the natural sciences". According to this definition, the new modes of access to phenomena through digital footprints are not those of the natural sciences, and therefore do not lead to a naturalization of the cultural sciences. They therefore maintain a bifurcationism, that is, still according to Andler, the assertion of a clear-cut distinction from the natural sciences. Nevertheless, the imprinted bifurcation is twofold: both with the natural sciences, because the epistemology of digital footprints does not induce a processing of social facts purely in the manner of the natural sciences, but also with the cultural "traditional" sciences, precisely insofar as they replace (or add to) the classical modes of access to human phenomena, and make possible both a naturalizing and a culturalizing approach.

The epistemology of the digital footprint, and of the data that derive from it, is an epistemology of the cultural sciences, whose target empirical domain is the human fact, and whose revisited index paradigm (due to being deprived of its idiographic dimension) traditionally belongs to this region of sciences. The exploitation of these digital footprints is therefore based on a conceptualization of these footprints that must be specifically constructed to acquire scientific legitimacy (*a priori*, that of the cultural sciences) and depends both on the material and semiotic nature of these traces, the scientific project pursued and the approach adopted to bring them together.

Indeed, the conceptualization of traces is not an operation that can be done once and for all forms of traces, or even for all forms of digital footprints. We can even go further and affirm that this conceptualization is systematically made *ad hoc*, at the time of the traces being constituted in data, even if a first more general conceptualization may pre-exist this constitution. At this more general level, we have seen that there can be as many ways to approach digital footprints as there are authors mobilizing them, and, on the other hand, each source (like Twitter) has intrinsic specificities. This conceptualization is to be reintegrated into a methodological continuity that also involves an epistemic project, a conceptual framework, tools and methods of analysis and interpretation. We will therefore question the existence of such continuity, required for the establishment of computational sciences of culture, and the characteristics of the components it mobilizes.

2

Toward an Epistemic Continuity Anchored in the Cultural Sciences

So far we have established that digital data have a potential epistemic value that must be able to be confirmed, and that by their technical format and quantitative character, they can also be computationally manipulated and computed. Because of the origin and semantic content of the data, derived from traces of human (or presumed human) activity, the theoretical and methodological framework in which these computational processes are carried out is rightly so that of the evidential paradigm, historically favored by the cultural sciences, but applicable to any data conceived as a linguistic trace. For these sciences, data play the role of an observable that, in order to generate new knowledge, must be subjected to analysis in the form of computational processing. In this *de jure* configuration, data theory and its processing is that of the discipline that governs the experiment as a whole: the observables are understood in terms of disciplinary norms that allow them to be placed in a theoretical framework. This framework also provides or agrees with an instrument theory so that the same norms govern the observation, analysis and production of scientific results. Our epistemological paradigm will also have to ensure this epistemic continuity, while respecting two additional constraints: it must be based on the exploitation of digital footprints (as opposed to other observable ones) and consider them as representations of human facts.

A variety of more or less fruitful research projects in the historically constituted cultural sciences have attempted, explicitly or not, to construct such an epistemology of the digital footprint and to turn it into theoretically charged data, but without realizing the hypothetical configuration of the computational cultural sciences. As we shall see, none of them presents all the required components; nevertheless, they reveal, in their contributions as well as in their shortcomings, different methodological strategies that will be exploited in our paradigm proposal. Concretely, several criteria must be examined to confirm the hypothesis of an epistemic continuity between the observable, the tools, the method and the general theory:

– the observables must belong to a theoretical framework to which they are related using the evidential paradigm as we have conceptualized it for the cultural sciences;

– the method of analysis of these observables must belong to the same paradigm;

– tools and methods must be compatible, usually resulting from a common genesis between the strategies to approach reality and the tools to apply this strategy.

We will also have to ensure that the observables mobilized are indeed digital footprints and that they have a status as an evidential representation of the human fact.

In order to identify relevant methodological strategies, we will examine these different research projects. We will thus see the theoretical and practical difficulties of historically constituted cultural sciences in appropriating digital objects. These difficulties are examined in particular through the example of the digital humanities, whose extensive disciplinary ambition will enable us to draw a crucial dividing line within the cultural sciences: those disciplines whose mode of access to reality is the field, and those whose disciplines concern the corpus.

In *field-based disciplines*, on the one hand, the advent of digital technology has made it possible to transpose existing methods, which are still based on the paradigm of the representative sample. We therefore examine in detail this transposition, which is performed through reconstructing the epistemological continuity between the observables and the theory, and which can be reused for our methodological paradigm. In *corpus-based disciplines*, on the other hand, digital technology is leading to a technical revolution of the text, which must be dealt with in a conceptual and practical way, through the acquisition of specific know-how or the construction of an interdisciplinarity. Although it does not mobilize digital footprints strictly speaking, textual statistics applied to the social sciences thus fulfills the criteria of a digital reconceptualization of text and its use in the service of an understanding of cultural (and not simply textual) facts. It manifests a form of continuity between the digital text, its analysis and its interpretation that corresponds to what we are trying to construct from the digital footprints.

At this stage, the missing step is the conceptualization, not of digitized or imported data, but of natively digital footprints, addressed here through the example of the web. It will thus be seen that there have been several projects to conceptualize the web as a trace or source of traces, which have been constructed by considering it first as an object in itself, then as an index intermediary. As a result, no research project within the cultural sciences proposes a complete epistemic continuity between the digital footprints, the tools and methods and the conceptual framework, but each analyzed element provides a part of it. Thus, by putting them together, our methodological paradigm can benefit from an epistemological viability that will need to be complemented with technical feasibility, which is discussed in the next chapter. First, we will look at how cultural sciences are mobilizing digital technology, on the one hand, and its traces or data, on the other hand.

2.1. Digital technology in the cultural sciences

One cannot deny how much the classical players in the cultural sciences have observed, problematized and questioned the advent of digital technology in general, and of the "deluge of data" in particular, for their discipline: all the theoretical and empirical work on digital technology and its role in culture, society, the media, politics, etc., over the last 20 years could be pointed out against such a denial.

However, there is a substantial difference between intellectual reflection *on* digital technology and the mobilization of digital technology for knowledge production. This second option remains a rare occurrence in the academic cultural sciences. The computational cultural sciences that we have conceptualized, and which aim to produce knowledge using digital technology, are an example of digital instrumentation by the cultural sciences in the same way as writing, mathematics or physical measuring devices, which guide the natural sciences. Nevertheless, the work undertaken by researchers in the cultural sciences has on the whole not constructed a real epistemology of the digital footprint, which would provide them with a meaning anchored in an epistemic project, based on an actual practice of knowledge production using digital data–driven knowledge production.

The reasons for this non-result probably lie in the fact that such an epistemology must first of all be able to give itself an object, and that it must be empirically accessible to it, at the risk of envisaging it in a purely hypothetical way and missing it: without confrontation with reality, reflection on a highly mediatized and politicized object runs the risk of being encumbered by an affective charge that substitutes for the object what one believes or fears it to be. The epistemologies of different historically constituted scientific disciplines have rarely been constructed *a priori*, as a metaphysics of science can do, but *a posteriori*, reflecting the data, tools and practices of an era. Given that the rational discourse on the exploitation of big data can also be difficult to establish without being based on effective research practices with big data, the existence and accessibility of these experiments is the main condition for the success of such a discourse. Faced with the rarity of these practices, reflection struggles to make them an object.

This scarcity of effective practices in what we have problematized as the computational cultural sciences can in turn be explained by the epistemological difficulties they pose through technical, economic legal and ethical limitations. From a technical point of view, they often require a significant skill level to produce research data, on the one hand, and to manipulate it technically, on the other hand. In the case of big data, mastering these technical issues constitutes a research field in its own right, which is difficult for researchers in the cultural sciences to master: as we have seen in the analysis of their mythology, for many, big data only consist of the design and use of these computational data processing techniques. This technicality poses specific interdisciplinarity issues that we will discuss later.

Moreover, the configuration of players that we have already mentioned several times poses economic and legal obstacles to such practices. Data and tools are often owned by companies that either require payment for access or simply do not offer it. In these configurations, big data analysis is simply reserved for companies; even if researchers had the desire, and the theoretical and practical apparatus, to process such data, they would technically not be able to access it – or would have difficulty doing so. The creation of data and tools also requires skills and material resources that cultural researchers do not necessarily, if ever, have. Finally, some technically accessible data are subject to legal or ethical issues such as the protection of privacy and the processing of personal data. While the natural sciences have been striving in recent years to remove the obstacles to research posed by the ownership of data, particularly through initiatives to open up and share data, the cultural sciences have in common with the medical world the sensitive nature of the data itself, irrespective of the ownership of the person who established or collected them. The exploitation of personal data for research purposes then gives rise to conflict in terms of two legal and ethical requirements: that of respect for privacy (and intellectual property), on the one hand, and that of providing public research with the necessary means to pursue its work, on the other hand. The French bill *Pour une République numérique* (For a Digital Republic) is similar to the second requirement by authorizing the reproduction of digital data by researchers in the context of "text and data mining use for public research purposes, excluding any commercial purpose"[1]. Ethical issues related to personal data, the question of consent and potentially problematic uses of data (and processing) nevertheless remain topical despite legal relaxations in favor of researchers.

Regardless of these technical, economic, legal and ethical limitations, much cultural science research related to digital data analysis is more reflective and critical in nature than experimental. There is an abundance of digital research fields developed in this context, such as digital humanities, digital studies, cultural studies, software studies, critical data studies, and many others, which share the common feature of being created more as a prospective and critical reflection on the digital and data than as an effective work with these elements.

The digital humanities are the emblematic example of these imaginative projects, which mainly produce discourses on techniques without uses of those said techniques, causing a gap between their ambitions and the means they give themselves. They are, so to speak, the counterpart anchored in the cultural sciences of the more general mythology of big data. We will examine its ambitions, its structuring and its relationship with technology.

1 French bill *Pour une République numérique*, Amendment 180; see http://www.assemblee-nationale.fr/14/amendements/3399/AN/180.asp [accessed November 16, 2017].

2.2. Field and corpus: two modes of access to reality

The digital humanities are usually described as a project relating to the articulation between the humanities and digital technology, both understood in a very broad sense. In both French and English, the notion of digital humanities has more of a programmatic than a descriptive function. The emblematic documents on the subject are manifestos, suggesting that it is more a matter of developing a program or a set of ambitions for researchers in the "humanities" than an analytical notion with which to retrospectively analyze a phenomenon in a sociological or epistemological approach. The digital humanities program focuses both on understanding digital humanities issues, the mobilization of digital technologies for research, but also the broader issues of organization, collaboration and interdisciplinarity between researchers, which digital humanities devices should make possible. This program is now widely questioned in all these aspects, and its speculative nature is well known and criticized. Digital humanities research is increasingly critical of itself, in particular with regard to the digital humanities' political and ideological motivations. Pierre Mounier, who is also a recognized player in the field, thus denounces the "political utopia" character (Mounier 2015) of such a project, as well as the discrepancy between the ambitions of this utopia and the means and forces involved. Éric Guichard (2013) describes more broadly the rhetoric of an era "saturated with revolutionary discourse", largely ideological; one could also point out the disproportions between the ambitions of the digital humanities (Berry 2012; Burdick *et al.* 2012) and the concrete transformations of the disciplines concerned. English language writers themselves agree that we should not dwell on this watchword, the use of which corresponds to a tactic of appropriating the problem:

> "We wave the banner of 'Digital Humanities' for tactical reasons (think of it as 'strategic essentialism'), not out of a conviction that the phrase adequately describes the tectonic shifts embraced in this document. But an emerging transdisciplinary domain without a name runs the risk of finding itself defined less by advocates than by critics and opponents, much as cubism became the label associated with the pictorial experiments of Picasso, Braque, and Gris." (*Digital Humanities Manifesto 2.0*)

This tactic, as well as the rhetoric of big data, serves, among other things, to raise the profile and funding of research; it also plays a role in recognizing and rallying researchers from different fields who are interested in a common problem. The imprecision and apparent disorganization of the project is not considered a conceptual weakness but an "operational strength" (Mounier 2015) that allows for exchange and interdisciplinarity.

Nevertheless, it is difficult to define what this common issue is, as the digital humanities can concern at the same time reflection on digital technology, the use of digital tools, the role of digital technology for the "humanities" and generally speaking any articulation between the terms humanities and digital technology. In particular, the French digital humanities are marked by a strong heterogeneity in terms of the disciplinary field and therefore epistemic culture, as they integrate, according to the French-speaking manifesto of the digital humanities "*l'ensemble des Sciences humaines et sociales, des Arts et des Lettres*" (the human and social sciences, arts and humanities together)[2]. This means that they consider that we can bring under one umbrella term:

– on the one hand, the humanities in the English-speaking world, i.e. disciplines that access reality through books and archives, or whose very object of research is precisely one of these media (such as media studies) and which are therefore particularly interested in these objects' changes with digital technology;

– on the other hand, the human and especially social sciences, whose mode of access to reality, qualitative or quantitative, is mainly the direct observation of the event, and not its trace.

Concretely, they mobilize a set of historically constituted disciplines that can be divided according to their mode of access with reality, with, on the one hand, disciplines centered on the study of texts and archives, and, on the other hand, those based on field research (Table 2.1). These families of disciplines are distinguished by the level of mediation and thus of formalization of their relationship with reality: in *corpus-based disciplines*, reality is always already mediated by a medium that brings its own grammar, form and format, and thus always already constitutes a transformation of the object studied. These disciplines are strongly anchored in the evidential paradigm. One never studies the historical event, but a material copy of a text, which is itself a trace of the event. This format prescribes possible uses and manipulations within a reading and interpretive culture. In the

2 See http://tcp.hypotheses.org/318 [accessed November 20, 2016].

field-based disciplines, on the contrary, reality must be seized, captured and translated with regard to a material constituted *ad hoc* for analysis and interpretation. For ethnography, the observation of the phenomenon must be formulated, recorded and presented as grammar by the researcher to constitute its meaning, either by taking notes during the observation, or by conducting the interview that leads the witness to a verbal and linguistic formulation of his experience of the phenomenon (which may moreover be precisely the phenomenon being studied itself). In quantitative methods, perhaps less linguistic and more formalized, the researcher must again produce their observables, governed by statistical norms. While there are several standardized observation, interview and survey techniques, they do not allow for the mechanization of the translation of observations, which is always a matter for each researcher's own know-how. Thus, in field-based disciplines, the researcher must always *construct* the data there, whereas in corpus-based disciplines they must be *found* and delimited.

Corpus	**Field**
History Arts Language and literature Law Information and communication sciences	Sociology Economy Geography Demographics Psychology Anthropology

Table 2.1. *Some examples of disciplines classified according to their mode of access to reality*

The dividing line we are drawing here, and the realities on both sides, are more blurred and complex than what we have outlined, and of course there are many exceptions. Within the human and social sciences, for example, the field of cognitive sciences covers both entirely naturalized practices, permeated by the imperialism of the natural sciences, such as experimental psychology, and fields of intellectual reflection such as psychoanalysis, which are much more closely related, from an epistemological point of view, to the critical work of the humanities than to the search for objectivity in the social sciences. This distinction, nevertheless, reveals a heterogeneity within the cultural sciences that refers both to distinct modes of access to reality and to specific relationships with the instrumentation of the disciplines, and in particular, as we shall see, to the instrumentation of digital technology.

According to this mode of access to reality, the advent of digital technology is indeed taking place in different ways, either by transforming the traditional observables of the disciplines, or, on the contrary, by providing them with new observables, or at least new media for the observation of phenomena. From this point of view, the French language digital humanities are silent on the complexity of the transformations of the cultural sciences through digital technology, and do not specify which part or all of these transformations are targeted by them.

The English language roots of the digital humanities are less ambiguous: they are often digitization projects with digital philology issues. The founding example is Roberto Busa's *Corpus Thomisticum* (digitization of Thomas Aquinas' texts) and one of the most vivid examples is the TEI (text encoding initiative) project, which aims to promote a format for digital documents that integrates the problematic aspects of text production. Digital humanities in the English language sense are thus resolutely corpus-based disciplines and work on a relationship with the text that is all the more crucial as it is their mode of access in the real world.

This question of disciplinary scope is crucial as it touches upon a major dividing line within the cultural sciences. Indeed, field-based disciplines adhere quite widely to the idea of a certain naturalization of their object, from which the construction of certain objectivity becomes possible. As we have seen, Durkheimian sociology posits social facts as things and is not anti-naturalist. Without necessarily denying the singularity of their object, and in particular the intrinsic reflexivity that characterizes it and which we mentioned in the previous chapter, the field-based disciplines consider their practice as scientific (in the sense of the natural sciences), and endeavor to evaluate the work through the prism of the requirements of rationality and validity criteria specific to their discipline. This gives rise to a material and conceptual structure that makes it possible to create observables, to measure phenomena, in short to build a coherent and valid access to reality from which hypotheses can be explored and validated. From this point of view, the positioning of field-based disciplines is, as we saw in the previous chapter, an epistemological bifurcationism that refuses to reduce the cultural sciences to the natural sciences (and particularly to physics) but nevertheless intends to propose itself as a science that combines a certain naturalization of its objects with a critical and reflexive distance.

Conversely, the position claimed by the English-language humanities, a good number of critical studies, and works of postmodernist obedience reject any scientific imperialism (Dupré 2002) coming from the natural sciences and present themselves as an intellectual investigation autonomous from them. Their ambition is by no means to construct a mathematical or computational objectivity, to derive laws or quasi-laws, but to account for the singularity of the objects they give themselves. As a result, they are often part of an epistemology where the pluralism of possible interpretations of a text is part of their discipline's data.

Field-based disciplines and corpus-based disciplines articulate different modes of access to reality, distinctly transformed by digital technology. The resulting epistemologies should also be examined separately, although parallels can be drawn. In order to highlight their specific relationship with digital technology, only outlined so far, we will now examine in more detail the mode of access to reality brought about by digital technology as conceptualized by these two families of disciplines: on the side of the field-based disciplines, we examine what Richard Rogers (2008) has called "virtual methods", i.e. the transposition of traditional qualitative and quantitative survey methods, and on the side of the corpus-based disciplines, several efforts to conceptualize the web as a corpus or corpus source.

2.3. Virtual methods, a reconstruction of access to the field

In the field-based disciplines, it is the web that has been considered relevant over the last 20 years or so for measuring social phenomena and opinion movements through quantitative surveys; for these, it constitutes an additional mode of access to reality, in addition to, or even replacing, more traditional channels. The so-called "electronic" survey has become dominant[3] in quantitative methods of collecting opinions because of its almost immediate nature, the manipulations it allows and its economic interest (it costs much less to produce than its alternatives). The digital medium is used in two ways:

3 Three-quarters of quantitative surveys in polling organizations were conducted via the Internet in 2015 [Online]. Investigation, Syntec Etudes. Available at: http://www.syntec-etudes.com/fichiers/20170320182258_Marche_francais_des_Etudes_2015.pdf [accessed November 30, 2017].

– various channels accessible via the Internet, such as e-mail or social networks, can be used to recruit respondents;

– the web itself serves as a medium for the questionnaire itself.

Online surveys do not develop new methods or a new epistemology: they are virtual methods (Rogers 2009) that transpose existing practices. They are not based on an epistemology of the trace but on a nomothetic approach to social phenomena, naturalized by quantification. The survey is based on an epistemology of representativeness that can be found regardless of the collection method: telephone, face-to-face and now online.

With the introduction of online surveys, field-based disciplines need to show that there is continuity with the collection methods, and that the norm of representativeness is preserved. Practitioners must therefore be able to demonstrate the ability of a sample of individuals to exhibit the same characteristics as the population from which it is sampled. Nevertheless, sampling as a criterion of data validity is subject to a certain number of biases linked to its very principle, depending or not on the way the questionnaire is administered. Thus, on the one hand, the standard of field-based disciplines is not always respected and, on the other hand, the introduction of the online survey implies ensuring that it has at least the same biases. These biases, which are well known to quantitative methods in the social sciences, reduce the representativeness of the data, and thus undermine their epistemic value upstream of the analysis that is made of them. They can be grouped into three types:

– *biases relating to the sampling method*: in the absence of a complete database of the French population (in the case of a survey targeting the French market), it is not possible to randomly select a sample from the total population. The quota method, widely used by polling institutes, introduces biases according to methodological orthodoxy. In theory, only a random sample can be considered representative; in practice, truly statistically random samples are difficult, if not impossible, to construct. As a result, the quota method is a very widely used and generally regarded as a second-best solution, even sufficient; it is in fact considered more reliable than the non-representative samples used by social scientists due to the lack of access to quota panels of individuals such as those available to polling firms;

– *non-response rate bias*: the non-response rate describes the proportion of individuals who, when asked to complete the questionnaire, did not do so.

The reasons for this choice can be various (the person feels that they have nothing to say; they have a physical or mental disability that prevents them from accessing the questionnaire or responding; they are opposed to the principle of the survey generally; they are dissatisfied with the company's performance and do not wish to share information; etc.), but the population of respondents and non-respondents differs in a number of ways. The reasons for non-response may in fact be precisely the type of information that the company is trying to identify. In addition, open-ended questions are sometimes optional in the questionnaires, which further increases the non-response rate to these questions;

– *biases due to the questionnaire's administration method*: the respondents' characteristics and the content of their answers vary according to the questionnaire's administration method. The academic literature on this subject (a little dated because it often predates the development of the web, or is contemporary with the penetration of computers in Western homes) is more concerned with demonstrating the differences between collection methods than the superiority of one over the other. Thus, the advantages and disadvantages of the different channels are also well known:

- *face-to-face interviews* are particularly costly, especially when the survey is carried out at several different times and places, or when it takes place indoors and not in the street (an uncomfortable situation for the respondent, especially for more sensitive topics). The physical co-presence allows richness in the exchange, not only verbal in nature; however, this richness is lost in the transcription from oral to written material, which transforms the respondents' words. The interviewer has a better perception of the respondents and their responses than the analyst, due to data that disappear in the formal mode of the questionnaire: hesitations, explanations, reformulations, non-verbal communication, etc. (Lallich-Boidin 2001). Moreover, the field surveys show a notable discrepancy between the methodological orthodoxy expected from the administration of the questionnaires (both face-to-face and by telephone) and real practices; the re-formulation of questions and the constitution of a personalized relationship are all elements that theoretically destroy the scientificity of quantitative methods, but which can in fact produce it by leading the respondent to propose meaningful answers. Moreover, the face-to-face method is known to create social desirability; in other words, a tendency in the respondent to give answers that give a good image of themselves, or more in line with what they believe to be the social norm (Frippiat and

Marquis 2010). Finally, surveys conducted in institutes are most often carried out by interviewers in precarious situations, who often work for the institute and are not paid, and whose time constraints reduce the quality of the questionnaire's administration, to the point of inventing the answers (Marc 2001; Caveng 2012);

- the *telephone* theoretically allows the use of the only sampling method considered to be truly valid, namely random selection, which is done in terms of telephone numbers. It has, to some extent, the same advantages and disadvantages as the face-to-face method in terms of orality, but the absence of physical co-presence reduces the personalization effects of the exchange and its consequences; the relative anonymity of the telephone could thus reduce social desirability. Nevertheless, the non-response rate, which is constantly increasing, biases the sampling, on a population that is less and less representative, notably due to the decline in home telephone use, with mobile use posing other problems (Witte 2009);

- the *Internet* is particularly ambivalent in terms of the populations it reaches. Although households are not fully served, with 65% in 2009 in the EU-28 (Frippiat and Marquis 2010), the rate continues to rise (it reached 85% in 2016 in France)[4] and this medium makes it possible to reach previously inaccessible populations: people who are reluctant to talk on the phone but also groups of individuals united by a common theme or shared characteristics. Internet users are not evenly distributed sociologically, but contrary to intuition, older populations, not young people, may be overrepresented (Loosveldt and Sonck 2008). However, the most striking feature of this collection method is the self-selection bias, due to the fact that the questionnaires are widely distributed (by e-mail, on social networks) to panels where respondents choose whether to register and then to answer, presumably according to their interest or their ethical or political involvement in the issue. On the other hand, the Internet enables a better control of the collection itself, with the tools for measuring and analyzing behaviors specific to the web. Finally, it should be noted that the concept of Internet surveys shields a complex network of collection modalities (Figure 2.1) that generate varying levels of representativeness.

4 According to the digital barometer of the Arcep 2016 [Online]. Available at: http://www.arcep.fr/uploads/tx_gspublication/presentation-barometre-du-numerique-291116.pdf [accessed April 14, 2017].

Divided between its advantages and disadvantages, in the end the Internet is nothing more than "technical potentialities that increase the researcher's control over certain aspects and reduce it on others" (Frippiat and Marquis 2010).

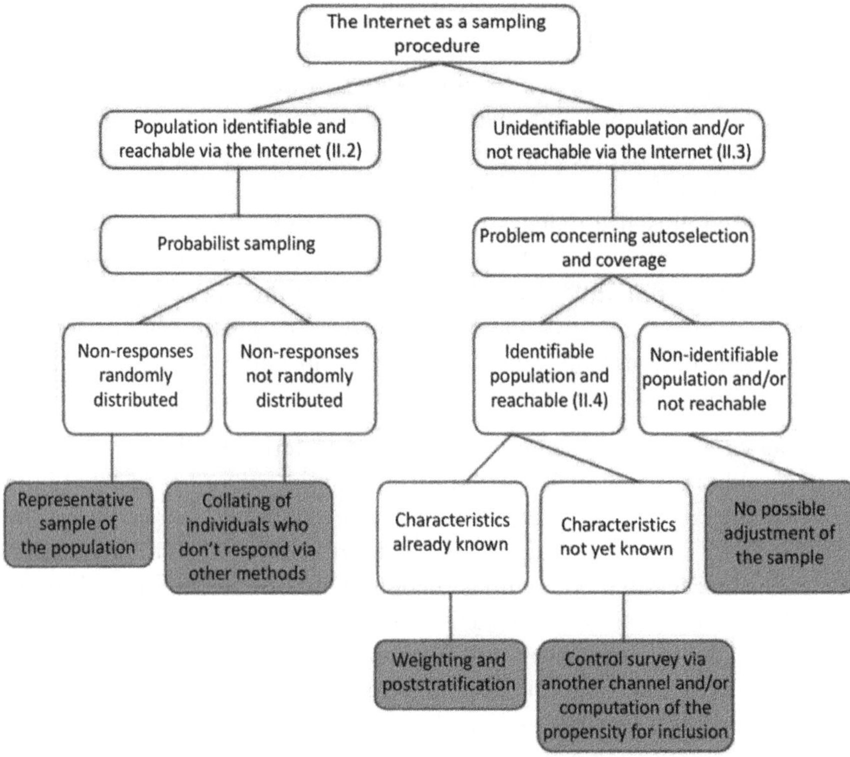

Figure 2.1. *Different sampling modalities in online surveys (source: Frippiat and Marquis 2009)*

Internet data collection remobilizes the written medium, as in postal surveys that have more or less fallen into disuse, and thus constitutes a breach with the previous innovation in survey history, the telephone: the history of data collection methods is not linear. However, the fact that these methods are commensurable does not mean that they are equivalent. As we have seen, each of them has their own specific biases. The development of Internet opinion research has also given rise to a fairly rich and recent literature on survey methodology in general. The emergence of a new channel of inquiry allows us to look back on previous modes with a new perspective. Rather than opposing the new mode to the traditional modes, this comparative mobilization makes it possible to integrate the Internet into the channels for collecting opinions and to ensure methodological continuity with existing ones. Comparison is possible horizontally (to identify the specificities of each mode, rather than comparing with a reference mode) precisely because there is no reference mode against which the others would be evaluated. While there is methodological orthodoxy in theory, none of the modes actually applies it in practice. The possibility of effectively random sampling via random digit dialing (RDD) may have given a certain prestige to the telephone survey, which was used as a reference in a comparison with an online survey conducted in 2004 (Schonlau *et al.* 2004). In this study, data collected online were adjusted using the results of the telephone survey, making it a *de facto* baseline measure. However, the same could be said of face-to-face meetings, which have also served as an element of comparison with the Internet (Loosveldt and Sonck 2008).

Other comparisons are possible. Their advantage is that they allow pollsters to explain the elements on which the comparison is made and to define methodological invariants and modular parts. One of these invariants is the object itself: comparing two methods in terms of their ability to measure the same phenomenon is an implicit assumption of the identity of the object measured by these different methods. From a statistical point of view, the samples formed can be compared numerically, either among themselves or in relation to a reference population (if available). The challenge is then to neutralize the biases linked to the mode of collection by a form of computation that makes commensuration effective. In practice, an example is the propensity score (Schonlau *et al.* 2004), which compares a first sample to a reference sample; the purpose of this comparison is to weight *a posteriori* the first sample. In the study in question, the reference sample was obtained by RDD and then resampled with quotas for ethnic origin (this is a U.S. study, which legally allows this type of variable to be included in a questionnaire), age, poverty level, etc. In order to carry out the commensuration, it is necessary that both surveys have common questions, constituting the same measurement; according to the answers given to these questions, each individual is provided with a new variable, obtained by computation, which allows the first sample to be adjusted with the reference sample. We are therefore in a mode of comparison that only indirectly uses the reference population and its known characteristics. The assumed representativeness of the reference sample, of which we have a probabilistic knowledge, serves as an proxy in the construction of the sample's statistical representativeness where it is not known. Simplifying the process a little, it can be said that it corresponds to the following reasoning:

– the reference sample is representative of the general population (starting assumption);

– the reference sample is characterized by a set of quantified properties E;

– the new sample is characterized by a set of numerical properties F;

– the difference between E and F is computed and then neutralized by computing weighting scores to be applied to F so that the two samples have the same properties;

– then the new sample is representative of the population.

This reasoning is not an inference in the sense of from the general to the particular, or in the terms of classical statistics, from the population to the sample; it is an inference from one individual who is instituted as a representative of the general to another individual who is sought to invest in the same representative properties.

For some researchers, doing without an inferential relationship with the general population is not acceptable in theoretical terms; in practice, access to this population may be difficult or impossible. Rarely is there a general, unbiased register of individuals. In France, INSEE figures are often referred to, but their relationship with the general population is also a construction, widely analyzed in the sociology of quantification following Desrosières' (2010) work on national referencing. The reference population, which is not the general population, is a convention against which surveys can situate themselves and compare with each other. The interest of the reference population is that its characteristics are more easily known through numerical measurements that serve as a norm for the constituted samples, and from which these samples can be adjusted. The need to know the characteristics of the reference population is not a necessity for all researchers: on the one hand, Frippiat and Marquis (2010) assert that operating without a reference population "should therefore mean that we condemn ourselves to abandoning any desire for representativeness" while Witte and Howard (1999), quoted by Couper (2000), write:

> "while the survey did not yield a random sample and the selection probabilities are unknown, 'this does not mean that the survey cannot yield representative social science data'."

This last quotation highlights an important point: while knowledge of the reference population is desirable *a priori*, it is not always possible.

Moreover, this knowledge is not binary: some information about the general population may be available, but not all of it. Using this information, it is possible to adjust the sample based on the comparison between the general population and this reference population (and not a reference sample as discussed above). However, adjustment techniques of varying degrees of sophistication are also subject to criticism, particularly in the context of Internet surveys: while it is possible to adjust proportions (based on the principle of quotas) according to responses or other variables, this does not mean that the sample will be more representative or more comparable with the general population (Loosveldt and Sonck 2008). Moreover, the differences between the different collection methods are not only measured in terms of statistical representativeness to the general population; the interviewers are also concerned about the quality of the responses and the propensity of Internet users to answer the questionnaire "well", i.e. without exaggerating or mitigating their answers (Frippiat and Marquis 2010).

The question of representativeness remains at the heart of pollsters' epistemological problems. It reflects a conception of social phenomena that has two interesting characteristics:

– on the one hand, the survey is a statistical representation of reality based on numbers and approximation. The individual exists only as part of a whole in which he or she embodies certain characteristics; we are therefore searching for general laws (or quasi-laws) rather than seeking to characterize what makes an individual specific and unique. On the other hand, while the approach is somewhat nomothetic, analysis of variance and other statistical approaches to the study of deviations from the norm highlight the specificities of a subpopulation in relation to the norm, in a more idiographic approach;

– on the other hand, while this representation is statistical, it is nonetheless conceived as a correspondence to reality, with which it shares some but not all of the features, with the problem of determining whether these features are sufficient to address the research question at hand. Thus, the pollster may well know that their sample is not homogeneous to the general population in terms of age or gender, but nevertheless use it knowingly, insofar as he/she is studying a phenomenon on which he/she also knows that these parameters have no impact.

Quantitative methods in sociology inherit at least in part their knowledge theory from the mathematical techniques they mobilize: the conception of truth as a statistical correspondence is not linked to the object or the disciplinary field but to the way of understanding it technically. It is at work here in the same way as it can be in other fields of use closer to the natural sciences, notably in biostatistics (which is, moreover, the field of invention of the propensity score). We would thus have a transdisciplinary epistemology organized around the concepts of the individual and population, which are in fact common to biology and quantitative sociology. Statistics would not play a purely instrumental role, where it would only be a technique in the service of science, but would in itself constitute a way of forming knowledge, both from an operational and theoretical point of view.

However, although the web is a new way of measuring social phenomena, its specificities are mobilized only in a very superficial way, in order to ensure continuity with existing practices. As such, it appears both as a practical opportunity (it costs less, allows for better control of collection methods) and as a response to the erosion of the representativeness of surveys, whose response rate has been steadily declining since Gallup. In this context, however, it is only a medium, not a source. Online surveys do not produce digital footprints but data about individuals via the web.

However, these virtual methods present a certain number of lessons for the conceptualization of digital footprints, notably in terms of the construction of an epistemological continuity with previous methods. Indeed, we can see that there is a certain amount of work dedicated to the evaluation of this continuity between collection modes, and to the development of criteria for comparison. For example, the change of medium (written versus oral) is not overcome by demonstrating the commensurability of the written and the oral method, but by comparing the results produced by one and the other, respectively. Virtual methods have equipped themselves with tools such as the propensity score to compare the representations of reality produced by the different collection method: this comparison is made *a posteriori*, on empirical examples, rather than by discussing the respective principles of the different approaches. Representativeness is the criterion against which these representations are assessed: how the sample is produced is secondary to its correspondence to the norms. In other words, it can be said that it is the justification of the representation's validity that allows for epistemological continuity and the inclusion of this representation in the discipline's norms. Overall, this can be considered a confirmationist epistemology where a result is strengthened if it is consistent with previous results.

Moreover, the relationship with the methodological norm is not entirely strict: the imperfections of the different collection methods are known and accepted. It is therefore not expected of a collection method that it removes all forms of bias, although a decrease in bias is of course considered an improvement. Since compliance with the norm is never perfect, the solution is to document deviations so that they are known and taken into account in subsequent analyses.

By comparing the web to other collection methods, the field-based disciplines achieve their "digital conversion" (Doueihi 2008) in a conservative manner, preserving their norms and ways of representing reality. To our knowledge, the advent of big data has not led to a massive appropriation of digital footprints by field-based disciplines, for which the non-representativeness of traces is an intolerable obstacle. The attachment to norms is moreover seen by some sociologists as a danger to their discipline, which would be seen "driven out from its jurisdiction" by online platform publishers. Ten years ago, Savage and Burrows (2007) already anticipated the risk of such a retreat into methodological orthodoxy:

> "We can emphasize our superior reflexivity, theoretical sophistication, or critical edge. Fair enough – up to a point. Yet the danger is that this response involves taking refuge in the reassurance of our own internal world, our own assumed abilities to be more 'sophisticated', and thereby we chose to ignore the huge swathes of 'social data' that now proliferate".

By refusing to appropriate the "social data" or digital footprints, the field-based disciplines carry out their digital transformation with a certain technical ease, but without epistemological revolution. As we shall now see, this transformation is taking place in a very different way in corpus-based disciplines, whose medium has been reinvented by digital technology, and is leading to a rethinking not only of the tools, but above all of access to reality through new observables and new methods for approaching them.

2.4. The challenges of the technical revolution of the text

The challenges brought about by digital technology are indeed quite different for corpus-based disciplines. In addition to the epistemological revolution it introduces, digital technology also constitutes a more significant technical obstacle in these disciplines, because of the relationship they have with technology. This difference in relationship is not unlike those of Snow's "two cultures" (1959), that of the humanities, on the one hand, and that of science and technology, on the other hand, although the dividing line between corpus- and field-based disciplines does not quite coincide with this distinction. As we have seen, the field-based disciplines are rather of bifurcationist obedience and therefore cannot be assimilated to science and technology. This dividing line, however, refers to the different relationship between technology and the digital world within the cultural sciences. The field-based disciplines have largely equipped themselves with tools that produce results of a quantitative nature, and have gradually achieved their "digital conversion" in a manner comparable to the natural sciences. For these cultural sciences, which are already mathematized, digital technology appears as a means of multiplying possibilities, automating repetitive tasks, producing new observables, in short, a field to be conquered in order to extend the field of possibilities for knowledge production. There is no epistemological revolution due to the technical instrumentation of these quantitative cultural sciences.

Conversely, corpus-based disciplines see their fundamental objects transformed by digital technology: with the digitization of archives, the document as a form is torn from its analog support to enter a digital format that still makes it already manipulable and computational, while its material support (the hard disk) is separated from its consultation support (the screen) (Bachimont 2010b). The researcher no longer has access to the document itself, but to its representation, which must, in order to play its role properly, faithfully present the determining characteristics of its object. Just as the written word cannot be conceived as a pure transcription of the spoken word, the digital document is not a reproduction of the book or the archive.

As Christian Vandendorpe (1999) has clearly shown, the text is not pure content: it also possesses semiotics, which have undergone their own transformations, and whose current form is a form of sedimentation or palimpsest. This semiotics integrates orthographic and typographical norms, as well as conventions of cross-referencing, indexing, and arrangement in lines, paragraphs, and numbered pages: everything that may appear to be given in the printed book is in reality the result of a slow detachment from orality and then from handwriting, which is not without impact on the content itself. The advent of a graphic form allows for a variety of layouts (columns, boxes, etc.) and formatting (bold, italics, typography, etc.). It introduces the new possible forms of writing dear to Jack Goody (1979): the list, the table and the formula, to which Bruno Bachimont (2010b) proposes to add the diagram. All of these changes play a role in the perceptual experience of reading, its comprehension, memorization and even appropriation: every printed book makes it possible to underline a passage, but the size of the margins affects the propensity and ease of writing comments and reading notes. In the same way, the advent of digital technology (and especially hypertext, which allows you to refer to and navigate through the text) is transforming the format (or media) of text, with consequences for its content: the text thread is delinearized into sequences, zones, in fragments; its closure and autonomy are given back to question; its display form is variable depending on the display device (computer, screen, resolution, etc.); the text is also displayed in a different format (e.g., a different type of text, a different type of image, etc.); the text can propose or require interventions from the reader, and become interactive; the textual form is no longer necessarily dominant and the illustration of the printed book is complemented by sound, video, a program, etc.; new non-textual or partially textual narrative forms such as video games become possible.

These few examples of changes in text in the digital world, which predate the advent of big data by a few decades, materialize for the researcher in two ways: the digitization of corpora transforms printed text into digital text, posing the need to determine what needs to be preserved in order for the digital text to be said to be a viable representation of the original text; new textual forms are presented to the researcher, and also challenge the norms and modalities of text in general.

The ontology of the source is thus being reinvented for a population of researchers marked by their spirit of finesse, their attention to nuances and details, and for whom such changes are therefore not without consequence.

The advent of digital technology for the humanities is a specific place of relation to technology, a place where technology not only plays the role of determining and conditioning the material possibility of activity, but is at the heart of the modalities of configuration of the activity itself.

Faced with this major challenge, many players in corpus-based disciplines see technology and digital technology more as a risk, a problem, or at least a subject for discussion, than as a space for tools and experimentation. It is in these contexts that we find the most resolutely technophobic positions. Some of these players embody Snow's humanistic, non-technical culture quite emblematically. To put it prosaically, anyone who has witnessed a conversation between a person with a purely literary background and a computer engineer is aware of a certain form of incommunicability between the fields of literature and technology. Very concretely, many eminent researchers in these fields are disoriented by the basic tools of the digital world, those that are not specific to the research activity: doing a search on the Internet, sending an e-mail and using a word processing tool are not necessarily self-evident and have been painfully adopted. This difficulty undoubtedly has explanations: training, temperament, apprehension, etc., which it is not for us to formulate here. However, it should be noted that it can be coupled with mistrust, with forms of technophobia according to which the mobilization of technology is always done in a way that is already problematic, in a tradition that is already longstanding and which is marked by authors such as Heidegger, Anders, Illich, or Ellul in France. These theoretical reservations about digital technology, coupled with a lack of practical skills in manipulating the object, are emblematic of the literary culture at work in the digital humanities, and of its difficulties in thinking of itself otherwise than as a project of reflection on, and not with, the digital technology. The men and women from humanities backgrounds involved in this project are thus poorly equipped to face the major ontological and epistemological challenge for their field of work: to rethink what supports their access to reality, namely the archive and the document, in the light of digital technology. However, there are several ways to facilitate this transition.

One way of preparing for this revolution in accessing reality is to modernize knowledge organization technologies, which we have seen that the big data themselves are part of. As such, the digital humanities are not always presented as a major theoretical project for the digital conversion of the humanities, but also as a more practical ambition to transform the tools for the preservation, processing and communication of knowledge. In France, platforms such as OpenEdition, Huma-Num, Cairn.info, Gallica and others are all used to publish, disseminate, share and consult knowledge for researchers. With the exception of certain aspects of Huma-Num, however, these are not tools for knowledge production, which is also reflected in the more dominant presence of other types of players than researchers. The new modes of collaboration and dissemination that these tools induce represent important changes from the point of view of the sociology of science, in terms of the organization and functioning of research practices, but are of little consequence from an epistemological point of view. Still with the exception of a few singular individuals who were able to summarize Snow's "two cultures", the figures of these platforms are more engineers (research or not), computer scientists and information-documentation or communication professionals (even marketing). Their problems are not so much about the production of knowledge as about its preservation, availability and circulation.

In this respect, a quantitative study conducted in 2015 (Schmitt 2015) highlighted the importance of archive and library issues in the research work actually published and claiming the digital humanities label (see Figures 2.2 and 2.3). It reveals that even in an academic context, the digital humanities are not perceived as a revolution in the production of knowledge in the social sciences, and do not correspond to the computational cultural sciences that we have previously conceptualized: they are, once again, part of the infrastructure of research rather than its practice. The gap between the ambitions and the reality of academic practice in the digital humanities is particularly marked in the French-speaking digital humanities, which are very much focused on examining the transformations in the world of publishing and information-documentation. Conversely, the English-speaking digital humanities are interested in natively digital computational techniques such as knowledge engineering, language processing and geographic information systems, which make it possible to develop new knowledge production tools. The English-speaking side thus appears to be more advanced in its reflection on humanities tools, with, it seems, the bias of experimenting with and on existing computational tools, even if in a somewhat unstructured and opportunistic manner, rather than problematizing them *a priori* without actually using them.

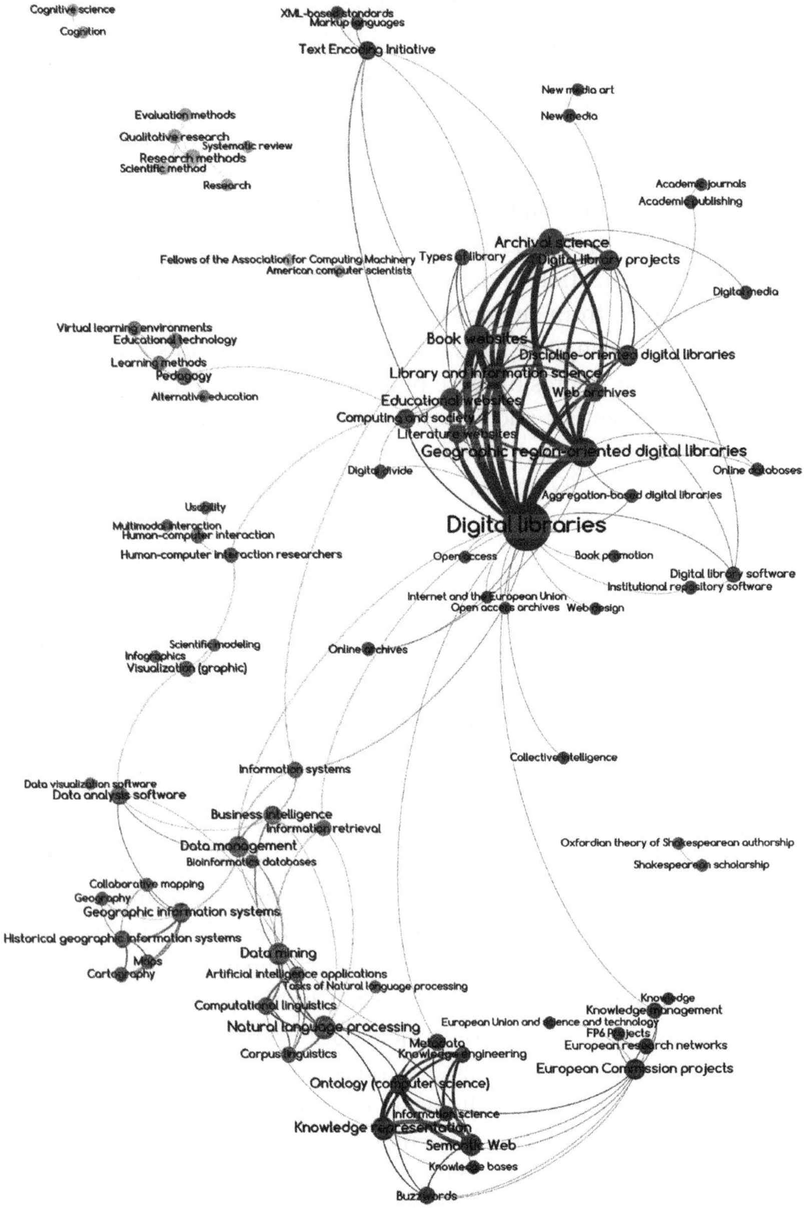

Figure 2.2. *Thematic mapping of the English-speaking digital humanities, according to Schmitt (2015). For a color version of this figure, see www.iste.co.uk/schmitt/data.zip*

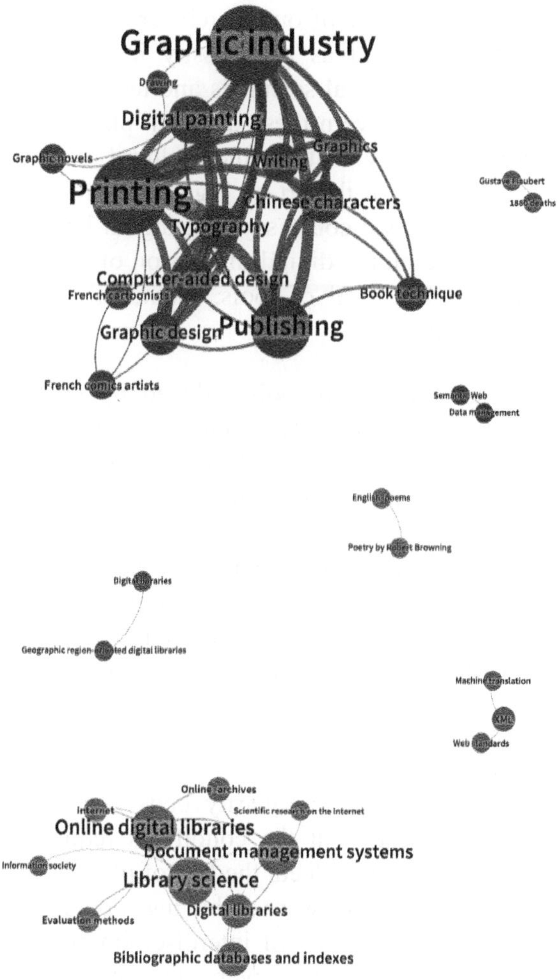

Figure 2.3. *Thematic mapping of French-speaking digital humanities, according to Schmitt (2015). For a color version of this figure, see www.iste.co.uk/schmitt/data.zip*

Another way of integrating "new" digital tools into the knowledge production of corpus-based disciplines is to rely on a division of labor that brings together cultural researchers and computer scientists. Indeed, the digital humanities have a recurrent ambition of promoting interdisciplinarity between the human and social sciences, but also and perhaps above all with computer science: interest in digital tools would unite the human and social sciences with a common issue, and would lead to an encounter with computer science. From the point of view of our search for epistemic continuity, this interdisciplinarity has emerged as a necessity in order to overcome the division of labor between cultural scientists and technical profiles, so that a common epistemology can govern these different players' activities. On the first point, interdisciplinarity within the cultural sciences, Dacos and Mounier write in their state of the art on digital humanities (2014): "At the highest level of generality, we could say that digital humanities refer to an interdisciplinary dialogue on the digital dimension of research in the human and social sciences, at the level of tools, methods, objects of study and modes of communication".

The reflection on objects and tools induced by the advent of digital technology could thus be conducted jointly by the various disciplines mobilized in the cultural sciences, united by the same challenge of thinking about its relationship with technology and digital technology. Nevertheless, the possibility of a common reflection is called into question by the tension we have highlighted between corpus and field-based disciplines, and the respective relationships they have with technology: there are differences in epistemic culture between a historian and an economist that the best intentions in the world can hardly hope to bridge. This first point therefore seems unconvincing to us and at least limited by the two cultures of the humanities and social sciences.

On the second point (interdisciplinarity between cultural sciences and computer science), it appears that the conditions required to give rise to interdisciplinarity rarely occur. Indeed, the fact of placing an order for a web application, buying a piece of software or having it developed by a research engineer does not create a situation of interdisciplinarity but a hierarchical relationship between two types of players, the suppliers and the buyers. Although design research in recent years has regularly stressed the importance of collaboration and co-creation principles for the successful design of digital tools, this collaborative configuration does not correspond to a scientific dialogue between disciplines. In order for such a dialogue to take place, it is necessary for IT to be convened as a scientific discipline. Yet, "artifactmanship" (Bachimont 1996) or "interactive artifactmanship" (Lassègue 1996) refer to a broad field that ranges from theoretical research on information to multiple fields of application, including computer science as a sector of economic activity. Developing a web application does not involve computer researchers but engineers and developers who use tools and methods originally based on the principles highlighted by computer research: between these two activities, there is a distance that can be compared to the one that exists between establishing the principles of classical thermodynamics in the 19th Century and installing a radiator in a university. In the digital humanities, computer science is generally not called upon as a scientific discipline, but is instrumented as a technique at the service of knowledge production: moreover, few teams bring together researchers from both disciplinary fields. However, as Bénel (2013) points out in an article on interdisciplinarity in the digital humanities, "there is no interdisciplinarity without the commitment of researchers from two (or more) disciplines, no successful interdisciplinarity without mutual enrichment".

The mistrust of digital technologies and the difficulties in constructing an interdisciplinary configuration between computer science and cultural sciences largely explain the still rudimentary character of the development of digital humanities. In corpus-based disciplines, the upsurge of digital technology involves a technical revolution coupled with an epistemological revolution that renews both the mode of access to reality and the tools for exploiting the observable, raising challenges far greater than those faced by field-based disciplines.

However, there is one notable exception to this observation, that is linguistics. While the mode of access to the reality of linguistics is resolutely the corpus, its approach is rather naturalistic on the whole and more compatible with the culture of science and technology. There is at least one branch of linguistics that is highly naturalized and hybridized with digital technologies. At the intersection of textual and quantitativist cultures, fields such as computational linguistics, but also stylometry, distant reading in history and textometry, propose to make the text considered as data computable. The particularity of computational linguistics is that it is, like computer science in general, both a field of research in itself and an applied science, or even a technology, that can be mobilized by other disciplines, including literary analysis and history, but also sociology. The theoretical framework of computational analysis is that of the target discipline (and not linguistics), which governs at the same time the logic of constituting the observables, the method and the tools: there is here an epistemic continuity that is both digitally instrumented and compatible with the cultural sciences, whose flaw is that it assumes the existence of pre-existing homogeneous corpora, whose coherence it does not take care of, and therefore cannot be applied as such to digital footprints.

In this way, it makes it possible to revisit historically and culturally attested units, as Roberto Busa did with *Corpus Thomisticus*. Another emblematic example of this rediscovery of familiar objects in the field of literary analysis is the textometric experiment applied to a text by Maupassant reported by Rastier (2001):

> "While it had taken me ten years to understand the importance of the number ten in Maupassant's short story *Toine* (the author, 1989, book. II, chap. V), the test of the reduced score instantly put it in front of me, and even allowed me to take advantage of an occurrence in the first line, which had, I confess, escaped me, although it would have strengthened my point."

In this example, the computational analysis of Maupassant's text makes it possible to reconstitute almost instantaneously knowledge that is already available; one can imagine that the same approach would make it possible to produce new knowledge on a less familiar corpus. The validity of this knowledge rests as much on the result of computation as on François Rastier's ability to give a linguistic and literary meaning to this result. Computational linguistics thus makes it possible to rediscover established corpora, and to reprogram cultural science objects through their digitization and their newly manipulable character.

This textometric approach can be applied in field-based disciplines such as sociology: text statistics for the social sciences, or statistical analysis of textual data (SATD), gives the corpus the role of an intermediary to observe social (and non-textual) facts. The corpus becomes a medium to access the field, summarizing the two families of disciplines that we have distinguished above.

This approach is used in particular to analyze transcripts of qualitative interviews and responses to open-ended questions in opinion polls. Software such as Alceste (Reinert 1990) or Prospéro (Chateauraynaud 2003) mobilize the conceptual framework of quantitative sociology to conceptualize linguistic observables and computational transformation operations of these observables compatible with the discipline's norms. Max Reinert is thus inspired by the French school of statistics developed by Jean-Paul Benzécri and the distributional linguistics of Zellig Harris. There is thus a method of articulation between linguistics, statistics and sociology, which pre-exists the software. Linguistic data are generally derived from answers to open-ended questions: they therefore inherit a quantitative epistemology based on the notion of a representative sample, which makes them compatible with the requirements of quantitative sociology. To exploit them, Reinert and Chateauraynaud develop an instrument theory (the software) that inherits from their epistemic culture. The instrument makes it possible to remove linguistic units and compute linguistic frequencies that have the status of quantitative observations, and which can therefore be analyzed and interpreted according to the logic of quantitative sociology. This analysis is possible, on the one hand, because the data correspond to the discipline's norms, and, on the other hand, because there is an epistemic continuity between these data, the software and the method that includes the use of the software and the interpretation of the results.

Ensuring epistemic continuity also alleviates the problem of instrument theory command by software users. This problem is relatively classical in the philosophy of science (Franklin 1994; Chalmers 2003; Adam 2004; Schindler 2013), with several positions ranging from the need to recognize the theoretical norms that preceded the development of the instrument in order to be able to use it, to the possibility of using it as a black box as long as one knows how to interpret the results it produces. It should also be pointed out that the epistemological debate focuses on the risk of circularity of use to prove an instrument theory built on the basis of this same theory. From our perspective, the question of whether one needs to know, for example, how a microscope works in order to use one naturally does not call for a binary answer. Asserting that only a microscopist could use a microscope, because only a designer would have this complete command of the instrument theory, would be intolerable in terms of the usability of the object. Conversely, the idea that anyone can see something under a microscope is contradicted by experience, as any budding biologist who has handled a microscope that is not adjusted to his or her sample will confirm. The question of whether the instrument's user should master the instrument theory therefore depends on the object, the disciplinary context, the instrument's technological maturity, etc.

In the case of textual statistics software for the social sciences, the instrument is provided with a method of use (presented in a scientific publication, for example) that is derived from the instrument theory without necessarily explaining it; this method is the subject of several publications presenting the general approach, or a use case for the software. The disciplinary continuity between the instrument's designer and its users gives the proposed elements a certain intuitive intelligibility once the technical operations to be carried out have been taken into consideration.

The statistical analysis of textual data thus combines the theoretical and methodological framework of the cultural sciences with the ability to mobilize numerical data and computational processing tools. It is therefore an interesting candidate for the computational cultural sciences program. Indeed, it presents a continuity between the data, the tool, the method and the theoretical framework that corresponds to the criteria we established for this hypothetical discipline. Its shortcoming from the point of view of the computational cultural sciences arises from the nature of the observables that it manipulates: the statistical analysis of textual data remains subject, in terms of the mode of access to the real, to the norms of the various disciplines that mobilize it. The analysis must be done on a representative sample (in quantitative sociology) or a homogeneous corpus (in corpus-based disciplines). It cannot therefore be mobilized as such for the exploitation of digital footprints; neither the corpus nor field-based disciplines have a proposal for the constitution of a standardized set.

This absence of a proposal does not mean that no research work has been carried out to mobilize digital footprints in the cultural sciences. On the other hand, it shows us that there is no existing candidate offering both an epistemology of the digital footprint and consistency with the tools, methods and theoretical framework: for our methodological paradigm, we will need to combine several candidates or components. To this end, we now examine research projects that propose an epistemology of the digital footprint that is not general, as we formulated it in Chapter 1, but applied to a specific, empirically constituted object.

This object will be, again, the example of the web. Through this example, we will see that digital footprints are indeed a human fact that interests these disciplines. Nevertheless, the trace is considered above all as an object in itself, and not as a representational intermediary to access the fact of humanity as a whole. It is only later, in the history of "web sciences", that this now better known object ceases to be simply a "virtual" object and begins to be considered as a way of accessing "reality".

2.5. From the web as an object to the web as a corpus

Web traces have not always been considered as sources for the analysis of sociocultural phenomena in general, whether digital or "analogical". The web can be understood as an object of study in its own right, with its own archiving methods and historiography. It is in itself an abundant object, made of contents, languages, protocols and serving to study itself through its own material positivity. In accordance with the propensity of the English-speaking world to name new fields of research around an object, the study of the web is part of a discipline, web science: "Over the past few years, there has been a growing recognition that the ecosystem that is the Web needs to be treated as an important and coherent area of study – this is Web science" (Shadbolt *et al.* 2013).

The web is a technical device, made of choices that can be studied or modified: web science sees itself both as a field of study of its object and as a field of improvement and modification of it, the web not being fixed from a technical point of view:

> "Physical science is an analytic discipline that aims to find laws that generate or explain observed phenomena; computer science is predominantly (though not exclusively) synthetic, in that formalisms and algorithms are created in order to support particular desired behaviour. Web science has to be a merging of these two paradigms; the Web needs to be studied and understood, and it needs to be engineered." (Berners-Lee *et al.* 2006)

Whether it is the evolution of its formats (major revision of HTML with version 5 in 2014)[5] or major innovations such as Linked Data (O'Hara and Hall 2012), the web is a dynamic object, which can be seen from a synchronic as well as a diachronic point of view. In terms of approaches, numerous representations of the web are possible, mobilizing a kaleidoscope of disciplines. The question of the mathematical or logical structure of the

5 See https://www.w3.org/TR/html5/ [accessed November 16, 2017].

web has mobilized a number of researchers in different fields, with varying degrees of conscientiousness. The work on web topology by Barabási and colleagues (1999, 2013) has had a great deal of influence, particularly on the graph analysis methods and tools applied to web; in contrast, attempts to intuitively define the shape of the web, such as a bow tie, a teapot or a cauliflower (Metaxas 2012), have had less academic and media attention. Beyond the anecdotal, this type of work reflects a proliferation of research areas that are far from forming a coherent whole and in which it is difficult to find one's bearings. In addition to this, the web, like any technical object, is the medium for planned or unplanned uses, and one can be as interested in what it represents culturally and socially as in the refinement of its technical materiality.

From a sociocultural point of view, the originality of the web compared to other technical environments is, as we have seen, that it keeps track of almost everything that happens there. The web is, so to speak, made up of what it leaves behind and which, unlike ancient ruins, seems never to fade. For the cultural scientist, this means that he or she does not need to attend the events that take place there, or to reconstruct them through testimonies, to keep track of them. The web is its own trace, its own archive, which does not mean that its study is devoid of historiographical and philological issues. As Monnin (2012) and Brügger (2012) have pointed out in particular, the default registration is not synonymous with stability: the *Le Monde* home page on one side, or TF1 on the other, an example of content that changes from one hour to the next, is displayed differently depending on the user's hardware and can also be personalized for the user. The digital medium is not degrading like paper, with a gradual loss of the information contained; however, digital formats are evolving and can quickly become obsolete.

Since exhaustive archiving of the web is not feasible, it is necessary to ask the question of the units to be archived and to propose an, at least instrumental, ontology of the web, i.e. to define its objects: page, site, resource, hypertext link, document, content, etc. Even less than in medieval philology is there an "original" document, which could be reconstructed from its variations. The web page is not a document that can be established; the impermanence of its form and content is constitutive. It is debatable whether one can attribute to it an essential existence beyond its various representations. It is indeed a graphic, textual, computational and technical object, which must be reduced to one of these dimensions in order to be archived and studied in a specific format, for example:

– screenshots to study it graphically;

– a full-text index to study it textually;

– a copy of the page's source code or database to study it technically.

All archiving is therefore necessarily partial and determined by methodological decisions, which are themselves formulated with regard to a certain number of foreseeable uses. What we have mentioned at the scale of an object such as the page is found at the scale of the web in general. It is not a question of archiving the entire web, but of developing collection strategies that follow a consistent logic. Targeted collections, such as Fouetillou's (2007) on the European Constitutional Treaty, aim for a "web locality" that is articulated in terms of themes instantiated by search keywords and reference websites. From these referring sites selected by experts in the field according to editorial criteria, the collection is made using snowball sampling, following the hypertext links present in the pages of these sites, so as to delimit a space of pages around these referring sites, whose distance is measured in number of links away from the referring sites. It is a synchronic collection, which constitutes a corpus at a given moment, and is not based on the temporality of the web but on its reticular spatiality and the applications it offers in terms of graph analysis. Conversely, the legal submission of the web proposed by Ina collects pages from a predetermined list of a few thousand sites, but at regular intervals, with a long-term inscription (Mussou 2012). The Internet Archive presents an even different strategy, with an initial ambition more in the order of library or document collection, based on curation; today this ambition has evolved in particular because of its collaborative dimension, by which any visitor to the Internet Archive can put under surveillance a website, which will now be archived at regular intervals. Search engine indexing robots are based on still distinct collection strategies, which combine the previous ones with other specific techniques.

Web archiving in its spatiotemporality is an issue that mobilizes multiple disciplinary cultures within the cultural sciences, such as history, philology and media studies. It is usually done in the service of a specific project, with the idea of studying a particular object through a "web locality". Historically, early initiatives such as the Internet Archive in the 1990s were influenced both by well-known worlds such as the library, but also by an imaginary world of the web, in which it was not just a formless spatiotemporality to be drawn upon, but an object conceptualized and essentialized as a territory. Yet, as Musso (2010) points out: "A territory is not simply a space, but the collective representation of a space-time, a place of history and of "rooted" projects, anchored in a space".

This imagination of the web as an object-territory carries its own richness and has permeated both a number of research areas, but also the way in which the web has been studied to a certain extent. In cybercultural studies (cited by Rogers 2010) and cyberspace studies (Graham 2013), the web is an object in its own right, considered in its entirety, whose materiality is made up of the traces that serve to study it. In these two fields of research, characteristic of the late 1990s, we find each time an imaginary world of spatiality that postulates that the web is a physically or virtually separate space, disconnected from the "true" geographical space (Andrade 2010). The metaphor of the parallel world appears as a way of culturally and linguistically appropriating a new technology. Rey (2012), quoted by Graham (2013), argues that cyberspace was a necessary fiction to overcome the cognitive dissonance caused by the idea of instantaneous, yet remote, communications made possible by an intermediate space. As in the imaginary world of nanotechnology (Loeve 2009), science fiction discourses are a constitutive element of the conceptualization of the object.

The cyberpunk literary genre thus refers to a certain number of works of fiction emblematic of this need to appropriate technology. The expression "cyberspace" was coined in 1984 by the science fiction author William Gibson in his novel *Neuromancer* where he describes it as a:

> "A consensual hallucination experienced daily by billions of legitimate operators, in every nation, by children being taught mathematical concepts... A graphic representation of data abstracted from the banks of every computer in the human system. Unthinkable complexity. Lines of light ranged in the nonspace of the mind, clusters and constellations of data. Like city lights, receding."

Other works imagine virtual spaces, such as the "infosphere", the "datasphere" or even the "matrix", which are all reincarnations of the same ideologically and politically charged imagination. Indeed, behind the "artist's viewpoint" of cyberspace à la Gibson, we find a utopian and libertarian universe emblematically represented by the "declaration of cyberspace's independence" by the poet and activist John Perry Barlow (1996), which presents the web as a new territory, without a master, freer and more just, independent of the sovereignty of States, with its own culture, ethics and civilization.

This imaginary world, artistic and political, goes beyond the framework of academic work on the web, but has had a lasting influence on the way they represent their subject. The question of the virtual is not so much an epistemological question as an ontological one: the virtual characterizes the object itself. Cyberspace is not so much a virtual object as a form of fiction. The idea that there would be a radical separation between the web (or any other device allowing us to be "online") and the "real" world is today contested, and at the very least considered obsolete. Nathan Jurgenson (2012) thus denounces the digital dualism that consists of considering "virtual" and "real" as ontologically separate, as if online social networks and the people who write on them were two distinct realities. He contrasts this dualism with the idea of a digitally augmented reality, taking the example of protest movements such as the Arab revolutions that did not take place separately on the Internet and in Arab countries, but in a reality that included both spaces. The shift from a rather documentary web to a web populated by social interactions has probably facilitated or accelerated the rejection of the digital dualism carried by the imaginary world of cyberspace, as it is difficult to maintain an ontological distinction between online social interactions and social interactions in general.

This evolution of mental representations of the web is now reflected in the way we study the web. While there is still talk of "space" online, it is now in a more abstract sense. Online spaces are no longer virtual, and the social exchanges that take place in online communities are not ontologically different from the social exchanges that sociology has always known; knowing someone on the Internet is a way of knowing someone in general. Historically, this separation presents itself apodictically, as a postulate and not as an explanation: influenced by an imaginary world, nothing justifies it more than from a conceptual point of view. Overcoming this separation makes it possible to consider the web as a representation of culture and paves the way for digital research that sees the web as a trace of something else.

There are several research projects in the cultural sciences that raise the question of the exploitation of the web as a trace of the human fact, including digital methods and cultural analytics. These different fields have in common that they refer to groups of a few dozen researchers, organized in a research structure (respectively the Digital Methods Initiative in Amsterdam and the Software Studies Initiative distributed between New York and La Jolla, California). These structures, which are now about 10 years old, have, in our opinion, worked in two complementary directions: a conceptualization of the web and social networks from the perspective of cultural sciences, and experimentation with "house" tools for collecting and analyzing digital footprints. In both cases, it is not really a question of "founding a school of thought" and imposing norms for the use of the tools: the software is made available as is, with a sometimes laconic contextualization, without having to fit into the conceptualization of the web proposed by these structures. In other words, although these two projects are complementary, they exist relatively independently. It also seems to us that they correspond to two stages of these structures' maturity: first an ambitious phase of theorizing the object, which in both cases did not really succeed, followed by a more pragmatic phase of experimentation aimed at "doing in order to understand" rather than "understanding in order to do".

About 10 years ago, Rogers (2009) proposed, in a prospective rather than retrospective mode, Internet studies that would be diagnostic tools for cultural and social changes, whether they occur online or offline:

> "I would like to put forward a new era in Internet research, which no longer concerns itself with the divide between the real and the virtual. It concerns a shift in the kinds of questions put to the study of the Internet. The Internet is employed as a site of research for far more than just online culture. The issue is no longer how much of society and culture is online, but rather how to diagnose cultural change and societal conditions with the Internet.
>
> [I]n studying the online, we make and ground findings about society and culture with the Internet." (Rogers 2010)

In the same vein, Manovich (2007) inaugurated the term cultural analytics to designate new ways of knowing and understanding cultural phenomena:

> "We feel that the ground has been set to start thinking of culture as data (including media content and people's creative and social activities around this content) that can be mined and visualized. In other words, if data analysis, data mining, and visualization have been adopted by scientists, businesses, and government agencies as a new way to generate knowledge, let us apply the same approach to understanding culture."

These new avenues of research differ from the virtual methods mentioned above: Rogers insists on the natively digital nature of the data and the corresponding methods. There is no methodological continuity with the existing method: the object gives rise to new methods. There is therefore no question of reconstructing a representativeness of the data as in virtual methods: it is illusory to evaluate these new methods against the norms of conventional methods. Methodological norms such as the search for statistical representativeness do not make it possible to appropriate the web's digital footprints. The data sources, but also the tools and concepts to apprehend them, are renewed. Rogers (2008) contrasts the usual sociodemographic categories of the social sciences with the "postdemographic" classes specific to the digital medium, such as declared interests, subscriptions, media libraries and content produced by individuals. These categories, which are better suited to web data analysis, are no longer used to statistically adjust the data as sociodemographic characteristics used to allow, but to bring about new typologies of individuals, and productively offer them content (whether it be music recommendation, content curation or targeted advertising). They are associated with a redistribution of players who are no longer just researchers but also the platforms that collect these categories, and the multitude of users who feed and exploit them.

Another aspect of Richard Rogers' research project is the interest in the *medium*. In his inaugural lecture in 2009, he proposed as a motto to *follow the medium*. Because of the permanent transformations of digital objects, whose conceptualizations are rapidly disintegrating, he suggested that research should not focus on the objects to be studied but on the observables available at the time. In this empirical approach, it is determined *a posteriori* whether these observables are representations of the web itself (in its entirety or its parts) or of broader sociocultural phenomena. The epistemic value of the web data is determined "on actual results", after examination, and not *a priori* when a certain kind of data are chosen in relation to a predetermined research object.

However, this methodological empiricism remains rooted in the epistemic culture of the human and social sciences: it stays critical of sources, methods and tools. Starting from the medium rather than the object leaves room for methodological innovation, for opening up research questions, for an exploratory approach that starts from empirical foundations, but nevertheless returns to critical evaluation. It is also an empiricism that takes culture and society as a horizon, and does not explore data for its own sake, but rather with the idea of finding an epistemic value for them in relation to sociocultural facts; Richard Rogers sums up his approach in a provocative way by proposing to see society in Google search results ("we look at Google results and see society, instead of Google"; Rogers 2013). The web does not have the status of a separate object, which can be studied in its technical and cultural dimensions as such, but a status as a source of observation and study of the human fact as a whole.

This methodological empiricism, as we have seen, remains, however, incompatible with the methodological orthodoxy of the cultural sciences: Richard Rogers does not propose a solution to restore continuity with the paradigm of sampling and representativeness, nor does he propose an archive theory as such. In terms of epistemic culture, it is, notably through the idea of "following the medium", within the continuity of media studies:

> "following the medium is a particular form of medium-specific research. Medium specificity is not only how one subdivides disciplinary commitments in media studies according to the primary objects of study: film, radio, television, etc. It also refers to media's ontological distinctiveness, though the means by which the ontologies are built differ." (Roger 2013)

A medium is, by definition, an intermediate object, which links content and its reader (or viewer). Considering the web as a medium allows us to inscribe it in the disciplinary culture of media studies and to explore the object from the point of view of its materiality, its contents and its culture; this work, however, appears only as an intermediary, prior to an analysis of the way in which the media reality of the Web can be reinterpreted as a reality for the cultural sciences. This intermediary status is also reflected in his work, among which one of the best known is the provision of the Issue Crawler, a software tool allowing researchers to collect web pages without programming knowledge, and following a method that has been widely documented for the academic world. As such, we can consider that the second era or second research project of the Digital Method Initiative reincarnates, with a richer contextualization and more marked bridges toward the cultural sciences, the software supplier role that Microsoft can have and that we have highlighted through *The Fourth Paradigm*. Indeed, initiatives of this kind reflect the idea that it is better to create tools, experiment and then examine the theoretical and scientific consequences of what one has achieved, than to try to denounce or solve theoretical problems upstream, as can be read in a number of writings on the digital humanities. Through these initiatives, we no longer find a radical empiricism as in the mythology of big data, but an empiricism of the order of Claude Bernard's experimental method, which starts from observations and trial-and-error experiments and ultimately leads to more general and more theoretical knowledge.

In contrast to the more abstract conceptualizations at work in the early age of digital methods, or digital humanities, this experimental approach is decisive for the emergence of effective work based on digital footprints. It can be based on the cultural sciences, or in a much more empirical way. Indeed, there is a third way of considering the web, after the object-territory and the representational intermediary: by considering it as an artifactual brick or as a demobilized resource. In this case, it is not a question of modeling a representation of the human fact, but of relying on traces to build a computational artifact. This status occurs more frequently in computer science (whether for researchers or professionals), and consists of viewing the web as a timely source of large amounts of data for tool development. More concretely, the development of software and services based on machine learning requires large amounts of specific data.

For example, in the field of automatic language processing, a task frequently considered is that of determining the tonality (positive, negative, possibly neutral or mixed) of a document. For this, the machine learning approach is based not on the conceptualization of what is positive or negative in a document, but on the massive examination of examples. Thus, in an article entitled "Twitter as a corpus for sentiment analysis and opinion mining", Pak and Paroubek (2010) propose to consider Twitter as a corpus for sentiment analysis. They thus present several automatic classification techniques that are put into competition on the basis of the same data set (a corpus of tweets). The type of conclusion that emerges is not about the general feeling that emerges from Twitter as an object-territory, or the human fact virtually accessible through Twitter, the general mood of society, but about the ability of these different techniques to achieve satisfactory scores, and the interest of using Twitter for this type of comparison.

Article	Citations[6]	Data status
"Twitter as a corpus for sentiment analysis and opinion mining" (Pak and Paroubek 2010)	1,543	Demobilized resource
"What is Twitter, a social network or a news media?" (Kwak *et al.* 2010)	4,619	Object-territory
"Twitter mood predicts the stock market" (Bollen *et al.* 2011)	2,221	Representation

Table 2.2. *Three examples of publications embodying the three possible epistemological statuses of the data coming from Twitter*

The three statuses we have highlighted are conceptually distinct, but they are frequently amalgamated in practice. The same object and the same data source can be considered simultaneously with these three statuses. To illustrate this ambiguity, we note (Table 2.2) three publications in scientific conferences or journals, disseminated in a short time frame (2010–2011) and frequently cited in the literature, that use Twitter as a source of data, with distinct purposes.

In the first article, presented above, Twitter data play the role of resources for constructing an artifact and are not given any particular meaning beyond the practical function of a resource for construction. They represent nothing, they serve. In the second article, Kwak *et al.* examine data from Twitter to identify generalities about how it is used in order to better understand its nature and to determine whether the activities that take place are more informational or communicative in nature. Here, Twitter is its own object; the fact that tweets can be quantitatively processed makes them play a role in proving hypotheses about the object. Finally, in the last article (as in the one already cited, which aimed to predict the revenues of films when they are released in theaters), the object targeted through the analysis of tweets is completely exogenous to Twitter, which serves as its representation.

6 According to Google Scholar [accessed December 29, 2016].

Not only can the same data source have different statuses depending on how it is used, but there are also cases where the data status is ambiguous and multiple. Thus, the work led by Dodds and his colleagues (2015) integrates, like that of Pak and Paroubek, an analysis of a corpus coming from Twitter in order to highlight its tonality, but the conclusions go far beyond a reflection on the use of this type of corpus, and focus on the "positivity" in language. The tweets thus have in turn the status of an artifactual brick and a representational intermediary. In many cases, the presentation of research projects that use web data does not allow a decision to be made on the field covered by the work; there is no clear inscription in one of the articles of association, either in the article or from one section to another. This lack of clarity is not to be taken as an inability on the part of the reader to establish the data status in the planned publications, but rather as a real ambiguity in the content and purpose of this work. While studying the web, we often know what we are analyzing, but not always with a view to what end: the tools give experimental effectiveness to this type of approach, but there is no theoretically or historically anchored interpretative framework that allows us to systematically give status and meaning to the data.

2.6. Conclusion

In analyzing the place given to digital and traces in the cultural sciences, we have established that no research project proposes a complete epistemic continuity between digital footprints, tools and methods and the conceptual framework. We have thus presented several obstacles to this continuity:

– some cultural sciences are proving unable to mobilize digital technology in an operational manner, due to technical, methodological, legal, economic and psychological obstacles, or even cultural ones;

– faced with technical obstacles, many do not manage to collaborate with other players who have the required technical skills;

– others mobilize many digital footprints, but are not natively digital;

– still others mobilize natively digital footprints, but are at the origin of their production rather than considering traces still there from their point of view;

– finally, some do conceptualize digital footprints as an intermediate representation of the human fact, but without completing this conceptualization with explicit tools and methods.

As a result, no proposal from the cultural sciences has both all the required components of the computational cultural sciences and an epistemic continuity between these components: in particular, there is a systematic epistemic breach between the trace and what is done with it.

This breach is perpetrated when one considers a configuration that has been set aside until now, involving mobilizing techniques and methods that are exogenous to the cultural sciences. As we have seen in previous chapters, the big data phenomenon is not exclusive to the cultural sciences, but relates also to computer science and industrial information technology. In their power relationship with the latter, the cultural sciences are not really in a position to put computer science at their service and to make it part of their epistemology. With a few rare exceptions such as the Médialab of Sciences Po, which presents itself as "composed of a small number of academics and a large number of engineers, all of whom are considered publishers (whether of articles, software, or methods)"[7], cultural sciences and computer science do not form an interdisciplinary couple within which the instrumentation would be constructed in harmony with the method and theoretical framework. We must therefore consider that the epistemic breach between the traces and their instrumentation is an inevitable fact that cannot currently be overcome, but can be later, as we shall see from Chapter 4, by means of reconstitution of meaning processes.

The output from the cultural sciences will not be without consequences: the operations, processing and tools will have no rudimentary meaning compared to a pre-established epistemology; they will not benefit from the methodological know-how of the cultural sciences. The alternative to explore is that these computational practices will have given rise to a specific epistemic culture, giving rise to new methods carrying new meanings. Our paradigm would then work to recombine the cultures of cultural sciences and computational practices to articulate them together and build a common epistemology based on a fine understanding of these two cultures. To explore this alternative, we will examine data sciences considered as computational practices born from the multiplication of numerical traces, and more specifically the status of computational instrumentation in these practices.

7 See http://www.medialab.sciences-po.fr/fr/about/ [accessed September 21, 2017].

3

The Status of Computation in Data Sciences

Knowledge based on observation is generally mediated by techniques and tools that make these observations manipulable, intelligible and interpretable. In the natural sciences, observation with the naked eye has given way to instruments that make it possible to see the distant, the tiny and the invisible, while other instruments make it possible to reveal the composition and properties of matter, to test the mechanics of objects or to force signals to manifest themselves. Computation is one of these epistemic techniques, which manipulates not nature itself, but its representation through data in digital format.

In a context of knowledge production, the design and manufacture of instruments are based on theoretical principles that are compatible with this knowledge production: the instruments of mechanics, thermodynamics and chemistry are based on the same laws of nature as the branches of physics to which they relate. While their design also arises from so-called technological research work, their result has the status of an instrument governed by scientific problematics. As in our computational cultural sciences, which we have hypothesized and therorized, the tool is put at the service of the scientific practice, which ensures an epistemic continuity between observation, instrumentation and the theoretical framework. This continuity is a historically and logically constituted norm of articulation between science and technology.

As we will see, data sciences mobilize computation as an epistemic technique, but without articulating it with the natural sciences or cultural sciences. As a result, they occupy an ambiguous position in knowledge production, according to which they could be seen more as data arts than data sciences. Thus, on the one hand, they are crafts based on computation, generating a reduction of what is known to what is computationally manipulable and computable, and, on the other hand, they constitute methodological know-how that gives computation a specific status in relation to its previous mobilizations in the service of science.

To evaluate this specific status of computation in data sciences, and thus determine what computational manipulation does to the digital footprint, we follow several steps: we first examine what computation does to data and knowledge in general, and then more specifically in data sciences. We will thus see that the intention to mobilize computation presupposes a formatting effort which makes the data computable, but immediately imprints constraints and limits on what is accessible through these data. The mobilization of computing itself also generates a determination of what can be known by reducing this space to what is computable or even programmable. Finally, this mobilization is a cognitive activity that requires a certain mindset, a certain way of posing and solving epistemic problems, which must also be counted in the material conditions of possibility of knowledge production from computation.

These conditions of possibility are common to any mobilization of computation. On the other hand, the articulation between science and technology at work in the data sciences is singular compared to computational practices in the natural sciences. The classic relationship between science and computation will thus be presented through the notions of modeling, experimentation and simulation, before highlighting the methodological (and institutional) specificity of data sciences in their relationship with computational techniques: modeling standards are in fact governed by the exploration of the possibilities of computation, which determines the actions to be carried out without prior definition of the targeted knowledge or the understanding of the object to be reached. Data sciences are thus part of a paradigm that is no longer confirmatory but exploratory, which brings computational models back to techniques that can circulate and be mobilized indiscriminately, whatever the epistemic project and the nature of the questions it raises. These techniques are often the same as in the natural sciences, but they occupy a significantly different status.

3.1. Making data computable

As we saw in Chapter 1, the digital footprint has no preestablished meaning that would allow it to be subjected to computational processing without first establishing its status. Moreover, the constitutive gesture that transforms the footprint into data by assigning a theoretical charge is not definitive: it is the first step in the construction of the digital footprint's intelligibility. We will now show that this epistemic gesture is coupled with a technical gesture that makes the footprint manipulable by means of computation and makes it a data item in the strict sense of the word, i.e. a technical object inscribed in a format.

Thus, numerical data are not only the recording of an observation of reality, invested in with an epistemic value that can be rendered effective. It is also an informational object with technical materiality. The constitution of the footprint into data is a technical as well as an epistemological activity. This materiality constitutes the condition of possibility of all and any kind of computational processing: non-digital data cannot be subjected to such processing, and such processing has theoretical and practical limitations. The space of possible knowledge, which can be produced by analyzing these data, is determined by this computer materiality, common to all digital data in the natural sciences, in data sciences or in any other situation mobilizing this type of object.

From this point of view, it is not enough for the data to be loaded with an epistemic value: it must be integrated in a format that makes it manipulable and computable. In the same way that a list or table is not a linear text, computer data must be represented according to certain constraints for its preservation and transmission. JSON and XML are classic computing data transmission formats; the index and database are emblematic storage formats. A dataset is described and modeled: just as the columns of a table have names, the types of values stored are named and their relationships are completed.

Although these problems may seem far removed from the epistemological issues of data analysis, they are the *sine qua non* of this activity: if the format is not valid, if it is damaged, incomprehensible, badly described, the analyst will not be able to perform any processing until they have identified the problem and found a solution to fix it, or obtained the same data but in a valid format. This is a major limitation as many data that could be computationally processed exist in unusable formats: a PDF is a digital file but its contents cannot be manipulated as data. In Tim Berners-Lee's[1] five-level data quality scale, PDF is the first level, followed by Excel, CSV and two semantic web formats: resource description framework (RDF) and linked open data (LOD). This typology of formats is associated with gradual usability: "you get more stars as you make it progressively more powerful, easier for people to use"[2]. In a certain way, data are not data, at least in the sense of manipulable and computable information, as long as they do not materialize in a certain format that constitutes the material condition of possibility of their processing. Although the information represented is the same, the extent to which it can produce knowledge depends in practice on this format:

– conversion to a usable format may be too costly for the analyst, who generally works within a non-infinite economic and time frame, and will find the effort for conversion excessive. For example, transforming a PDF of several dozen pages into a CSV table is a long and tedious source of transcription errors;

– conversion to a usable format may simply not be possible due to incompatibility between the knowledge representations embodied in its formats. For example, Linked Data standards incorporate so-called semantic relationships between values, which do not exist in a data table. A text is not a list, which itself is not a graph; each of these representations corresponds to one or more formats that cannot be translated from one to the other without loss of information, if at all.

In summary, the format determines a space of "possibles" within the computable in general: to each format corresponds a set of possible manipulations, both theoretical (the space of possibility traced by the format) and practical (the already existing computational techniques that correspond to it, and to which the analyst has access). By transforming a PDF into an Excel sheet, it becomes instantly possible for the analyst to apply to their data all the mathematical formulas proposed by the software, including those that are not relevant to the data in question; between the computable and the

1 See http://5stardata.info/en/ [accessed November 16, 2017].

2 You get more stars as you make it progressively more awful, easier for people to use [Online]. Available at: https://www.w3.org/DesignIssues/LinkedData.html [accessed November 16, 2017].

computed, the temporal space becomes negligible. Unlike the mathematician facing the blackboard, the analyst no longer manipulates themselves but programs manipulations whose extent is determined by the format; they do not compute themselves but makes things computable. The determination of the computational possibilities space by the format concerns all numerical data. Whether the data are big or not, the extent of what can be known by computation depends initially on its computer representation.

Formatting is often a dual epistemic activity: first because, as we have seen, it determines the space of possible knowledge from the data, and second because it is a procedure involving a number of decisions that depend on the informational content of the data and not only on their format. Thus, an Excel table can contain a certain amount of information that is readable by humans but not by machines: comments added to cells, their formatting (bold, colored) cannot constitute the variables of a mathematical or logical formula in Excel. The formatting in particular often corresponds to semantics which (1) are not explicit for the machine and (2) are obscure for the analyst if they have not created the file themselves, or if a long time has elapsed between the constitution of the file and its analysis. In addition, this formatting can be inconsistent, especially when several people have worked on the same file or when the file is very large. The coloring of a cell in red may mean that it is important, or to be deleted: in the absence of other semiotic elements integrated into the file or accompanying it, the analyst who prepares their data will be unable to assign a stable meaning to it, and thus to materialize this meaning in a machine-readable format. In other words, this type of information will not be computable, and therefore will not be part of the knowledge production process.

Early formats in the scale defined by Tim Berners-Lee are particularly sensitive to this type of ambiguity or loss of information; however, many problems are common to all computer representations of data. These problems can be of various natures: missing information, ambiguous, partially redundant, contradictory, illegible, inconsistent, etc. In companies, it is estimated that the cost of formatting and cleaning data can represent up to 50% of a project's budget (Yakout *et al.* 2013). An emblematic figure in the processing of big data, a data scientist-type profile would spend, depending on sources and testimonies, between 60% and 80% of their time preparing their data[3]. In some cases, this preparation work even represents the bulk of the time spent analyzing the data, to which, once cleaned, elementary processes are applied by comparison, such as sums and averages. In these situations, the technical and epistemic difficulties lie not in the sophistication of the processing applied to the data, but in the constitution of these exploitable data from "raw" data, not yet cleaned or formatted. The construction of data usability can thus be seen as a technical and epistemic process in its own right, almost sufficient. Machine learning techniques have been developed to automate some of this work (error detection and resolution) but the choice of technique and its development can potentially be as time consuming as manual adjustments based on heuristics. The time required to manually configure and adjust these machine learning techniques may also exceed that of the computational processing that will be performed later, increasing their preparation time, while the execution time of these computations may remain negligible.

In the field of natural language processing, the task of making data computable lies at the boundary between data preparation and actual analysis. Since a text is not, by its very nature, predestined to be subjected to quantitative or logical processing, the constitution of the units on which the computation will be made is in itself a work involving analysis and interpretation, as much as a stage of preparing for the computation. Counting characters, words, sentences in a text is an operation that depends on how these units are defined: is a punctuation mark a character? Should the singular and plural forms of a word be counted as the same word? Does a line break mark the end of a sentence? Turning text into data implies modeling these units in a double step of formalization and formatting with joint determination of one by the other: the unit "word" will be both what we define and what we can technically cut out as such. Natural language processing is thus opposed to formal systems in artificial intelligence, which "rely on the linguistic interpretability of their symbolic signifiers to represent knowledge in the field and on their formality to be effective without there being a direct relationship between the two" (Bachimont 1996).

3 See, for example, https://www.nytimes.com/2014/08/18/technology/for-big-data-scientists-hurdle-to-insights-is-janitor-work.html?_r=0; http://visit.crowdflower.com/rs/416-ZBE-142/images/CrowdFlower_DataScienceReport_2016.pdf; http://www.forbes.com/sites/gilpress/2016/03/23/data-preparation-most-time-consuming-least-enjoyable-data-science-task-survey-says/#35b787147f75 [accessed November 16, 2017].

Conversely, tokenization is a simultaneously technical and epistemic task where the word is *de facto* defined as what is broken down as such.

The question of format and formatting cannot be seen as a purely technical issue, as it presents crucial epistemic aspects in the delimitation of the field of what can be known. This is the first stage of data discovery and manipulation for the analyst (assuming that they have not already taken charge of the constitution of the data from the footprints), it is also the stage where they receive a first idea of their content and the processing that they will be able to apply to them, where they formulate, according to the load that one wishes to give to this attitude, hypotheses or prejudices on the data, which will serve as a lever and a guiding thread for the choice of subsequent processing steps. Without this step of getting to grips with the data, the data have no meaning for the analysts, even virtually. Some data processing requires a certain format; by placing the data in this format, the analyst makes the data compatible with the corresponding processing. It is the act of formatting that gives meaning to the data, and frees the analyst from the vertigo and disorientation that inspires the rhetoric of big data.

Thus, if epistemological investigation is naturally inclined to focus on computational data processing techniques, the fields of algorithmics and machine learning, it cannot avoid examining the way in which information is constituted as data, and the way in which the apparently purely technical question of formatting and cleaning actually induces choices about the data that can actually be computed. Just as the logic for selecting footprints was, in Chapter 1, what constituted them as data for the analyst, formatting is the counterpart of this action for the machine. The epistemic constitution of the footprint is coupled with a technical constitution, without these being absolutely independent, since in the framework of the computational analysis of cultural data, technical feasibility is the material condition of possibility of the data and the boundaries of the knowable are included in those of the manipulable and the computable.

3.2. The field of computability

The recording of footprints on a digital medium has consequences on the nature and scope of the manipulations that can be carried out to produce knowledge: any knowledge resulting from such processing is dependent on the technical and theoretical limitations of such processing.

From a theoretical point of view, this computable field does not appear to be much more restricted than the knowable field: the distinction could be considered small enough to be neglected. The domain of what can be computed by a computer derives from what can be manipulated in mathematical or logical terms. This field is a restriction compared to the ambitions of the natural sciences, for example. Indeed, the Galilean sciences are meant to be mathematical, that is to say, they consider what is knowable as a subset of what is mathematicizable. Nevertheless, while some areas of contemporary physics exist almost exclusively under the Leibnizian injunction of the *calculemus*, most scientific theories are based on knowledge of a qualitative nature, including the conceptualization and definition of objects. It is not up to us to consider if this situation is temporary, in other words to consider qualitative knowledge as mathematical knowledge in the making, or if there is irreducibly qualitative knowledge. Therefore, in the state of knowledge, the knowable cannot be reduced to the mathematicizable.

Second, there is no exact equivalence between the mathematicizable and the computable. We know today that not everything that can be expressed in mathematical or formal language can necessarily be computed: there is in fact a class of mathematical problems that are said to be undecidable, i.e. it is not possible to determine a *priori* whether there is a computation procedure that leads to a solution in a finite number of operations. Historically, the problem of determining whether a problem is decidable was posed by the mathematician David Hilbert: the decision problem. The solution to this problem, established at the same time around 1935–1936 by Alonzo Church and Alan Turing, involves the affirmation of an equivalence between the formal problems envisaged by Hilbert and other forms of problems, among which it can be proved that there are non-computable ones. The equivalence thus defended by Church-Turing's thesis relates, on the one hand, to computation as defined by formal systems such as recursive functions or lambda calculus, and, on the other hand, to the informal notion of what can be computed by an effective finite procedure (Pégny 2013). Church-Turing's thesis thus asserts that everything computable in the informal sense is computable in the sense of computable recursive functions; his explanation states that any computable recursive function is computable by an actual procedure, or in other words, an algorithm. Therefore, any mathematical knowledge that can be expressed by the formal relation constituted by a computable recursive function can be considered as effectively computable in theory, it being understood that there are non-computable mathematical functions, i.e. formal relations that do not allow any knowledge to be obtained through computation.

However, Pégny underlines that there is a rather generally accepted distinction between the algorithmic form and the empirical form of Church-Turing's thesis: while the first, which we have seen, concerns itself with the informal notion of computation as an effective finite procedure whatever the material substrate where this procedure is carried out, the empirical form concerns itself with procedures that can actually be computed by a machine, including, but not exclusively, computers. In contemporary terms, it states that any computation that can be performed by a machine can be described as a recursive function. It is not obvious that this theory is true, but it has never been disproved in practice.

The examination of the different versions of Church-Turing's thesis and its consequences is ideally done with many nuances and subtleties in the assertions of equivalence between the different types of computation procedures: it crystallizes all the questions that prelude the emergence of theoretical and then practical computing from mathematical and formal problems formulated at the beginning of the 20th Century. Nevertheless, for our reasoning, it is sufficient to establish, through Church-Turing's thesis, that there is hardly any difference *in theory* between epistemic assertions that can be expressed as recursive functions and those that can be accessed by computer calculation. It is *in practice* that the knowable field is narrowed, moving from the mathematical to the computed.

Indeed, not every function that is theoretically computable is necessarily computable in practice. The limitations that arise when considering the computation's empirical aspects arise from the complexity of the procedure and are manifested through its temporal inscription[4]. The computability of an assertion is binary (some problems have a solution accessible through a finite procedure, others do not), but its complexity is gradual. Complexity theory is a subdomain of computer science as a theoretical computation science, which has highlighted categories of problem complexity, within which the problems posed are considered equivalent in terms of complexity:

4 There are other limitations to computability in practice, such as the properties of the computed values: for example, Pégny (2012) points out that a computation could not be made on a value composed of 10,250 digits because its size in number of digits would then be greater than the number of particles in the universe.

the complexity of a problem is established in theory but materializes in practice. Thus, NP-complete problems are a category of high complexity problems, effectively computable in theory but not systematically computable in practice. This distinction arises from the fact that a calculation on a computer is a physical phenomenon anchored in time and material constraints. The computation time depends on the complexity of the problem, the efficiency of its solution and the power of the computer on which it is carried out. The computer scientist who designs an algorithmic program with the aim of solving a concrete problem evolves within the negotiation space defined by these three parameters:

– they can try to reduce a problem belonging to a high complexity class to a simpler problem, less costly in terms of computing time and power, notably by means of approximating the problem;

– they may seek to improve the program itself, evaluating alternatives in terms of programming language, functions used, order of steps, etc.;

– they can, finally, try to access more computing power, either by getting a faster computer, or by distributing the computing effort over several machines.

At the interface between these last two points, there are also a multitude of strategies for optimizing the adequacy between the program (software level) and the machine (hardware level), which aim in particular to distribute the computation over several processor cores, to favor certain forms of memory over others (hard disk, SSD, RAM), other types of processors (GPU versus CPU), and to optimize the way, the order and the priorities with which these various physical elements are mobilized. They also refer to a change in programming practices, between a first period that strives to improve the program itself, to refine the algorithm, its use of memory, etc., and a more contemporary period where the abundance of computing power makes this work optional.

Although these different optimization techniques make it possible to negotiate a computation's practical feasibility, the success of these efforts is not guaranteed: what is computable in theory may ultimately turn out to be non-computable in practice, or computable following epistemically insufficient approximations or reformulations. Therefore, we have highlighted three successive limitation levels that algorithmic programming implies with respect to the generally knowable:

– not everything that is knowable is mathematicizable (there is qualitative knowledge that cannot be formalized in a mathematical language);

– not everything that is mathematical is computable in theory (there are undecidable problems);

– not everything that is computable in theory is computable in practice (algorithmic complexity makes some computations impractical for a given technological and material situation).

We will now show that there is a fourth level, which is not negligible, and whose causes are more psychological and metaphysical than purely epistemological. It can be formulated as follows:

– not everything that is computable in practice is computed in practice.

This fourth level, which we will analyze with the notion of "computational thinking", is an additional restriction compared to the computable in practice, but which also produces an excessive extension. Indeed, we will see through this notion that two additional constraints must be formulated:

– not everything that is computable should be computed (moral constraint);

– not everything that is computable necessarily produces something knowable (epistemic constraint).

Through this notion of computational thinking, we will see that the practice of computer science produces two excesses of the knowable field by the computable, a predilection for certain forms of knowledge production, and a belief in the inclusion of the knowable in the computable, with a programmed reduction of the knowable.

3.3. Computational thinking

So far, we have indeed seen the theoretical limitations of computation, and how the mediation of computation implies a reduction of what is knowable from computational observables. It is crucial, on the one hand, to be aware of these limitations, and, on the other hand, to keep in mind that not all knowledge comes from computation, and that there are other ways of producing knowledge. In addition to these practical limitations, there are also theoretical limitations: not everything that can be envisaged in terms of computational processing is implemented, either occasionally or generally. In practice, the mobilization of computation directs toward certain types of activities and epistemic projects. Thus, in companies in particular, a very large part of the work of algorithmic programming does not consist of finding a solution to a concrete problem but in optimizing this solution; most of the problems that arise have known solutions, but not perfectly adapted to the situation. Thus there is a certain self-fulfillment purpose of the computation practice, which consists of perfecting the way one solves an epistemic problem rather than conceptualizing new projects. This practical observation promotes a computational mindset that is not without epistemic consequences. This mindset is not, as Wing (2006) points out, a computationalism that would encourage thinking like a machine (and conversely, thinking like a computation), but a specific form of creativity: "Computational thinking is a way humans solve problems; it is not trying to get humans to think like computers. Computers are dull and boring; humans are clever and imaginative" (Wing 2006).

The ingenuity required to make computation possible, to increase its efficiency and to cut back on the use of computation time, sometimes millisecond by millisecond, for a task that will be programmed to run thousands of times, can be both beneficial and problematic. This computational thinking induces a predilection for efficiency over relevance, and for feasibility over what is ethically and epistemologically desirable. This mindset is marked by a search for the achievement of the possible which will promote:

– on the one hand, the production of computable knowledge rather than other forms of knowledge;

– on the other hand, the use of algorithmic techniques that are easily implemented and that save computational time regardless of the epistemic relevance of these techniques and the significance that can be attributed to their results.

The extreme risk in terms of relevance (although often reached in the intermediate stages of the development of a computational procedure) is to arrive at results that are computable but meaningless. Less radically, reducing an epistemic problem to a computable problem requires prior modeling, i.e. a simplification of the problem, to which we shall return below. Although his subject matter is axiologically charged, and illustrated with crude psychologizing caricatures of the figure of the computer scientist, Golumbia's book (2009) occasionally puts the finger on the computer scientist's tropisms which, for example, help to explain the gap of mutual incomprehension between researchers in cultural sciences and computer engineers mentioned above:

> "While philosophers use the term computationalism to refer to others of their kind who believe that the human mind is ultimately characterizable as a kind of computer, here I deploy the term more expansively as a commitment to the view that a great deal, perhaps all, of human and social experience can be explained via computational processes." (Golumbia 2009)

From this, we can better understand projects that predict socioeconomic phenomena based on big data such as the ones we have already mentioned: stock market prices or box office performance for movies, Twitter, flu epidemics from queries on the Google search engine, etc. We also better understand the Promethean figure presented by Pedro Domingos in his book *The Master Algorithm*. From an epistemological point of view, algorithmic programming traces an immense and unprecedented field of possible knowledge in relation to the already "unreasonable efficiency of mathematics" in the natural sciences (Wigner 1960); but there is also a psychological (or metaphysical) aspect, a representation of algorithmic programming by its practitioners within which there is a tendency toward a superimposition of what is knowable and what is computable in practice. Without going as far as the epistemological assertion that all computation produces knowledge (because computer scientists know, on the other hand, the tendency of computation to produce nonsense), we can nevertheless detect a form of moral injunction to compute everything that can be computed, mixed with a form of scientific mind, in the sense of an inclination to experiment and develop heuristics. There are thus two illegitimate extensions of Church-Turing's thesis: the first would involve considering any result of a computation as knowledge, and the second would consider as knowledge only that which results from a computation.

The computational thinking of computational practitioners should not be reduced to a common temperament that is fortuitous or that could be reduced to sociological causes, from an externalist perspective. It has a transcendental role in the practice of algorithmic programming: it is indeed part of its conditions of possibility but also determines its limits, in the sense that knowledge production is limited by the agent's epistemic capacities. This computational thinking also has a historicity already translated into the "national book" of computer programming, punctuated by figures such as Leibniz and his universal combinatorics, Charles Babbage and his analytical machine, Ada Lovelace and her "programs", and of course the work of Alan Turing.

In this way, we recognize an influence of the normativity of the natural sciences, conferring legitimacy on processes such as experimentation and trial-and-error research, in short a more or less systematic exploration of the field of possibilities opened up by the computable in practice. The epistemic use of algorithmic programming being quite recent (at least on the scale of the history of the natural sciences), its practice is often marked by a pioneering, or even a conquest spirit, following what can be seen as the discovery of a new world in the field of knowledge. In this metaphor, the old world is that of the natural sciences, which serve as a referent. It bequeathed its state of mind, in a version that strongly resembles that of Claude Bernard's experimental method, defined as follows: "The experimental method is nothing more than a set of rules sanctioned by the experiment and whose purpose is to guard against the errors that can result from the handling of facts and hypotheses in the construction of science" (Bernard 1947, quoted by Lassègue 1996).

In this configuration, it is no longer experiment on (and in) nature, but computation which plays the role of opposable reality. As we shall see below, the test of reality is no longer the stone that falls, the wall into which one bumps, but the computation in practice in what it delivers as effective knowledge of itself. Computational experimentation can thus quite naturally be translated into the terms of the experimental method in the natural sciences, as proposed by Jean Lassègue (1996):

> "The heuristic use of computers is similar to and can be combined with the traditional hypothetico-deductive experimental method in science. In this method, a hypothesis is made on the basis of the available information, the consequences are tested experimentally and a new hypothesis is formed on the basis of what is found; this sequence is repeated indefinitely. Using a computer heuristically is the same, except that computation replaces the experiment."

Nevertheless, it should be stressed here that computing in this case occupies a specific status as a tool for virtual experimentation, which is a particular example of the articulation between science and technology. More generally, arithmetic has a dual status as an autonomous, theoretical and practical artifact science, and as a transcendental empirical modality of other sciences:

– on the one hand, computer *science* is a *science of combinatorial possibility*, which establishes in a theoretical and practical way what is accessible by computation, the latter playing the role of the object of nature thrown in front of us, and whose properties and limits we seek to establish in order to found its objectivity. As such, algorithmic programming and optimization play the role of an art of the possible, i.e., a set of techniques and know-how to efficiently establish empirical knowledge related to this science;

– on the other hand, this art of the possible is an instrument at the service of other sciences, of which it is therefore the *empirical transcendental*, in the sense of empirical determination of the transcendental space of the sciences that it instruments. In other words, it empirically delimits the domain of what is knowable for these sciences.

As a result, computational thinking has a dual relationship with the natural sciences: on the one hand, it can be seen as a new form of scientific mind imbued with the normative nature of the natural sciences, without being limited to it; on the other hand, it becomes a component of the ethos of the natural sciences, in the sense that the acquisition of this mind set is necessary, or at least desirable, for the effectiveness of scientific practice in the computer age. Conversely, the cultural sciences do not benefit from this natural compatibility with computational thinking, especially with regard to what we have called corpus-based disciplines as opposed to field-based disciplines (and which could also be called, using Claude Bernard's vocabulary, experimental cultural sciences). Since the normativities of the natural and cultural sciences are heterogeneous in the bifurcationist hypothesis that we have adopted, the relationships that these normativities each have with computational thinking are also distinct.

As soon as computational thinking is integrated into the consequences of the mobilization of computation, and as soon as it is considered as an additional condition for the possibility of knowledge, computation imposes *a priori* additional constraints on the knowable in the cultural sciences. The obstacles to interdisciplinarity between computer science and cultural sciences, which we have raised in the context of our analysis of digital humanities, are therefore not only formal incompatibilities between unmeasurable scientific standards, but also obstacles of a psychological or even metaphysical nature between opposing conceptions, experiencing a mutual aversion between them when they are expressed in their respective extremes: an excessive demand for the conceptualization and problematization of objects and tools, on the one hand, and an unbridled injunction to experimentation and the realization of the possible, on the other hand. Put another way, it is a Pascalian incompatibility between a spirit of finesse focused on qualitative and comprehensive knowledge, and a spirit of geometry fond of optimality and efficiency. However, as Pascal wrote more than three centuries ago, it is still rare "that geometricians are astute and that astutes are geometric", which makes computational thinking a limitation, or even an obstacle, to what can be known in practice and by computation, in the cultural sciences in particular. This incompatibility endorses and reinforces the epistemic breach between the digital footprint and its computational processing, which must be overcome in order to make possible the computational cultural sciences.

Independently of this breach, we have, through the notions of format, computability and computational thinking, analyzed the question of computation and what is computable by algorithmic programming in a transcendental perspective, i.e. with the aim of elucidating the articulation between the knowable and the computable, and more specifically the domain of the knowable opened up by the computable. This perspective reminds us that computation is an empirical transcendental, i.e. that it constitutes above all the material conditions for the knowledge production that mobilizes it.

This status is valid regardless of the mobilization context. Nevertheless, the mobilization of computation in data science introduces two main differences with respect to this field. The first one, which is technical in nature, exacerbates the importance of computability in practice and optimization. Specific processes, which we will present later, make it possible to deal with the technical characteristics of big data: their volume, but also their incompleteness, their heterogeneity, the fact that they are manufactured and processed in along the way, and not all at once, etc. The effort required to integrate these difficulties accentuates the predilections of computational thinking, and its search for efficiency independently of the epistemic project that motivates computation. In companies, the injunction issued by consulting firms in big data to equip themselves with the tools to absorb these difficulties is often even adopted without any epistemic project: the purchase of servers or clusters, the implementation of distributed infrastructures capable of scaling up, the use of non-relational databases, etc., are frequently not followed by any use, because they are not driven by any explicit need. These companies, ordered to and convinced of the need to invest in "big data", thus acquire the means of processing without associating them with an objective, because they are unable to formulate an epistemic project based on these data. In this situation, there is computability but not knowability, with an inability to connect each to the other. The exacerbation of a technical problem (the management of data properties) has the epistemic consequence of failing to establish, to begin with, a knowable domain.

The second difference, particularly in relation to the mobilization of computation as an empirical transcendental in the natural sciences, concerns not the technical properties but the semantic content of the data: as we have seen, the epistemic value of digital footprints falls within the domain of the cultural sciences, while proceeding from a breach with the epistemic continuity of this domain.

To accurately highlight the specific status of computation in data sciences, we need to create a benchmark to show where data sciences are making a change. The comparison with the mobilization of computation in the natural sciences will enable us to characterize data sciences and to highlight their specificity compared to the usual mobilization of computation in an epistemic project, in this case scientific. We now look at how computation is mobilized in the natural sciences in the context of simulation, numerical computation and data processing of scientific instruments.

3.4. Computation in the natural sciences

There are at present three ways of using computation in the natural sciences known to the philosophy of science. Although they may partially overlap, they can nevertheless be analyzed independently and can be referred to as follows:

– *numerical simulations* generally have the function of proposing a computational representation, static or dynamic, of a physical or biological system;

– *numerical computation* allows us to solve complex mathematical equations on the computer;

– *data processing of digital instruments* is used to improve the quality (sharpness, accuracy, readability, etc.) of the data produced by these instruments.

In line with its predilection for scientific theory rather than experimentation, classical philosophy of science has been particularly interested in the forms and functions of numerical simulation, the practice of which generally arises quite directly from the problems of scientific modeling. The increasing use of computers in the natural sciences is renewing the question of the relationship between theory, model and experiment. A growing academic literature exists today on the subject, following on from the work on the role of models in the natural sciences.

However, the model on which simulation is based is not the same as theory. A scientific model is a representation of a phenomenon (and not the represented phenomenon, like the painter's model) whose function is not to describe the phenomenon exhaustively and in all its complexity, but from a certain point of view corresponding to the one being worked on. Thus, the molecular graphics well known to high school students, which represent molecules outlined by colored balls and stems, are not an exact representation of the molecule (they have neither solid balls, nor colors, nor rods) but they do effectively describe the number and nature of the atoms, as well as the atomic bonds of which the molecule is composed.

Sometimes, the point of view that one wants to have on the object does not allow one to reduce its complexity by modeling it, in the state of knowledge. Thus, in biology, there are frequently objects that escape modeling, or whose simplest model is the object itself: the liver and the brain are examples of objects whose functioning is not sufficiently known to be modeled and simplified, so that the only available model is the object itself.

It is easier to inscribe the model in an instrumental epistemology than a realistic one: a model must above all be functional from the point of view of the task that one seeks to accomplish, without necessarily describing the true one. This functional aspect gives it a certain autonomy from the theory in which it is inscribed. It can be used to prove an aspect of the theory from which it derives (or is inspired) by unfolding its consequences, but it can also be detached from it and function within the framework of other theories.

It thus represents the result of a compromise between the legality (the character of law) of the theory and the empirical and practical constraints (such as those of computability in practice) that may lead to simplifications of the initial model, or the introduction of equivalent models that are easier to compute. Negotiation can be played out between the intelligibility of the model, on the one hand, and its accuracy or computational efficiency, on the other hand. Moreover, a model must be manipulable, either literally, with our hands, like the models of wooden or plastic molecules that any high school student will have known, or within the framework of a specific formalism (graphic, mathematical, logical, computational) that defines the legal operations. Therefore, a model is something operational, which should enable experimenting and exploring possibilities within the formal rules defined by the model. In these terms, numerical simulation is what makes it possible to systematize and automate this exploration on a computer.

However, numerical simulation practices are far from being homogeneous and they can in turn serve a function of validating a scientific model of prediction, experimentation or support for a scientific experiment. According to Varenne (2007), who distinguishes in his vocabulary between *numerical simulation* (based on computation) and *computer simulation* (carried out on a computer), computer simulation practices historically emerged from two fields: work on formal models, on the one hand, and work on numerical simulation, where computation is carried out step by step by a human. The simulation is based on a symbolization of the computational objects that receive meaning before being processed by the computation itself. Computer simulation allows the consequences of a formal model, i.e. a set of formally defined objects and relations (in particular mathematical, statistical or logical) to be deduced automatically (by computer calculation). Simulation practices are therefore emerging from scientific fields where mathematics, formalism and computation already play an important role in the production and validation of knowledge. This formal model must first be translated into a numerical model (or computational model) in which the parameters are discretized and the relations computationally computable (Jebeile 2013). It is, in a way, the most concrete, formalized and least qualitative version of the different types of models that coexist and articulate with each other, namely:

– scientific theory, sometimes wrongly called a theoretical model (e.g. the standard model), is not a model, but the framework (including laws) within which models can be developed;

– the conceptual model is the scientific model in the common sense, the one that describes, in the terms of the scientific field in which it is inscribed, the objects and their relations;

– the formal model, which can be expressed graphically, logically or mathematically;

– the computational model[5], which describes variables, parameters, values, etc., and is based on a model of the environment.

Generally speaking, the function of the model is to act as an intermediary between theory and situation. From theory, it inherits laws, truth and scientific validity; unlike theory, however, it does not describe reality but a specific object. With regard to the situation, it represents an increase in generality by conceptualizing and characterizing the object through different situations. This increase in generality comes at the price of a simplification that makes the model manipulable, and is built from the characteristics one wants to explore, so that there can be several models of the same object. The model is a representation that serves as an interface between theory and situation in order to play several roles: to make the object intelligible through a representation, to produce new knowledge about it by making the hypotheses it materializes testable, or to experiment with what is known about the object.

While the development of a formal model of the target system is a prerequisite for simulation practices, there is also an inverse pressure of the computational model on the formal (mathematical) model or even on the conceptual (scientific) model. Barberousse and Imbert (2014) were able to point out the relatively small number of formal models used in science, and the fact that some models such as Poisson's or Lokta-Volterra equations are widely used. The same model will be used frequently within a given discipline, but also from one discipline to another: what is at stake is, in short, a standardization of science from the point of view of the mathematical models it mobilizes. Barberousse and Imbert suggest that these models are favored in particular because they can be solved numerically (i.e. via a computational model) and also influence the conceptual modeling of scientific objects. In other words, the authors suggest a predilection of

5 More precisely, there is no computational model per se, but an algorithm or program, on the one hand, and an implicit translation model from the formal model to this algorithm, on the other hand.

researchers for research objects that can be formalized mathematically and processed on a computer to the detriment of other objects that are difficult to manipulate formally and computationally: we find here in modeling practices in the natural sciences a form of computational thinking that promotes what can be solved by computation, and restricts the field of research to what is computable in practice (within a reasonable time).

The recurrence of certain models may suggest an ontological interpretation according to which a few quasi-universal mathematical models would suffice to describe the structure of reality, in a Platonic sense where this structure would be mathematical. On the contrary, the authors propose to attribute this recurrence to pragmatic motivations: the fact that a model can be solved computationally, but also the existence of ready-to-use implementations (notably in the form of software) of model solving algorithms; the popularity of certain computational approaches among certain laboratories or research journals explain their popularity. This pragmatic explanation defuses the ontological inflation of the mathematical and computational models in question, and restores them to an instrumental character where the tool influences research but does not necessarily govern it.

In the case of plant morphogenesis, which has been studied extensively by Franck Varenne, simulation based on the plant growth model enables the model to be validated by unraveling its consequences. Simulation therefore plays a deductive role in relation to the model and its different levels: it automatically determines what it implies. It is computational in nature but its rendering is visual: its result is the image of a tree that can be submitted to immediate visual validation, ensuring that the simulated image of the tree looks like a tree. If the visual result of the simulation intuitively resembles a tree, then the growth model implemented by the simulation is correct. In some cases, the simulation can be dynamic: the computation process consists of a representation of the plant's growth and makes it possible to visualize dynamically the various stages of the growth; the computation generates an animated image that corresponds to the growth model. Nevertheless, the representation of the plant is not necessarily dynamic: some models produce an image of the tree at the end of the computation but the temporal inscription of the computation itself is not a representation (in real time, accelerated or slowed down) of the temporal inscription of its growth.

Moreover, the simulation itself must be validated: the agricultural engineer Philippe de Reffye, studied by Franck Varenne, defended the need for an empirical validation of the equivalence between a computer simulation and its numerical counterpart that can be computed by hand, which corresponds to both an empirical control of the computation and a construction of the epistemic confidence we have in the machine. We also saw that the simulation could be intuitively validated based on its results and their visual consistency, without diagnosing the computation operations then considered as a black box. Finally, comparison between simulated and experimental data is a common form of validation. A validated simulation can have many scientific and technical applications. A simulation based on data describing the present makes it possible to predict the future state of a system: for example, simulations can be used to compute weather forecasts or determine climatic or economic trends.

An experimental status is frequently given to computer simulations: the data they generate are compared with data from experiments conducted in the physical world. For Norton and Suppe (2001, cited by Jebeile 2016), they are a source of experimental data and "simulation models can function as measuring instruments providing real-world data that face the same epistemological challenges as data models".

In cases where it is more practical, less costly, etc., to work on simulations, where it is simply not possible to intervene on physical objects, or where predictive results are sought (for which data from experiments cannot, by definition, yet exist), simulations substitute for experiments by providing data that have, like experimental data, the power to prove or reject a hypothesis. However, in order for simulated data to have this evidential power, the numerical model from which they are derived must itself be validated, otherwise their respective validation is based on circular reasoning where model and simulation data are mutually justified.

Overall, numerical simulation has strong links with both modeling and experimentation. Computation is used as a technique to deduce the consequences of the model and to act as a substitute or alternative to the experiment. The results of the computation are validated from a computational point of view but interpreted at the level of the formal and scientific model: the computational solution remains an intermediary to the understanding of more abstract representations.

The simulation also appears to be a complex object, which does not allow for a univocal point of view on its epistemological interpretation. Moreover, it has multiple links with another way of mobilizing computation in the natural sciences, namely numerical computation, i.e. the computational resolution of equations that generally represent physical objects. On the one hand, from a technical point of view, numerical simulations are a form of numerical computation, in the sense that they take the form of calculations that are performed by computers. Just as in the Galilean sciences with an instrumentalist conception of mathematics in relation to the natural sciences, scientific models are generally given a mathematical form, the simulation of a physical system is based on the translation of a physical model into a mathematical or formal and then computational model. In addition, a mathematical model can also be the subject of a simulation; as Franck Varenne (Varenne and Silberstein 2013) suggests: “A numerical computation of a mathematical model can therefore be conceived as a simulation of a mathematical model”.

Depending on one’s point of view, a numerical computation can therefore constitute all or part of a numerical simulation. Conversely, it is not uncommon for numerical computation to mobilize simulation techniques, or at least techniques that may have the dual epistemic function of solving equations and generating simulated data. Thus, Monte-Carlo methods are often presented as simulation methods (Barberousse and Imbert 2013; Jebeile 2013; Boyer-Kassem 2014) but they are also stochastic equation-solving methods based on random data generation, the synthesis of which provides a good approximation of the result of the equation. One of the clear distinctions that can be made between computation and numerical simulation is that the elements of the simulation, the data generated, have a function of representing the target system; in other words, they have a physical meaning, they mean something from the point of view of the natural sciences.

Thus, in Monte-Carlo methods applied to statistical physics, data points may (a) have a physical meaning (i.e. represent molecules, system states, coordinates, etc.) or (b) be merely computational intermediaries for solving a mathematical equation (these methods are, for example, often used for solving integrals) whose result can, by construction, be interpreted not only in a mathematical but also in a physical framework. In the first case, the mathematical and computational objects that constitute the method (parameters, variables, distributions, etc.) must be translated into objects that make sense in relation to the target system: in this way, the same method and the same computation can symbolize a gas, particles, an electrical signal, etc. Simulation techniques are usually developed in a specific context: Monte Carlo methods were originally designed for the description of physical systems containing a high number of particles, but are named after casino games (Metropolis and Ulam 1949) and can be used to describe a virtually infinite variety of target systems in statistical physics, quantum physics, climatology, population biology, genomics, etc.

With the distinction between numerical simulation and computation, we can see that numerical tools for the natural sciences have the capacity to circulate in different ways between disciplines and from one problem to another: either in terms of the simple computational resolution of the computation, or in terms of the formal model from which this resolution proceeds. Here again, it is the question of interpretation and the meaning of the computation that makes it possible to distinguish epistemic functions and distinct representational statuses for a particular simulation technique, and also to characterize, by differentiating between them, simulation techniques and numerical computation techniques.

To these two mobilizations of algorithmic programming in the natural sciences, we must add a third: data processing of measuring instruments. Many scientific instruments such as telescopes, microscopes, sensors and medical imaging devices have been computerized, and therefore render the measurements they make in digital formats, which can be processed computationally from the outset. It should be noted that very often these processes are, in scientific images as in other fields, actually integrated into the instrument. Thus, digital cameras do not directly record the signal from their sensor but compress, modify and adjust it, according to device-specific and user-defined parameters.

Nevertheless, in the context of scientific observation, there is a suspicion with regard to the processing of digital data that these transformations could take away from the data its character of observing reality and its evidential status: modifying the data from scientific measuring instruments and sensors would sever the link with the empirical phenomena that they allow us to construct. Israel-Jost (2016), who has worked on the role and modalities of scientific observation, questions the idea of the superiority of an observation that is supposed to be direct and neutral, and shows on the contrary that algorithmic transformations of data improve its readability and usefulness. It is thus part of a broader line of research concerning the place of measurement instruments in scientific observation (Hacking 1981; Humphreys 2004; Daston and Galison 2007) and the epistemic enhancers they occupy in relation to direct visual observation, which is no longer the preferred form of access to empirical natural phenomena.

In the field of scientific imaging (whether of microscopic organisms or galaxies), digital processing of data generated by the measuring instruments can be used to improve image sharpness, reduce noise or neutralize visual artifacts that may result from the measurement. It thus makes the images more precise, more accurate, more legible: it does not diminish but on the contrary improves their observational character. In the field of medical imaging, computational processing also makes it possible to produce a three-dimensional representation from a series of 2D images taken by MRI: without this processing, the analysis of the three-dimensional image would require a particularly complex effort of thought. The digital processing of scientific imagery thus provides a concrete example in the natural sciences of cases where raw data are not preferable to reprocessed data, or, on the contrary, where such processing is necessary to make the data usable. It also exemplifies another aspect of data preparation: the fact that the data processing algorithm model does not depend on the target object (galaxy, mitochondria), but on the instrument theory, so that the same processing operation can be applied to images of completely separate objects. As we have seen in the case of simulation with the example of Monte-Carlo methods, computational processing depends on the computer and mathematical theories on which it is based (formal level), but is (with some exceptions) independent of the scientific theory within which it aims to produce certain knowledge.

While we have essentially discussed in this section the status of computation in the natural sciences, at least some of the conclusions we reach can also be applied to the cultural sciences: there is a generality to the status of computation that is more specific to the naturalized sciences than to the natural sciences. In other words, it is with the method of accessing reality that the link between computation and scientific practice is defined. Combined with the ability of computational models to circulate from one epistemic context to another, this remark suggests that computational practices from the natural sciences also have the ability to circulate within certain cultural sciences, particularly in field-based disciplines.

What is more, simulation has a greater attraction for these disciplines: in contrast to matter or living matter, which can in many cases be studied and manipulated *in vitro*, in the closed space of the laboratory, social phenomena are generally understood “in their natural environment”, where observation does not modify them, and generally without intervention. This is the very principle of the field, which is based on direct observation of the phenomenon that is taking place. Yet, intervening in social worlds raises technical difficulties and ethical issues that the manipulation of particles or force fields does not pose: the use of numerical simulation would be a way for field-based disciplines to escape these difficulties and to facilitate research work by substituting numerical simulation data for field data.

In fact, the circulation of computational techniques is already taking place within certain particularly mathematical social sciences, such as economics, which also uses models derived from physics: for example, Brownian motion, which is a case of the mathematical modeling of a particle’s movement. It is also used in finance to describe the dynamics of a stock market price. Multiagent systems are common in population biology but also in quantitative sociology, where human population dynamics are modeled and simulated: in this context, “agents” are no longer living organisms but human individuals because of a reinterpretation of the epistemic function of the elements of the simulation model. The introductory manual to computational social science (Cioffi-Revilla 2014) contains several chapters dedicated to this type of approach, which also has its own research journal (*Journal of Artificial Societies and Social Simulation*).

Nevertheless, in the cultural sciences, the modeling-simulation pair is rather exceptional, located in a few disciplines with a largely mathematical field, almost “Galileean”, such as economics and quantitative sociology. As far as we know, they have not given rise to initiatives in corpus-based disciplines that do not have this mathematization tradition, and do not benefit from the natural compatibility between the spirit of the natural sciences and computational thinking. Moreover, where field-based disciplines directly access phenomena, corpus-based disciplines have always already mobilized an intermediary of representation, a footprint that symbolizes an absent and past phenomenon. It is therefore difficult to imagine what a simulation could be in a corpus-based discipline, especially for those interested in idiographic knowledge. On the whole, the cultural sciences appear to be only partially compatible with numerical simulation practices, leaving room for other mobilizations of computation.

There is thus specificity to the mobilization of computation in the natural sciences based on modeling practices that can be summarized in a few points:

– the link between science and technology is made by using computation as a tool; the scientific question is the first one. Scientific problems lead to computational solutions through models at different levels;

– a Galilean culture of mathematization and modeling is necessary to see simulation practices emerge within a scientific discipline. Under these conditions, there is little or no breach with the epistemology of the discipline, even if these innovations imply technical and methodological developments. Modeling is the starting point for mobilizing computation;

– regardless of the discipline's epistemic culture, formal models and computational techniques have the ability to flow from one follower to another, and therefore do not need to be developed by a practitioner of a given discipline in order to be used by that discipline. They can access a certain autonomy that allows them to move beyond the scope of the initial scientific problem;

– this ability to move beyond the initial problem is based on a process of decontextualization and then recontextualization of the computational model's objects, which must regain meaning in relation to the new scientific problem.

These characteristics propose both methodological answers for the development of computational cultural sciences and obstacles to its construction from the epistemic culture of cultural sciences. On the answer side, the circulation capacity of computational techniques from the natural sciences provides both concrete tools to exploit digital footprints, and a logic of decontextualization/recontextualization that makes it possible to give them meaning. On the obstacle side, the need for a culture of mathematization and modeling implies a shift from computational sciences to epistemic culture. Thus, if the conceptualization of the footprint fits well into this culture, which is capable of considering it, according to the bifurcationist hypothesis, from both an idiographic and a nomological angle, the mobilization of techniques that allow us to manipulate these footprints in order to extract a meaning from them takes place in another epistemic culture, confirming the epistemic breach between the footprint and its manipulation. Before considering, in the following chapters, how can we reconcile these two cultures and overcome the epistemic breach between footprint and computation, we now examine what computation does within the footprint in the context of data sciences, here considered as a stage or component of computational cultural sciences (1) possessing the epistemic culture required through the computational thinking that characterizes its practitioners and (2) constructed from the outset with a view to exploiting digital footprints (without, however, being conceptualized as such).

On the other hand, where the natural sciences mobilize computation as an instrument, by governing all the objects and stages of knowledge production, the data sciences reverse this logic: it is computation that is first and governs practices. Among the levels of modeling that articulate the link between theory and reality, only the computational model level remains. They should therefore be considered more as an art of calculation, whose computational models may invite formal and conceptual interpretation, than as a science in the strict sense of the word, where modeling is the primary tool. These data arts constitute a necessary component of the computational cultural sciences, a *sine qua non* condition for their effective realization, but their contribution must be limited to the contribution of techniques and know-how relating to computation and data. In these terms, this component can function autonomously, within a methodological paradigm that takes the already constituted footprint as a starting point and leaves downstream a space, a play for interpretation and decisive judgment on the meaning of data. We now look at the data sciences as historically constituted objects to highlight how they can effectively provide the computational component of the computational cultural sciences, without exceeding the extension of this field.

3.5. From exploratory analysis to data mining

Just like big data or digital humanities, data sciences refer as much to an informal set of objects and epistemic practices as to an associated mythology; it is therefore difficult to ascertain its precise domain. Like statistics, these are data analysis practices, but more specifically these emerged following the advent of big data, giving computation a particular status, and are part of a specific methodological paradigm. They are based, as will also be seen, on a melting pot of pre-existing techniques from historically distinct technical lines, including frequentist and Bayesian statistics, data mining and artificial intelligence. What they have in common is that they come from more fields of technological research, i.e. fields that intervene at the level of the computational or formal model, than from the natural sciences. They also correspond to rather loose groupings of various fields of research, schools of thought and techniques already developed, having evolved over time and been applied to distinct problems. We propose to examine what data sciences are doing within the digital footprint from three historical, methodological and technical frameworks: statistics, computer science and artificial intelligence.

First, we will see that data sciences are part of a methodological paradigm distinct from classical statistics, favoring an exploratory mode over the hypothetico-deductive mode around which the latter is constructed. This paradigm is fueled by computational practices resulting from an institutional and methodological circulation between the academic and business worlds, through individuals who prefer to work from a technological problem rather than from an institutional or disciplinary framework, and are thus distinguished from the epistemic culture of statisticians, but also from corporate computing, by the type of research called "interdisciplinary" that they practice. Finally, the development of data sciences is leading to a revival of artificial intelligence based on its techniques, which has the consequence of redefining its program and incorporating it into the interdisciplinary exploratory framework that characterizes them.

From a statistical point of view, first of all, the emergence of data science is at odds with the theoretical and conceptual evolution of the field. Initially highly descriptive and applied to empirical problems, statistics became, especially from the beginning of the 20th Century, an increasingly formal tool at the service of hypothetico-deductive approaches in the natural sciences. Nevertheless, this recent development does not reveal the complexity of the history of statistics, its schools of thought and points of view. For example, in modern statistics, the frequentist and Bayesian perspectives correspond to different interpretations of the concept of probability: while frequentists analyze the observed frequencies of phenomena to infer probability, Bayesians are interested in the degree of belief with which a phenomenon is considered likely to occur (Hacking 2002; Barbin and Lamarche 2004). Frequentist statistics became very active at the end of the 19th Century and in the first half of the 20th Century, notably with the contributions from Karl Pearson and Ronald Fisher, and were structured as a field of mathematical research based on the descriptive empirical techniques developed in the 18th and 19th Centuries (Beaud and Prévost 2000; Porter 2003), notably because of their formalization by

Kolmogorov in the 1930s (Lanciani 2011). Hypothesis testing, in particular, has become a preferred instrument of inferential reasoning and scientific deduction within the falsificationist framework defined by Popper (Spanos and Mayo 2015). At the same time, Bayesian approaches, which have fallen out of favor since the 18th Century, have experienced a revival of interest with the development of computers that make it possible to operationalize these approaches. Both frequentist and Bayesian frameworks have provided concepts and models that have survived their philosophical differences: while frequentist statistics were seen as deductive and Bayesian inductivists, Gelman and Shalizi (2013) have shown that a hypothetico-deductive interpretation of Bayesianism is possible, and Mayo and Cox (2009) have shown that frequentism can be inductive.

These philosophical developments accompany the practical changes brought about by the computerization of statistical methods and the new possibilities brought about by the fact that actual computation is much faster. The laws of probability, analysis of variance, correlations, etc., become tools for a variety of problems and theoretical frameworks.

In particular, the exploratory data analysis developed by Tukey (1977) constitutes both an alternative to the hypothetico-deductive paradigm and a form of return to descriptive statistics, but with a new epistemic function. Conceived before the advent of computing, Tukey's exploratory paradigm is undoubtedly one of the major inspirations for the computational analysis of big data: where descriptive state statistics were mainly used to produce a quantitative summary of the data, the exploratory approach introduces the idea of discovery, experimentation and identification of regularities but also anomalies, in short, anything that can lead to the emergence of unexpected knowledge. The notion of data analysis was first raised in 1962 as opposed to statistics in an article entitled "The future of data analysis" but it was not until 1977 that he published his manual of exploratory data analysis. As Tukey wrote:

> "This book is about exploratory data analysis, about looking at data to see what it seems to say. It concentrates on simple arithmetic and easy-to-draw pictures. It regards whatever appearances we have recognized as partial descriptions, and tries to look beneath them for new insights. Its concern is with appearance, not with confirmation."

The data are no longer a sample whose epistemic scope is mastered and which serves to falsify a hypothesis, but a given, in the sense of a territory to be explored, regardless of the nature and origin of the data, which can be studied as an autonomous object. Nevertheless, the exploratory approach is constructed next to, and complements, the "confirmatory" approach, and not in its place:

> "Once upon a time, statisticians only explored. Then they learned to confirm exactly – to confirm a few things exactly, each under very specific circumstances. As they emphasized exact confirmation, their techniques inevitably became less flexible. The connection of the most used techniques with past insights was weakened. Anything to which a confirmatory procedure was not explicitly attached was decried as "mere descriptive statistics", no matter how much we had learned from it.
>
> […]
>
> Today, exploratory and confirmatory can – and should – proceed side by side."

Tukey's ambition was thus to restructure an approach that he did not present as his invention, but as the original form of statistics. He emphasized that this was not a formal approach but a set of globally elementary techniques; the guide thus contains techniques ranging from a trick for very simple tasks such as determining a number's digits without getting it wrong, presented with a level of detail that stretches to instructions such as "put your left hand on the sheet of paper with the index finger pointing to the right". These techniques are associated with a certain state of mind that can be characterized by curiosity, humility and the search for simplicity. Tukey's guide thus has Bachelardian overtones of a "new scientific spirit" manifesto, carried by a set of values that a data analyst must possess. The analyst must also demonstrate a form of agnosticism with respect to the techniques employed, which do not have a formally defined epistemic function out of context. As such, the first technique presented in the guide is remarkable for its simplicity, its effectiveness and its absence of recourse to a computing machine. This is the stem-and-leaf plot, which simply consists of copying a series of numbers in such a way as to group them by unit, by tens, by thousands, etc., according to their numerical amplitude. Figure 3.1 shows a series of prices ranging from $150 to $1,895 ($250, $150, $795, $895, $695, $1,699, $1,499, $1,099, $1,693, $1,166, $688, $1,333, $895, $1,775, $895, $1,895, $795), grouped in hundreds. The stem and leaf representation is constructed by writing about a hundred per line (from 1 to 18), then distributing the values in the corresponding lines, removing the numbers from the 1 to 18 indicators from the 100. For example, $250 becomes $50 on line 2, $795 becomes $95 on line 7, and so on. The result is similar to a histogram representation because the more values in a line, the longer that line is. This visualization, which can be done with paper and pencil, makes it possible to see the dispersion and distribution of values; it makes it possible to identify the most frequent values, the general appearance of the data and the presence of outliers. The median of the values can also be estimated roughly but without computation. It thus constitutes a first description of the data, independent of its meaning, but through which footprints can be identified.

UNIT = $1
STEM-and-LEAF
two-digit leaf

1**	50
2	50
3	
4	
5**	
6	95, 88
7	95, 95
8	95, 95, 95
9**	
10	99
11	66
12	
13**	33
14	99
15	
16	99, 93
17**	75
18	95

Figure 3.1. *Excerpt from exploratory data analysis (source: Tukey 1977, p. 9)*

Another important aspect of the exploratory data analysis highlighted in this example is its requirement for demonstrativeness, which will be established by emphasizing data visualization:

> "The greatest value of a picture is when it forces us to notice what we never expected to see."

With exploratory data analysis, visualization acquires heuristic value. It is not only used to demonstrate and communicate results to peers, but also to make the data intelligible, to surprise the analyst and make them formulate new hypotheses: it is both a tool for discovery and demonstration. Exploration is therefore not just about going through the data, but about representing it visually in different ways so that you can get an idea of it and get to know it more and more precisely. As a tool of discovery, data visualization plays a hermeneutical, almost cabalistic role in revealing what is hidden in numbers.

I		II		III		IV	
X	Y	X	Y	X	Y	X	Y
10.0	8.04	10.0	9.14	10.0	7.46	8.0	6.58
8.0	6.95	8.0	8.14	8.0	6.77	8.0	5.76
13.0	7.58	13.0	8.74	13.0	12.74	8.0	7.71
9.0	8.81	9.0	8.77	9.0	7.11	8.0	8.84
11.0	8.33	11.0	9.26	11.0	7.81	8.0	8.47
14.0	9.96	14.0	8.10	14.0	8.84	8.0	7.04
6.0	7.24	6.0	6.13	6.0	6.08	8.0	5.25
4.0	4.26	4.0	3.10	4.0	5.39	19.0	12.50
12.0	10.84	12.0	9.13	12.0	8.15	8.0	5.56
7.0	4.82	7.0	7.26	7.0	6.42	8.0	7.91
5.0	5.68	5.0	4.74	5.0	5.73	8.0	6.89

N = 11
mean of X's = 9.0
mean of Y's = 7.5
equation of regression line: $Y = 3 + 0.5X$
standard error of estimate of slope = 0.118
$t = 4.24$
sum of squares $X - \overline{X} = 110.0$
regression sum of squares = 27.50
residual sum of squares of Y = 13.75
correlation coefficient = .82
$r^2 = .67$

Figure 3.2. *Values and statistical representations of data sets from the Anscombe quartet (source: Tufte 2008, p. 13)*

A classic example of the added intelligibility provided by graphical representation over statistical representations such as mean or variance is that of the Anscombe quartet (Anscombe 1973, cited in Tufte 2008). In this example, four data sets (Figure 3.2) composed of two *x* and *y* variables have the same statistical properties (number of values, mean and variance of *x* and *y*, correlation between the two, equation of the linear regression line, etc.). However, when plotting the scatter plot of these four sets, it becomes apparent that they do not look at all the same (Figure 3.3).

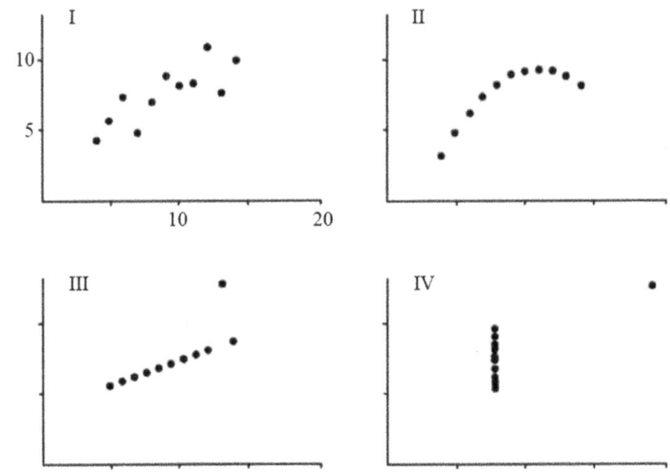

Figure 3.3. *Data set scatter plots of the Anscombe quartet (source: Tufte 2008, p. 14)*

As will be developed in Chapter 6, data visualization benefits from the epistemic value attributed to direct observation, and from the evidential character (in the sense of what is beyond doubt as well as in the sense of evidence) of what can be seen with the naked eye rather than by purely statistical representations such as mean and variance. This obviousness of what is visually represented is an epistemic virtue that is reflected in our ordinary language, where we can see with the naked eye that something is obvious because *it can be seen* and where we understand the world around us with our gaze. What can be shown need not be demonstrated: in common sense, observation renders reasoning useless and constitutes its own evidence. Data visualization takes full advantage of the epistemic virtue of observability. It is thus based on common sense, sufficient to see what is seen, but also on the art of observation developed by a trained eye: the data analyst and also the one who knows how to see clues in the data, what the ordinary eye cannot spot. Data visualization is part of an epistemology of the eye as conceptualized by Lorraine Daston and Peter Galison (2007), but also of the art of *trained judgment* developed in the same book as one of the epistemic virtues that underlie scientific truths.

However, the expertise at work in exploratory data analysis is not just about vision. It is a trained judgment but also a trained manipulation, a game between seeing and doing. The combination of intuition, experience and command of the statistical tools at the analyst's disposal are necessary to instrument the inventiveness with which they gather, sequence and represent data to identify interesting angles. In the absence of a formal (or informal, but at least teachable) method, the analyst must invent methodological and graphical solutions to each new data set using the toolbox proposed by Tukey. With this inventiveness by which intelligibility is coupled with sagacity, the analyst must detect the nonsense that can be introduced by visualization. A representation can indeed be misleading: if, for example, the visualization tool used automatically truncates the axis of a histogram, the difference between two series of data will appear disproportionate, creating a false impression of meaning. In the absence of standards such as the *p*-value in hypothesis testing, this sagacity also consists of being able to distinguish what is significant from what is not, which is information or statistical noise.

Exploratory data analysis is thus presented as an art, both as a non-formalized, prescientific skill, the execution of which depends on the analyst's quality, and as an aesthetic work through which data visualization plays a rhetorical role of seduction and argumentation. As a skill, the art of identifying leads and clues is a constituent aspect of exploratory data analysis that can be linked with the evidential paradigm at work in the cultural sciences and which we have already discussed. Like Ginzburg, Tukey uses the metaphor of the detective and the police investigation:

> "A detective investigating a crime needs both tools and understanding. If he has no fingerprint powder, he will fail to find fingerprints on most surfaces. If he does not understand where the criminal is likely to have put his fingers, he will not look in the right places. Equally, the analyst of data needs both tools and understanding. It is the purpose of this book to provide some of each."

Tukey's guide is thus presented as an investigative manual for data analysts. This is based, as Ginzburg writes, "on details that most people do not notice". Exploratory data analysis techniques are the tool of this observation work: like luminol, they reveal what we cannot see with the naked eye, they highlight what we cannot see by looking at the data themselves, but at a given graphical representation. The mediation of data visualization combines with the data analyst's judgment to identify clues. This "detective" singularizes elements that present additional meanings in relation to the whole: irregularities, anomalies, surprising elements in relation to pre-established knowledge. Statistical and graphical techniques to represent data synthetically are not so much to describe the data as to provide a framework for comparison to highlight variations. Averages and regularities are the benchmarks, the frame of reference from which the analyst looks for statistical difference.

As a result, nothing that comes to light with data analysis comes to light automatically: techniques linked with the exploratory approach empower an analyst whose judgment is the key to understanding the data. Nevertheless, unlike the Ginzburg detective or art critic, Tukey's clue is already a quantity singled out as significant, and not a unit, a singular object: it is not a single branch broken by the beast that the hunter is tracking, but an exceptional, statistically significant number of broken branches that may be an indication, for example, of the movement of an animal population. The index of exploratory statistics is a quantity that derives from a norm within the data, rather than an element that stands out from the background of reality. Moreover, the form of restitution of the evidential paradigm is narrative, argumentation, i.e. in the terms of Ricoeur (1983) a temporal synthesis of the heterogeneous; conversely, that of exploratory analysis is initially a spatial or topological synthesis, based on the graphic rhetoric of data visualization, although a narrative of the data can be proposed later, as we will see in Chapter 6.

The exploratory paradigm developed by Tukey predates the computerization of data analysis and statistics. Alongside transformations brought about by the development of computer science in the natural sciences, he too nevertheless built up a computational form in the meantime: if we thus have to search for the genealogy of the spirit of the data sciences, it is with Tukey, through data mining, that we have to look for an origin. The exploratory approach has thus found applications in the business computing world in the form of data mining and knowledge discovery. Although data mining is not necessarily presented as an exclusively industrial technique, its main applications are in marketing, finance and fraud detection; examples cited in the literature generally relate to the analysis of consumer data (Fayyad *et al.* 1996). Data exploration is conditioned by the existence of structured databases in data warehouses that follow conventional models and are used to aggregate the "business" data produced and/or available to the company: it emerges from the development of business intelligence in the 1990s and its function is to facilitate decision making in companies.

The term knowledge extraction, or more exactly knowledge discovery in databases, is attributed to Gregory Piatetsky-Shapiro and defined as "knowledge discovery is the nontrivial extraction of implicit, previously unknown, and potentially useful information from data" (Frawley, Piatetsky-Shapiro, and Matheus 1992); it is notably a question of identifying patterns, subsets of similar elements and anomalies. This field is based on the notions of exploration, discovery and on the idea that the object studied is the data itself and not what it represents. It is a data-driven approach in which knowledge must be the end product, and in which data mining is only one step among others such as selection, pre-processing, and interpretation. Like Tukey's exploratory data analysis, knowledge discovery is a general approach that is more about purpose and mindset than about specific techniques. It is the methodological paradigm of data science.

Within this paradigm, data analysis per se is based on techniques derived from business informatics, natural and cultural science research, statistics or artificial intelligence. These categories are themselves simplifications of the fundamental or applied research fields leading to these techniques. We now examine, through the main techniques of data sciences, the status of interdisciplinary research that makes possible this indifference to historical theoretical frameworks and this ease of circulation between epistemic projects.

3.6. The institutional and theoretical melting pot of data science

The various computational techniques used in data mining have been the subject of numerous attempts to classify them according to their origin, function or theoretical basis. Thus, the *Mining Massive Datasets* guide (Rajaraman *et al.* 2011) organizes data mining algorithms according to the operations performed on the data (clustering, outlier detection, similarity search, etc.) as well as the nature of the data (streaming data, large sets) or epistemic problems (recommendation, advertising, web analysis), which can also be different; thus, the search for similarity is one of the techniques used to generate recommendations that can be applied to advertising targeting problems. Similarly, the guide *R and Data Mining: Examples and Case Studies* (Zhao 2012) proposes groupings both according to the type of operation performed and the algorithm's technical lineage: thus, clustering, decision trees and regression are three types of classification techniques, but are the subject of different chapters. At a more conceptual level, Diakopoulos (2015) proposes to organize data science techniques according to the type of decision made by the algorithm: prioritization, classification, association and filtering.

In reality, from the point of view of the operations carried out on the data, we identify three main families:

– *prioritization*, which assigns a rank;

– *classification*, which assigns a category;

– *clustering*, which assigns similar elements.

Filtering in the sense of Diakopoulos is a form of binary classification that breaks down a set between filtered and unfiltered. Association is a form of grouping, while prioritization includes what Diakopoulos calls prioritization. Nevertheless, when the question is examined from the point of view of the epistemic problem posed, these different families can be mobilized alternately or in a complementary manner. For example, a search engine prioritizes search results, but it may also rely on identifying terms similar to the search terms, or return all results matching the same thematic category as the search terms. If these families constitute entry keys into the universe of data analysis algorithms, no attempt to classify these algorithms will be satisfactory because of their constant circulation and their versatility in terms of technical and epistemic problems, or in other words, their ability to belong to all and none of these families at the same time. Historical background, research community and theoretical framework do not determine in any way the cases and functions of these techniques which are, on the one hand, indifferent to them and, on the other hand, circulate from one framework to another.

At the lowest level, there are libraries or specific implementations that enable the effective use of an existing algorithm, e.g. the APriori algorithm developed by Agrawal and Srikant (1994). The APriori algorithm is defined as an association rules algorithm, i.e. a technique that enables the identification of frequently associated elements. Historically, it is known for its application in mass distribution where it enables identifying products frequently bought together by analyzing supermarket checkout history. Being frequently associated can be seen as a way of measuring some form of similarity between elements, or at least a way of grouping elements together according to a certain systematic logic. In addition, there are countless techniques for automatically grouping elements in the family of unsupervised classification algorithms. The notions of supervised and unsupervised classification come from the field of machine learning, itself considered as an application or an extension of the general project of artificial intelligence. Although association rules and unsupervised classification are two technically distinct algorithm families, operating according to different principles, they can be related in terms of their function, i.e. to achieve or highlight similarities between elements, regardless of the meaning initially associated with these elements (products, people, words, etc.).

Through the example of automatic clustering, we can see that, from the point of view of epistemic functions but not historical origins, there are strong overlaps between data mining techniques developed in industry and machine learning techniques developed by researchers. Moreover, as discussed in our analysis of the mythology of big data, the processing of big data calls into question the relevance of this industry/research dichotomy. Indeed, we are seeing the emergence of actors who escape this dichotomy and base the richness of their work on this freedom. For example, the sociologist of science Shinn (2000) conceptualized the notion of "transversal regime" to describe practitioners whose work is organized around a project rather than around specific disciplines or organizations. These practitioners can be at the same time academics, engineers, contractors and consultants, while also escaping all these categories. Along with the disciplinary regime, which maintains membership in a discipline, and the transitory regime, in which the practitioner "crosses the boundaries of his discipline" to borrow from neighboring disciplines, the transversal regime is one of the three research regimes put forward by Shinn. The interdisciplinary regime can, for example, take the form of "technico-instrumental" research. This type of research:

> "...is based on concrete practices that include design, construction, endless odd jobs and analysis to justify the basic principles of the instruments, adaptation to improve their performance, research and monitoring to define the extent to which a generic instrument can be generalized, testing and modification to check whether the principles of generalization hold, and transfer of the instrument to users for final adoption and implementation."

Marked by opportunism and the rejection of allegiance to a particular organization, the figure of the technical-instrumental researcher frequently moves from industry to research and vice versa; their intellectual production takes the form of concrete instruments, scientific publications, reports, patents and conferences. The "artisan" of technical-instrumental research is concerned with instrument design more than a theoretical activity, and strives to produce generic tools, which can have multiple applications. Today, this figure could probably resemble certain types of influential entrepreneurs who speak indiscriminately to an academic, professional, or amateur audience, with an ability to mediate without being placed in a category.

The concepts developed by Terry Shinn are particularly useful in describing the actors who design and develop the algorithms for big data processing. To understand the origin of these techniques, we must not only analyze the circulations between the institutions defined by classical sociology of science, but also consider out of context these categories to understand how these techniques emerged. Just as the techniques themselves move from one institution to another, actors also navigate between changing institutional contexts. These material conditions correspond to a theoretical framing (or lack of framing) that has a direct influence on the design and intended uses of these techniques.

If we now look at the most "influential" algorithms in data mining, we can see that almost all of them are the result of transit or transversal trajectories. To illustrate this, we refer to a survey (Wu *et al.* 2008) presented at one of the major data mining research conferences, the 2008 International Conference on Data Mining (ICDM) organized by the IEEE. This survey is based on the contributions of the winners of two awards, the ACM KDD Innovation Award and the IEEE ICDM Research Contributions Award. The IEEE and the ACM are the main organizations of computer researchers, here mobilized in the field of knowledge discovery and data mining. These winners identified a number of techniques. Those with fewer than 50 citations in research articles were eliminated. The list was then put to the vote of a multitude of actors in the field (organizers and participants in research conferences) whose votes concurred. Although this survey does not necessarily make it possible to identify the main techniques of mass data processing in general (and does not take into account only industrial players), it nevertheless gives a good idea of recognized techniques in the field.

In the "top 10" highlighted by this survey, we find the APriori algorithm that we have already mentioned, as well as other families of techniques. Half of this top 10 consists of supervised classification techniques (C4.5, CART, SVM, kNN, Naive Bayes), which is indeed the most common problem in machine learning. Also present are methods for unsupervised classification (k-means), parameter estimation (EM), sorting (Page Rank) and boosting (classifier optimization: AdaBoost).

As the APriori algorithm embodied an example of the flow of an industrial problem towards more generic uses, the k-means is an example of a technique's trajectory resulting from research in cultural sciences. It is the work of a psychologist, James McQueen, who was interested in the mathematical modeling of human activities; in the article describing his method, he presents several applications on both behavioral and textual variables derived from psychological observations of student populations (MacQueen 1967). Finally, the disciplinary circulation of a technique can be done by its designers themselves: a documentary indexing technique that is now commonplace, Latent Semantic Analysis, which was patented in 1988 and published two years later in a information science and technology journal (Deerwester *et al.* 1990), was later reworked by its designers for use in psycholinguistics (Landauer and Dumais 1997), with the theoretical ambition of better understanding language acquisition in children. The corresponding article is published in a psychology journal, *Psychological Review*.

It was at Bell Laboratories, where Turing, Shannon and Tukey also worked, that Vapnik and his colleagues developed Support Vector Machines (SVMs), which are among the top 10 in the ICDM. SVMs are extremely popular in data mining because of their simplicity, efficiency and the quality of the results they provide. As a result, they quickly supplanted neural network-based techniques when they first appeared. Vapnik's ability to migrate between institutions (now working at Facebook), from research to industry, is reflected in his theoretical work: in 1998, he proposed the statistical theory of learning (Vapnik 1998) which provides a statistical basis for artificial learning and ensures theoretical continuity between these two often opposing cultures.

Another example of an individual who embodies a synthesis between these two cultures is Leo Breiman, a statistical researcher who became a consultant and then returned to academia. He is thus a perfect example of the researcher and techno-experimental craftsman described by Terry Shinn. Breiman is best known in the IT community for developing random forest techniques, surprisingly absent from the ICDM ranking. In a research paper on "two cultures" in statistical modeling (Breiman *et al.* 2001), he describes the mindset of the machine learning practitioners he worked with in industry when he was a consultant, and the emerging community of computer and physics engineers and researchers working on this type of approach from the 1980s onwards. As a result, Breiman is not only an emblematic actor of techno-instrumental research under a transversal regime at work in data sciences, and a significant contributor to this type of research, but also an observer, almost an analyst, of the social and epistemic conditions of the advent of data sciences from multiple technical and disciplinary lines.

In his article, Breiman regrets the conservatism of the "statistical" culture as opposed to the emerging culture of "algorithmic modeling". The opposition between these two cultures is evident in the reception of the article, which is commented on with virulence by eminent representatives of the statistical culture that it denounces, such as David Cox and Brad Efron. Whether this opposition is philosophical, cultural, generational, institutional or a mixture of these aspects is not evident from the comments, but it appears there with a force that goes beyond that of an exchange of arguments on computational techniques.

These two cultures thus partially coincide with the opposition between academic and industrial practices, and with certain predilections on both sides. They also refer to techniques that are more specific to them. While they are the subject of intense debate, it is probably also because the two cultures have many points in common, possibly described in different terms. Robert Tibshirani, Professor of "Statistics and Biomedical Data Science" at Stanford University, has thus examined a number of comparative elements between machine learning and statistics for the purpose of clarification for his students (Figure 3.4), suggesting that the same algorithm can be interpreted in machine learning as in statistics. Indeed, if these two cultures can be opposed in such a precise way, it is because they are part of a common task, the (now systematic) computational analysis of data. It is at the level of the conceptual framework, the epistemic culture and the research community that the differentiation between these two cultures is played out.

Machine learning	Statistics
network, graphs	model
weights	parameters
learning	fitting
generalization	test set performance
supervised learning	regression/classification
unsupervised learning	density estimation, clustering
large grant = $1,000,000	large grant = $50,000
nice place to have a meeting : Snowbird, Utah, French Alps	nice place to have a meeting : Las Vegas in August

Figure 3.4. *Lecture notes by Robert Tibshirani, Professor of "Statistics and Biomedical Data Science" at Stanford University*

Breiman's article thus crystallizes a balance of power between two epistemic cultures at the very beginning of the 2000s, before the emergence of the big data phenomenon. Today, the articulation between these two cultures has become more complex:

– some statisticians simply consider data science to be a buzzword for statistics, and therefore they are data scientists[6];

– some statistical techniques such as logistic regression are often described as machine learning techniques[7];

---

6 See http://simplystatistics.org/2011/11/22/data-scientist-vs-statistician/ [accessed November 16, 2017].

7 See https://en.wikipedia.org/w/index.php?title=Machine_learning&oldid=951683773 [accessed November 16, 2017].

– other statisticians feel threatened by the increasing proportion of their work that can be automated[8];

– practitioners of data science do not generally oppose data science and statistics, but consider statistics to be an indispensable skill for a good data scientist[9].

On the other hand, if statistical techniques and know-how are indeed absorbed by data sciences, the epistemic culture of statistics seems no more soluble in that of data sciences than in that of machine learning, with which it does not quite coincide. The opposition traced by Breiman persists from the point of view of the "philosophy of data" practiced by these two cultures.

One way to understand the incommensurability of these two cultures is to compare them to the incommensurability of Kuhn's scientific paradigms. Statics and data sciences would then correspond to their own theoretical frameworks, within which formal and computational models are developed that can circulate from one framework to another. It is not the models but the theories that are incompatible. Thus, as a theoretical framework, Newtonian physics and general relativity are immeasurable: they correspond to mutually contradictory representations of the world. Nevertheless, in terms of its models, Newtonian physics is not invalidated, but perfected by general relativity. Its equations are less exact, but are often sufficient approximations to represent a target system; for example, taking into account the curvature of space-time to model the flow of water in a bathtub is a sophistication that adds complexity to the analytical model without providing any interesting precision. In the natural sciences, two theories can be incommensurable while leaving the possibility of translating the models from one into the other.

Similarly, statistics and data science can be seen as two mutually contradictory mathematical and computational theories based on different standards of validity. Nevertheless, as we have seen for numerical simulation techniques and tools in the natural sciences, techniques and models developed within distinct theories can, because of their operational nature, circulate, regardless of the underlying theory. The models are used in an

8 See http://bulletin.imstat.org/2014/09/data-science-how-is-it-different-to-statistics%E2%80%89/ [accessed November 16, 2017].

9 See https://blog.mixpanel.com/2016/03/30/this-is-the-difference-between-statistics-and-data-science/ [accessed November 16, 2017].

a-theoretical way, for their only computational effectiveness, and not for the object they may have initially represented.

The contribution of statistics to data sciences, through its methods and techniques, is therefore not an isolated phenomenon: several historical lines mobilizing computational or pre-computational data processing have been aggregated in the melting pot of data sciences. While the contribution of statistics is made at the price of an epistemological decapitation, which removes statistics from its theoretical standards, the contribution of the field of artificial intelligence seems to be made in a less conflicting way, due to its own history and in particular to the way this project has revised its ambitions over time.

3.7. The contribution of artificial intelligence

The initial artificial intelligence project can be summarized as an artifact design project aimed at a better understanding of human intelligence, both at the biological level, the physicality of the brain and at the cognitive level, the functioning of the mind. As Bachimont (1996) and Lassègue (1996) have pointed out, this is not originally a technological project for the development of computing tools for the cognitive sciences, but a cognitive science project that aims at a better understanding of objects such as the mind or intelligence through the construction of tools for modeling and simulating these objects. It should be understood as a science of the artificial mind. As such, it produces and mobilizes psychological or neurological theories such as computationalism, connectionnism, cognitivism and behaviorism. The Dartmouth Conference of 1956, generally considered as the birthplace of the artificial intelligence project, had the following purpose: "The study is to proceed on the basis of the conjecture that every aspect of learning or any other feature of intelligence can in principle be so precisely described that a machine can be made to simulate it".

This was a machine-instrumented investigation project, whose mobilization requires the formalization of the objects studied. The main themes of artificial intelligence were already included: reasoning, language learning, the construction of artificial neural networks, the relationship between machine and programming, and the relationship between machine and mind. It was also an artifact project, which aimed to build intelligent machines.

The Dartmouth conference symbolized the meeting of two research fields that had been active since the 1940s: cybernetics and formal systems. With McCulloch and Pitts, on the one hand, to which we shall return later, but also Wiener, cybernetics was already advancing on the questions of the relationship between thought and computation, and the modeling and construction of artificial systems, following approaches more or less oriented toward modeling or engineering. Just as the concept of control applied to the living and the artificial, the concept of intelligence applied to humans and machines alike. On the other hand, a mathematical research project, led in particular by Hilbert and then Gödel, led to the work of Turing and a mechanical conception of reasoning.

Nevertheless, artificial intelligence is a vast and ambitious project, which from the outset brings together diverse research and more or less homogeneous working hypotheses. The same researcher can evolve their approach and hypotheses. Thus, the same Turing, who answered, as a mathematician, the problem of Hilbert's decision in 1936, wondered, some 15 years later, about the nature of thought and the consequences of the hypothetical development of thinking machines. Even before the Dartmouth conference, the 1950 paper "Computing machinery and intelligence", published in the psychology and philosophy journal *Mind*, set out a research agenda for the science of the artificial mind. In this article, Turing begins by returning to the ambition to create "machines that think" by removing the relevance of the very question of whether a machine can think, and replacing it with the question of a machine's ability to mimic human behavior. This was the famous "imitation game", now called the "Turing test", then posed as a thought experiment to reformulate the question of the articulation between thought and machines.

Turing aimed to imitate human cognitive abilities, excluding the human body, later embodied in some robotics research. While he initially considered as a machine any artifact similar to humans, including someone who could be bioengineered, in every way similar to someone "born naturally", his thinking then turned more specifically to digital computers or, as we would simply say today, computers. If the reformulation of the capacities of these machines into imitation capacity rather than thinking capacity may at first sight seem like a reduction of this ambition, it is on the contrary a way of circumventing a certain number of objections relating to the thinking and consciousness of the machines. The artificial intelligence project is thus redefined as an artifact project not of thinking machines, but of machines capable of imitating human cognitive abilities in a convincing enough way. Formulated in this way, this project is the subject of extensive speculation on the part of Turing, who went as far as to wonder how his machines and humans could befriend each other, or how to integrate "machine-children" into the school without the other pupils making excessive fun of them. Finally, the conclusion of the article proposes a number of options for future work in artificial intelligence:

> "We may hope that machines will eventually compete with men in all purely intellectual fields. But which are the best ones to start with? Even this is a difficult decision. Many people think that a very abstract activity, like the playing of chess, would be best. It can also be maintained that it is best to provide the machine with the best sense organs that money can buy, and then teach it to understand and speak English. This process could follow the normal teaching of a child. Things would be pointed out and named, etc. Again I do not know what the right answer is, but I think both approaches should be tried.
>
> We can only see a short distance ahead, but we can see plenty there that needs to be done."

Turing outlined a research program that would appear to be remarkably successful. Speech recognition, pattern recognition, natural language processing, conversational agents, expert systems and machine learning are all fields of research whose success is considered necessary to build machines that learn, perceive, speak, understand and reason.

The perceptron imagined by Rosenblatt in 1958 was one of the first if not the first example of a machine actually built to carry out this program. It reflects the duality between science and technology of the original project of artificial intelligence, in that it is both a theoretical description of the brain as an information storage and processing system, and the design of a computational model corresponding to this definition:

> "The theory to be presented here takes the empiricist, or "connectionist" position with regard to [the] questions [that we must answer to understand the capability of higher organisms for perceptual recognition, generalization, recall, and thinking]. The theory has been developed for a hypothetical nervous

system, or machine, called a perceptron. The perceptron is designed to illustrate some of the fundamental properties of intelligent systems in general, without becoming too deeply enmeshed in the special, and frequently unknown, conditions which hold for particular biological organisms. The analogy between the perceptron and biological systems should be readily apparent to the reader." (Rosenblatt 1958)

As can be expected from research in the field of cognitive sciences, published in a psychology journal, Rosenblatt's article first examines the different theories and positions existing at his time on the processing of information in the brain, and claims to belong to the connectionist school. Moreover, it should be noted that the very fact of conceptualizing the nervous system as an information processing system is also an implicit assumption, which could be discussed or formulated in other terms. The article then proposes a functionalist model of the brain, freed from its biological substrate, but imitating its structure, and whose ambition is to reproduce and represent its functioning: Rosenblatt concludes with the explicit hope that his model will help to better understand "information processing systems, human as well as artificial". He was more specifically interested in perception, visual recognition and learning. It is not a purely conceptual model, but a computational model and a formal procedure, i.e. an algorithm, with its software and hardware implementation, including the Mark I perceptron (see Figure 3.5) developed in the 1950s at the Cornell Aeronautical Laboratory.

Figure 3.5. *The Mark I perceptron at Cornell Aeronautical Laboratory (source: Cornell University Library)*

This model is designed to be dynamic: following the idea that the nervous system reconfigures itself according to the visual stimuli it receives, a perceptron reconfigures itself according to the information sent to it. We can thus consider the perceptron as the founding algorithm of machine learning, i.e. a formal procedure capable of modifying the model's structure according to the information sent to it, or as we will say today, of learning from data. This ability to learn is the perceptron's major contribution to the artificial neural networks imagined by McCulloch and Pitts (1943), who proposed a more sophisticated model of the neuron from a logical-formal point of view, but incapable of mimicking the plasticity of the brain and learning from the information received.

If we compare Rosenblatt's objective with that of Turing, we will note that it was no longer a question of building a machine that would imitate a human's behavior in a way that would be convincing enough for a human evaluator, but of making something that resembles the brain from a functional point of view, with the need to propose a model of the said brain. In terms of cognitive science, Rosenblatt was a cognitivist and representationalist where Turing was a behaviorist, embodying several conceptions of the brain in their time.

Severely criticized by Minsky and Papert in 1969 in their book *Perceptrons* for its inability to effectively learn elementary logical functions, the perceptron is, however, the first transformation of a technical lineage of artificial neural networks in which we first find supervised techniques, such as the recurrent neural networks introduced by Grossberg (1988), and the convolutional neural networks introduced by Fukushima (1980) and then the unsupervised techniques from the very end of the 1980s (LeCun 2014). This lineage has long been out of favor both for the weakness of its results, the insufficient computing power of computers and the dominance of the symbolist stream and AI knowledge engineering, and due to the availability of simpler and more efficient machine learning techniques such as SVM and random forests. In particular, this disfavor led to a reduction in the theoretical scope of artificial neural networks, which therefore does not date back to the advent of data sciences (unless the history of these fields is rewritten retrospectively). In the early 1980s, in Fukushima's work (1980), for example, the artificial intelligence and understanding of the brain project is still in active mode: "If we could make a neural network model which has the same capability for pattern recognition as a human being, it would give us a powerful clue to the understanding of the neural mechanism in the brain".

By the mid-1980s, the tone, the mood, had changed. The concepts of brain and nervous system were disappearing, and research objectives were in the realm of logical-mathematical and computational development. In a 1989 article considered influential by LeCun, Hornik *et al.* (1989) describe their ambition in the following terms:

> "This paper rigorously establishes that standard multilayer feedforward networks with as few as one hidden layer using arbitrary squashing functions are capable of approximating any Borel measurable function from one finite dimensional space to another to any desired degree of accuracy, provided sufficiently many hidden units are available."

Similarly, the work of Rumelhart *et al.* (1985), who read and cited the work of Minsky and Papert, is a refinement of techniques:

> "The major theoretical contribution of the work is the procedure called error propagation, whereby the gradient can be determined by individual units of the network based only on locally available information."

This lineage has come back in force following the appearance of the big data phenomenon, because of a configuration that benefits from these technical improvements, a computing power and a volume of data never before seen.

The major difference between the artificial neural networks used today in data sciences and those of Rosenblatt or McCulloch and Pitts is, as we can see from the end of the 1980s, that they are now stripped of their initial theoretical ambition for researchers and practitioners of these techniques: there is no trace of a willingness to create a general artificial intelligence, nor of explanatory research in cognitive sciences[10]. It is no longer a question of representing, but at best of reproducing and imitating cognitive abilities such

10 However, the imagination associated with artificial intelligence is alive and well, with its share of enthusiasts and worried people. During the months when the first version of this book was written, media and commercial discourse shifted from "big data made X possible" to "an algorithm made X possible" to "an artificial intelligence made X possible" to describe an identical process. Whether the process in question is at least based on machine learning or on a set of manually formalized rules rarely intervenes in the choice of the vocabulary in question.

as vision, speech or language. This is the essential change that makes it possible to understand the difference between artificial intelligence as a scientific, technological and artifactual project and machine learning as a field of research and technological application. If one can be seen as a technoscience producing artifacts with explanatory intent, the other loses that explanatory intent. As Turing's 1950 paper foreshadowed, more specialized fields such as robotics, natural language processing, knowledge engineering or computer vision also developed. Moving from a general program to a set of specialized fields means at least postponing the project of a strong artificial intelligence, similar to human intelligence, which would comprise the assembly of the results of these different specialized fields. In practice, these fields have also changed from scientific research with an explanatory purpose to technological research with an instrumental purpose. Theoretical and even philosophical questions are usually dismissed unless a practical problem can be solved without returning to a more conceptual level. With the efficiency of machine learning techniques in these fields, industrial applications are within reach, which also favors applied instrumental development (producing and perfecting technical objects) at the expense of fundamental development.

More prosaically, artificial neural networks are used essentially like any classification algorithm, in the same way as SVMs or random forests. Data mining techniques from the development of data warehouses, neural networks inspired by the original artificial intelligence program, and other machine learning techniques have had distinct historical developments, but do not present strong theoretical or functional distinctions: there is little good justification for proposing a classification of the techniques mobilized by data sciences that follows these historical distinctions, especially since these lineages crossed many times before the appearance of data sciences. The work of Piatetsky-Shapiro and colleagues (1996) on Knowledge Discovery in Databases (KDD), mentioned above, was published in *AI Magazine* and the journal *American Association for Artificial Intelligence*. They point out that the term has become popular since 1989 in the fields of artificial intelligence and machine learning; it also describes KDD as a field emerging from the meeting of existing fields, including AI:

> "KDD has evolved, and continues to evolve, from the intersection of research fields such as machine learning, pattern recognition, databases, statistics, AI, knowledge acquisition for

> expert systems, data visualization, and high-performance computing."

As early as the 1990s, the distinction between artificial intelligence (in the sense of a set of machine learning techniques) and data mining (or KDD) became indistinct. Artificial mind science is hardly at work in these developments anymore, even if some researchers or engineers remain vectors of computationalist beliefs. The development of data warehouses historically coincides with the appearance of unsupervised machine learning techniques (including artificial neural network techniques) also used for searching these data warehouses. The appearance of new data in companies, the development of a melting pot of techniques, constitutes a first conjunction between new data, a set of techniques and an improvement in computing power, which could be seen as a first age of big data and data sciences. In any case, the development of data mining integrates the different characteristics of data sciences as the art of computation: know-how based on autonomous research of computational techniques, a pre-eminence of computational models over conceptual models, the insertion in an exploratory paradigm and a circulation of techniques independently of the epistemic project made possible by these different characteristics.

3.8. Conclusion

Computation or computational analysis is a necessary component of the methodological paradigm for making big data intelligible. It is part of the computational cultural sciences, but it is not the totality of them: it is surrounded, upstream, by a theoretical and technical framework that makes it possible to confer an epistemic value on the data and to constitute a coherent unit of information (a corpus), and downstream, by the work of interpretation and recontextualization that we will discuss in the following chapters.

On the epistemological level, the mobilization of computation engenders a double restriction from the knowable to the computable:

– the data must become computable, in terms of format and medium, to involve the data sciences;

– the computable and the computed determine the field of the knowable and constitute a subset of it through the mathematization of epistemic problems.

In other words, there is a dual determination of knowledge and data by computation, which defines the conditions of possibilities of producing one from the other. To this dual theoretical determination is added a practical restriction of what is knowable, through a specific epistemic culture, computational thinking, which directs the production of knowledge toward objects that can be subjected to modeling and computation.

This dual determination is common to all mobilizations of computation in data processing to produce knowledge, whether in the natural sciences, field-based disciplines or data sciences. In the cultural sciences, the mobilization of computation is mainly the result of modeling work, from which computation occupies a status close to that of an observation or experiment. Numerical simulation, in particular, makes it possible to produce data that replace experimental data obtained through measurements of scientific instruments with simulated data. The computation is then integrated into an epistemic continuity that ranges from theory to experimentation through the model. Conversely, data sciences have a status of know-how without a theoretical framework, which does not assign a specific meaning to the data. They intervene at the level of the computational model and not at higher levels. They take the data for itself, as it constitutes the territory to be explored by means of computational techniques whose theoretical and institutional origins are multiple and without consequence on practices and results. As such, they constitute a melting pot of techniques that acts as an exploratory toolbox for a variety of epistemic projects. These projects may be defined in advance, or may emerge from exploration, and will not receive final meaning until later.

Data sciences do not provide standards or a conceptual framework that would allow the result of the computation to be interpreted as some representation of reality. This means that the epistemic value of the data, obtained prior to the computation, is suspended by it, and that the meaning of the results, while being consistent with this epistemic value, must be reconstructed by attributing a meaning to the computational transformations of the data. In these terms, the function of the epistemic project is not so much to provide a rudimentary framework for data processing as a set of working hypotheses that emerge and evolve over the course of exploration. It is the common thread that makes it possible to explain a corpus constitution logic, to guide the preparation, formatting and exploration of data, and finally to formulate a meaning that can be communicated through interpretative know-how.

It is indeed up to the practitioner to discover the meaning of the data from their epistemic project by iteratively mobilizing imagination and computation following an exploratory paradigm. The epistemic value of the data is a possibility updated by these two operations of the equipped mind, put in suspense by the computation. As we will now see through a concrete case of big data exploitation, this art of interpretation is present at all stages of the constitution and restitution of the meaning of data, whether this restitution is narrative, visual or software-based in nature. Although this art of interpretation is, finally, largely based on the methods of cultural sciences, it is in a completely different institutional framework of a software company, which we will return to.

4

A Practical Big Data Use Case

So far, we have highlighted the practices associated with big data and their computational processing. The mythology of big data is contradictory to the practical modalities of exploiting digital footprints from the web, while the digital humanities hypothetically represent a configuration realized in practice by data sciences, themselves loaded with the mythology of artificial intelligence. The status of data and processing techniques constitute both elements of epistemological questioning and steps in the processes involved in knowledge production using digital footprints. The status of the data arises with the constitution of the corpus, while what data sciences do to the data materializes during their actual processing. In explaining these two components, data and computation, we have also highlighted the simultaneous need for a third component and a third step to bring intelligibility to the data: the question of interpreting computation results, and the role of hermeneutics in the production of valid knowledge.

Moreover, the way we have examined the data and the computation has so far remained rather general, with an ambition to describe the characteristics common to all computational processing of digital footprints. While the analysis of the general conditions of knowledge generation in this context has been a significant part of the research work presented here, the examination of a more specific case has also been a significant component, the presentation of which we have delayed until now. In order to give weight to this generality and to show how it branches out by anchoring itself in reality, we are now going to present this more precise case by describing how the problems of corpus constitution and data cleaning, the processing modalities and what they do to the data, concretely materialize in a given situation. We will thus be able to confirm and qualify what we have developed so far, while showing that each situation also presents specific epistemological problems, which cannot be considered as universal properties of digital footprint processing, but which illustrate instead the density of the methodological ramifications implied.

This more specific case is based on a "field based experience" – the modalities of which are described below – which allowed us to observe and participate several times in a digital footprint process. While being more specific, it also retains a certain generality with respect to a single process that would have been observed as a unique event; it is in fact a summary of the repetitions of the process. It also illustrates several points that we have developed so far: these are, of course, digital footprints relating to human behavior, which are computationally processed using techniques inspired by artificial intelligence, decisional computing and statistics. These digital footprints are not exploited by researchers in cultural sciences, but by a software company on behalf of customers. This company, on the one hand, has the technical culture to manipulate such data, and, on the other hand, carries out these operations for non-academic purposes.

This case, however, has unique characteristics in relation to the archetypical situation we have drawn so far. Indeed, the analyzed data are textual in nature, which mobilizes techniques and problems of format and representation of additional data compared to the so-called structured data. Moreover, their analysis is carried out in a distributed manner among several epistemic agents who occupy different functions and are thus understood, as we shall see, within the framework of a social epistemology.

4.1. Presentation of the case study

This case study is based on several years of experience in an organization that processes massive amounts of data, the software publisher Proxem. In its communication, Proxem presents itself as a player in big data and thus constitutes an example of a representative for this mythology; in terms of activity, Proxem is a technological start-up specializing in natural language processing, a branch of artificial intelligence dedicated to the analysis of digital textual content, and which is one of the techniques used in data sciences. In terms of mythology as in terms of practice, Proxem is a player in the computational processing of digital footprints.

I was part of the Proxem company between 2012 and 2019; my various roles led me to analyze, understand, design and develop tools for processing textual data. The nature of the data, the complexity of the processing and the difficulties in deriving meaningful results, assessing their reliability, and linking these results to customer needs triggered a reflection that was the starting point for this book. This reflection has been individual, with the present research work, but also collective, through exchanges, discussions and experiments by my colleagues. I was thus able to observe their practices, their working methods, their way of approaching a problem, but also to exchange and actively contribute to their activity, without holding a purely contemplative position.

The case presented is thus part of an ethnographic approach, insofar as it draws its legitimacy from its anchoring in the field, but also from a logic of strong intervention in the phenomena observed, which goes beyond the framework of participant observation. The idea was not to be a data scientist, and to describe from the inside the practices of this type of actor, but to be part of a collective work over several years mobilizing data scientists, software engineers, business engineers, communicators, linguists, managers, directors, etc. It is therefore not an ethnography of the data scientist, which would allow us to identify the essence of this figure, but research in a structure that intervenes on data science issues, whose complexity is sought to be shown, and in particular with regard to the diversity of actors, functions and epistemic positions which collectively address this issue. Therefore, this intervention can be seen as action research, carried out in a structure in keeping with the intent of this book, and which consists both in research on digital footprint processing aimed at producing a new understanding of this object, and in productive work that integrates this research into client projects and software design; action and production are mutually nourishing and transforming as they intervene in each other. In Lewin (1952), in fact, understanding is achieved through modification: the description or observation of practices is considered insufficient, whereas action really enables the modified object to be understood.

The concept of action research, which has many ramifications (Jouison-Laffitte 2009), describes well, in its classic form, the mutual agreement concluded with Proxem concerning my research work and its articulation with my roles in the company. While being based at Proxem gave my research substance to draw upon in order to problematize its object, this research work had to provide the company with a methodological contribution, allowing it to improve its software service and product offerings, and ideally constitute, in the form of a proprietary method, a marketable product in itself. The agreement put me in a privileged position to observe the company's practices and illustrate data science processes. The detailed knowledge of these practices allowed me to adapt my contribution to the company's specificities and to propose an intervention adapted to its problems. Thus, as Robinson (1993) advocates, there has been a convergence between the theoretical interests of the research being conducted and the expectations of the firm with respect to it.

All references to software design, language processing, customer project management, etc., which will follow here and in the following chapters, are nourished by this field experience that takes the form of observations, informal interviews, internal training, exchanges, contributions, practice, discussions, etc. Until 2015, the entire team was located in the same room, which allowed me to physically witness almost all of the exchanges between team members through physical immersion. I saw and heard them working, I could see their screens, the tools they used, and so on, and see what it is like to work for a software company. I acquired an understanding of what, for example, a release day in the software industry brings both from my colleagues' explanations, from their conversations with each other before, during and after the operation, from my access to the notifications in the internal monitoring tools of the different stages of the operation, from my access to the software before and after, and from repeating these points until I acquired a certain vision of the variability of the operation, how it could go well or badly, what it implied, etc. In addition, access to other information outside the company, via professional events, meetings with customers and prospects, and informal and friendly exchanges with other players in the sector, confirmed my colleagues' testimonies.

The guiding principle of the case study we will present is the process of analyzing a certain type of data. As we have mentioned, this is not the presentation of a single project in its singularity, but already a summary of different projects carried out for Proxem's customers. This summary does not come from observing the progress of the projects alone, but details the functioning of the tools used, the motivations of the methods and ways of doing things, and the explanations of the different participants, so as to describe but also to explain this process.

Moreover, this summary is nourished by my own research work, the academic knowledge acquired, alongside my work duties, on linguistics, natural language processing, statistics, quantitative and qualitative methods in the social sciences, textometry, etc., to which I refer in this summary when it sheds additional light. The mobilization of this academic knowledge has in fact led to a better understanding of this process, to the inclusion of methodological lines of thought that were known or unknown to my colleagues, and that facilitated my contribution to the process.

The process in question includes the following steps:

– creating and cleaning data;

– textual data analysis;

– interpretation, visualization and restitution.

While the first two, discussed in the preceding chapters, had partly stabilized by the time I joined the company, the final stages were still emerging. My action research thus brought about theoretical, methodological and practical answers to develop them, building interpretative know-how nourished by my academic knowledge on data analysis in the cultural sciences. This knowledge allowed me to move from an empirical and practical contribution to the data analysis process to a more formal contribution making its methodological and theoretical modalities explicit and formulated and transmitted within the company. As my contribution focused on the final stages of the process, it was imperative to have a clear understanding of the previous stages in order to make sense of them. In other words, where my colleagues were mainly involved in the constitution of the data and the computation, steps discussed in the previous chapters, I contributed to the interpretation of the results of the computation, which will be analyzed more specifically later on.

In what follows, the presentation of the process is therefore not so much the raw description of a series of events, as a reconceptualized reconstruction, based on several examples, of the typical procedure for data processing in the organization. The reconstruction is based both on empirical observations and on theoretical contributions, and on comparisons with other epistemic practices, with the aim of clarifying the procedure. It thus mixes, on the one hand, observations of practices and descriptions of these practices by their practitioners, and, on the other hand, an epistemological contribution that formalizes these practices, links them and inscribes them in research traditions in order to clarify their meaning.

Proxem is a software publisher founded in 2007 by François-Régis Chaumartin, entrepreneur and software engineer and holder of a PhD in linguistics (since 2012; see Chaumartin 2012). The software publisher markets semantic analysis solutions based on natural language processing technologies. Proxem offers several areas of application for its technologies and services, called "expertise". The company's three main areas of expertise are defined as follows:

– *customer experience*, where Proxem helps companies analyze the discourses of consumers and clients;

– *human resources*, where documents associated with a company's employees and candidates (job offers, CVs, annual interviews, etc.) are analyzed;

– *market intelligence*, for which the web presence of economic, public and market stakeholders is analyzed.

The commercial offer of the company is also structured in products of a different nature:

– a *software solution* of "exploration and visualization of textual data" available by subscription, which allows its users, since March 2017, to:

- collect text content from the web or load it into the software from an Excel table;

- extract information from this content and structure it according to a "thesaurus", also called a "coding plan" or "concept dictionary";

- quantify the information and visualize it in an interactive way;

- share results in the form of exports, dashboards or customized reports;

– a range of *services* including training, support, software configuration and the production of customized analyses.

From the moment I joined the company in February 2012 (more than a year before the start of the research work materialized by this book), I had multiple roles which evolved over time. In particular (but not exclusively), I was involved in:

– the structuring and promotion of commercial offers;

– the preparation of study reports and the design of a method for producing these reports;

– design and analysis of software usage.

4.2. Customer experience and coding of feedback

For the sake of brevity and readability, we will only present the process related to expertise called "customer experience": presenting the complete course of a typical project of this nature provides a better illustration of the concrete uses of data sciences at Proxem than attempting to aggregate practices related to the various expertise on offer, each governed by specific standards. In particular, "market intelligence" expertise is based on the constitution of data corpora from the web, an exercise that is still weakly stabilized in the company (therefore difficult to conceptualize) and that raises technical and epistemological issues that we will not develop here in order to focus on the role of technical instrumentation and interpretation in the data analysis process.

Customer experience, previously called customer knowledge, is the company's oldest and most stabilized expertise, and the one from which others were essentially derived; we present it as it was proposed by Proxem in 2017. Among the roles that I hold or have held at Proxem, a role as a research analyst, then as a research manager, have enabled me to be in direct contact with the recipients of the projects that fall within the scope of this expertise, and thus to understand their business, their problems, their expectations and their criteria for the acceptability of the work carried out by Proxem.

Before being a field of application for Proxem's technological and methodological skills, customer experience is in fact a concept that stems from marketing, which designates the relationship between a company and its customers, and conceptualizes it from the point of view of the subjective experience that customers have of the company through its various components (its products, its points of sale, its communication, its identity and its reputation). Proxem has developed its knowledge of this notion through contact with customers and prospects who expressed a need on this subject in order to promote its technologies in terms that are intelligible to these players. It is a concept that partially overlaps with issues of user experience (which focuses on the specific use of a product), market research (which aim to analyze the market, i.e. the meeting point between supply and demand) or communication studies (which analyze, in particular, the perception of the company and the brand by consumers). Customer experience is an issue generally managed within a market research department by positions created specifically for this need such as "customer relationship managers", or positions that existed prior to the conceptualization of this issue, such as call center managers or regional division directors.

The main tasks for the "customer experience" representatives are, in their own words, as follows[1]:

– *collecting information* on customer experience and satisfaction, i.e. developing "customer knowledge" and tracking its changes;

– *addressing customer expectations*, i.e. improving customer satisfaction, implementing actions to prevent negative experiences from reoccurring or reducing their frequency, recontacting strategic customers individually, setting up and administering customer service, whether by telephone, physically or digitally.

As part of their duties, customer experience managers must therefore deal with a lot of information, often of a textual nature, from their own customers. To this end, they may use external service providers (survey companies, consulting firms, software publishers) or develop a dedicated system internally. These may be one-off surveys or satisfaction barometers, such as the so-called "exit poll" surveys, through which the customer is questioned immediately after an action such as a purchase, a subscription or a visit to the store. For example, if they buy a product on a merchant site, the company responsible for the site sends an e-mail after receiving their order to ask them if they are satisfied with their purchase and if they have any comments. Other Proxem customers survey their customers immediately at the point of sale: one restaurant chain, for example, has equipped its

1 At the end of 2017, an additional mission was expanded to optimize and even automate the request processes using technologies such as "response assistants" or "chatbots".

employees with tablets that allow them to take notes by questioning the customer after a meal.

These *customer listening* devices are more or less formalized; for example, many companies have adopted the Net Promoter Score (NPS) methodology, which has been patented by the management consulting firm Bain & Company and has also been the subject of several books (Brooks and Owen 2008; Reichfeld and Markey 2011). In this method, the customer must rate their experience from 0 to 10, and explain the rating in a few words. From the aggregation of these scores, the methodology enables the calculation of a score (Figure 4.1) that evolves over time, as well as a number of indicators materialized in dashboards. As we will see in Chapter 7, there is a benchmarking system (Bruno and Didier 2013) that allows the company's performance to be scored and measured, its evolution to be monitored and finally, the players, points of sale, regional divisions, etc., to be compared.

Figure 4.1. *Example of an NPS score visualization in a dashboard form. The NPS score is a quantitative measure of customer satisfaction expressed on a scale of –100 to +100 and is computed from the average score of satisfied customers minus that of dissatisfied customers*

NPS-type devices produce a lot of free text responses, in this case due to the open-ended question that enables the user to explain their score. In other devices, the open-ended question may be more or less optional, and there may be more than one: a question may be associated with each product or used to express customer satisfaction in two stages:

– "what did you like", "what did you appreciate?";

– "what did you dislike?", "what could be improved?".

Proxem's role in customer experience approaches is to proceed with the codification of answers to these open questions, also called "customer feedback". In qualitative methods in the social sciences, coding is usually a manual task that aims to organize the feedback by assigning them a "class" or "code", i.e. a topic covered in the message; feedback can be multiclassified, i.e. it can be assigned several codes. The set of codes constitutes a coding plan (see Figure 4.2).

For example, the feedback "a good team full of good advice" [sic] can be categorized with the codes *Quality of staff* and *Quality of advice*. By repeating this categorization of each piece of feedback, coding makes it possible to study all the responses of a survey or device by determining the frequency of the codes. At the end of this operation, the code becomes quantitative information that can be crossed with other variables, whose evolution can be measured and visualized in a dashboard.

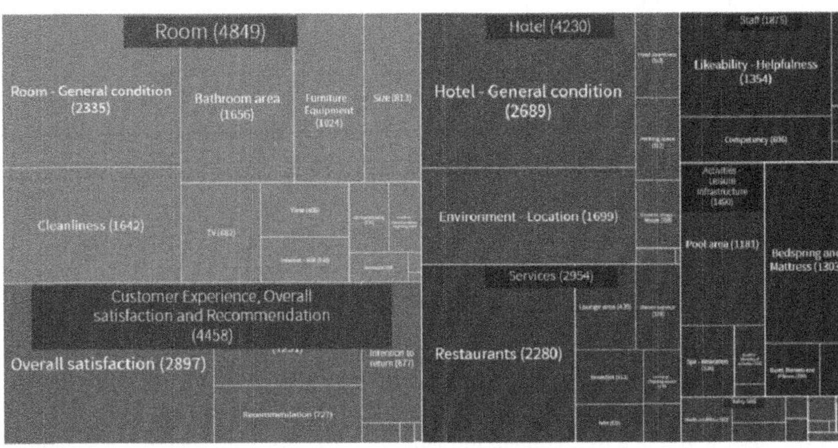

Figure 4.2. *Example of a "treemap"-type visualization of a coding plan. The codes are labeled and prioritized in a two-level organization. In terms of the visualization, the area covered by each zone represents the number of corresponding customer feedback. For a color version of this figure, see www.iste.co.uk/schmitt/data.zip*

4.3. From the representative approach to the "big data" project

Customer relations managers who come from market research backgrounds or training are particularly sensitive to the way respondents are surveyed, and in particular to the wording of these questions. They consider that two differently formulated questions measure different realities, in keeping with the methodological tradition of opinion polls and quantitative surveys in the social sciences. They are also sensitive to the representativeness of the survey, which must, through sampling, offer a faithful reflection of all the company's customers or its market (made up of current customers but also potential customers, prospects, and non-customers). In Chapter 2, we traced how this representativeness is considered in the academic and business world: for customer relationship managers as well, it determines the epistemic value attributed to the data. The satisfaction survey data analyzed by Proxem therefore inherits at first glance an epistemology of the data that comes from the world of opinion surveys. The selection and sampling biases and those introduced by non-response are known to the people in charge of the customer relationship; they are not attributed to Proxem and constitute a limit known and accepted by its customers, which occurs upstream of its contribution.

Moreover, the exploitation of these surveys is a secondary use of data marked by an epistemic breach between the conditions of data constitution and the conditions of analysis. The Proxem analyst, like the research officer of a polling institute, is always already deprived of knowledge of the initial conditions, unlike the pollster who collects the information. Ideally, the data are documented (most often informally and orally by Proxem's client) to reconstruct the context of the survey from a spatiotemporal, methodological and epistemic point of view. Nevertheless, this oral transmission may be incomplete and, like any communication, may be subject to misunderstandings. Reconstruction of the epistemic context of the survey facilitates, at the end of the process, the interpretation of the data computed by Proxem, but is not always possible.

Generally speaking, the entire customer population is difficult to access: Customer Relationship Management (CRM) tools rely on databases built up in an often erratic manner by successive participants on the basis of aggregations that often generate loss of information, duplications and missing information: for example, for a given customer, we will have their purchase history including age, preferred store, etc. but not for others. Loyalty card customers are often overrepresented, as they usually have to fill in information to obtain the card, which is not the case for the general customer population; the fact that they have chosen to have a loyalty card obviously makes them a specific population, not representative of the general population, more strongly attached to the brand[2]. The reference population for opinion polls is the customers who have made a purchase over a specific period of time, not all of the company's customers. Some surveys are set up only for e-commerce site customers, not in-store and are therefore representative, at best, of only this subset of customers. Opinion polls are criticized for the more extreme, emotional reactions they can achieve; cold surveys are said to be imprecise, more difficult to interpret. Generally speaking, all these specificities linked to the survey mode, and which can be reconstituted by documentation and recontextualization, are in practice overwhelmed by the aggregation of these different surveys in the CRM databases.

This aggregation has significant consequences on the epistemic value of data: while the representativeness of each type of survey is difficult to reconstruct individually, the representativeness of the aggregation of all surveys compiled according to heterogeneous standards is simply not attainable. There is no procedure for estimating and reconstructing it, for a given aggregate, other than by redrawing the database into homogeneous units.

This aggregation is therefore a crucial breaking point in relation to the epistemic continuity of textual data processing. It is put forward by Proxem as a justification for its position as a player in the big data processing of various data. This is a breaking point from the point of view of opinion poll standards, but also more specifically in relation to traditional coding, which values and relies on an at least presumed homogeneity of the corpus of textual data. Indeed, a textual corpus must traditionally be "regulated on the linguistic map" and present "a strong thematic stabilization" (Cailliau and Poudat 2008) to enable a statistical approach to the text (as in lexicometry).

In the aggregated approach followed by Proxem, thematic stabilization does not come from source's uniqueness but from the similarity between the pragmatic contexts of various sources of textual data: aggregation is justified by the fact that the context of feedback utterance is that of a client seeking to convey a remark or problem to a company. This intention to communicate is what makes it possible to make feedback commensurable with each other,

2 Contrary to what one might think, satisfaction is not always higher among loyal customers because, correlatively to their attachment to the brand, they also often have higher expectations and are more sensitive to the disappointments that the brand can cause them.

regardless of their origin. Homogeneity therefore does not come from the way the data themselves are constituted, but from their aggregation as an epistemological gesture that constitutes the whole, which nevertheless allows the aggregate to become a corpus. This axis of commensuration will then be the axis of data interpretation, which will be analyzed from the point of view of this communicational relationship between the customer and the company. The justification for this commensuration is empirical: whether customers express themselves by e-mail, in writing or by telephone, Proxem has found that in practice the themes addressed are sufficiently homogeneous to be able to apply the same coding plan to different sources aggregated into a corpus. This commensuration is also possible from one project to another: the themes identified are sufficiently stable from one company to another and from one sector of activity to another to allow at least partial overlapping. It is then possible to compare the results obtained for a Proxem client with other previous results to constitute an empirical standard at the scale of an industry sector, and no longer at the scale of a single corpus.

4.4. Data preparation

The epistemological gesture of data aggregation and commensuration is coupled with a set of technical gestures by which textual data are effectively made manipulable by Proxem employees. More specifically, data processing is carried out by a team of computational linguists, i.e. people with technical skills in computer science and linguistics. These people are capable of using linguistic analysis software, but also of developing or upgrading such software. Within the company, they also have a role as project managers, i.e. they are in charge of understanding the customer's expectations, responding to their requests, organizing and respecting a work schedule, and finally ensuring the quality of the analyses.

Among the operations prior to the linguistic processing of the data, the first stage of their work is to import the data. This step is far from being purely technical as it depends on a number of ad hoc choices (made at the time of a specific project) and systematic choices (made at the time of the tool's design, and therefore common to all projects). It is indeed necessary to enter the data provided by the customer into the model practiced by Proxem; this step corresponds to the cleaning phase considered crucial in data sciences.

The data are generally received in the form of an Excel file where each row corresponds to an individual and each column to one or more questions. Questions are often renamed or represented by a code; the computational linguist in charge of the project must then "decode" the file to reconstruct the questions and answers and make sense of them. Sometimes the coding is not consistent: for example, on one part of the table, the gender is coded as "M" or "F", and on another part as "1" or "2"; it is not uncommon to encounter other numbers or letters (such as "G" or "H", which could be reinterpreted, but also "B, "K", "00", etc.) lacking an assigned semantics, in the same column for "gender". It is then up to the computational linguist to decide whether she[3] can recode these outliers, or must convert them to missing values. As in any form of data processing, the management of missing values is problematic: in our example, for example, the male/female ratio can be computed only on those individuals for whom it was possible to determine gender; if we want to compare what men and women talk about in the survey, we will then work on a subsample of the data that does not represent 100% of the opinions expressed. These missing values are a problem that appears as soon as the data are acquired, cannot be solved by the computational linguist and affect the accuracy of the subsequent analysis.

When the questionnaires are long, the computational linguist may also have to select a subset of the closed-ended questions deemed more interesting for the project: this selection is subject to operational and commercial negotiation, the maximum number of columns taken into account being specified in the contract between the customer and Proxem. These closed-ended questions are then converted into feedback metadata, i.e. information that characterizes the author of the feedback. The way in which this metadata is then organized is also discussed between the computational linguist and the customer, or is organized internally depending on the availability of the various parties involved. For example, it is not unusual to find one or more geographical location columns with different granularities (IRIS INSEE code, city, zip code, department, region, etc.), some of which are specific to the company (regional management, store, geographical area theoretically covered by the store, etc.) that have to be reconciled, often at the cost of a loss of information: for example, if we have for some individuals their zip code and for others their region, we will have to bring everything back to the department to have commensurable

3 To date, Proxem's team of computational linguists is entirely female.

information. The categorizations appear in a hierarchical way in Proxem's tool; it is also possible to preserve these different levels of granularity: it will then be up to the software's user to take care not to compare elements according to different granularities. These problems of data heterogeneity can arise within the same file, especially when it has been manually compiled by different people, and even more so when the project is based on the aggregation of several data sources.

In traditional investigative processing, too, there is always an epistemic breach due to the division of labor. The person who interviews the respondents and transcribes their answers is not the one who designs the questionnaire or who will codify it. Some survey institutes outsource the actual administration of the questionnaire: not only different people, but also different companies collect and process the data. There is then a little back and forth between the institute, which designs the questionnaire, then analyzes the results, and the service provider which carries out the field work. As Caveng (2012) points out for the academic field:

> "Users of quantitative surveys hardly ever ask themselves about the actual conditions under which the data they process are collected. This 'indifference' to the terrain, which contrasts with the injunctions to critical reflexivity considered as a constitutive dimension of the ethnographic expedition and its scientific validity (Beaud and Weber 1998; Schwartz 1993; Olivier de Sardan 1995), can be explained quite easily. The operation of a quantitative survey consists of the manipulation of files from which the conditions for collecting information are absent. The type of processing as well as the division of labor involved in the production of these surveys tends to obscure the activity that, between the design of the questionnaires and their capture, has been deployed to obtain a result that appears as an inert set of rows and columns."

This division of labor leads to an almost nominalist consideration of the survey: opinion is not what is collected in the field, but what is materialized in the feedback reports. The actual terrain is unknown, made inaccessible by the investigative apparatus and the division of labor. For the analyst or coder, the observable variable they will have to manipulate is not the opinion itself, but the image offered by the feedback. Nevertheless, this does not lead to a devaluation of the data where they would be relegated to the rank of an arbitrary construction that cannot be exploited. On the contrary, the positivity of feedback (rather than of the field) gives rise to a positivist epistemology, reinforced by the use of certain qualitative data processing software (designed for the codification of feedback), which does not show an "inert set of lines and columns", but already preorganized, presemanticized elements.

It should also be noted that in qualitative surveys, where the analyst is usually also the pollster and transcriber, this breach between field and analysis does not exist, which allows for critical reflexivity in relation to the field and at least partly explains a more classical epistemology of the human sciences such as ethnomethodology or interactionism (Fielding and Lee 1997). These approaches, based on the fact that the object observed is the person and not the written feedback, are difficult to sustain in the case of quantitative surveys, particularly because of this division of labor between the pollster and the analyst, and the specific methodological framework of survey questionnaires. Thus, although the processing proposed by Proxem relate to data traditionally seen as qualitative (textual data), the epistemology that governs them is resolutely that of quantitative surveys with their positivism of the data due to a similar division of labor. When the computational linguist receives and imports feedback, she is always already deprived of direct access to reality, which can only be partially reconstructed by recontextualization. Nevertheless, the only sustainable attitude for the epistemic activity of computational linguists is to consider feedback in terms of positivity and to rely on this positivity to constitute knowledge. If, at the end of the linguistic analysis, it is possible to question the validity of the knowledge produced in the name of insufficient data quality, this quality is, for the computational linguist, data that cannot be modified or negotiated from the point of view of its epistemic value, and constitutes the starting point of the analysis.

4.5. Design of the coding plan

After the data have been formatted, the computational linguist's main job is to study the feedback data to highlight the main themes and structure these themes in a coding plan. This step is particularly difficult: depending on how the classes are delimited, they will aggregate more or less feedback units and will therefore be more or less important in the rankings. Proxem's computational linguists consider that there is no ideal coding plan that one would seek to approximate, and that the same set of feedback can be covered by distinct coding plans that do not necessarily resemble each other. The epistemology of Proxem's coding plan construction is thus similar to that of quantitative surveys: it is a back-and-forth movement between a principle of empiricity aimed at bringing about the themes of the data (bottom-up approach), and a principle of rational order aimed at identifying a coherent structure of themes (top-down approach). The construction of a coding plan is a difficult exercise of negotiation between these principles that must be applied with sagacity.

On the one hand, the coding plan is a social and theoretical construction that has no absolute and natural optimum: in contradiction with Socrates' ambition in Plato's *Phaedra* to break down an idea "according to its natural articulation", there is no categorization system that perfectly breaks down the domain concerned by feedback. The top-down approach is thus considered a particularly serious risk for survey analysis. The utopia of categorization has been widely analyzed in the sociology of quantification, particularly with regard to the classification of diseases (Bowker and Star 1999), phylogenetic taxonomy (Desrosières 2010) and socioprofessional nomenclatures (Amossé 2013). These are all examples of historically constituted and more or less stabilized typologies, although regularly called into question, which cannot be approached with a naturalistic or positivist viewpoint, but are nevertheless usable and used conventions.

On the other hand, the idea of making categories "naturally" emerge from empirical material is also a utopia: all unsupervised classification techniques give imperfect results that bring about a mixture of relevant and incomprehensible categories, i.e. results that are often heterogeneous and difficult to interpret. For example, Proxem's computational linguists rely on terminology extraction tools that highlight the most frequent words and expressions within a set of feedback; however, on e-mail analysis corpora, the expressions that dominate quantitatively are generally salutations, which do not refer to any theme in a coding plan. The results of this tool cannot be exploited as they are: on the other hand, they are a valuable aid for the computational linguist who is trying to extract the main themes of a corpus. As Bénel *et al.* (2010) also say, the information that emerges "does not in any way constitute a 'natural analysis' but rather an invitation to attentive reading. Their purpose is heuristic: a quantitative insight can suggest to the analyst the opening of an investigation".

The conflict between the two principles of coding plan constitution, to which we shall return, is accompanied by practical conditions common to the traditional analysis of quantitative surveys with open-ended questions and the work proposed by Proxem. The analyst naturally benefits from being familiar with the field being analyzed: at Proxem, computational linguists develop specializations over time in the expertise offered by the company, including customer experience. As we have seen, there is stability in the themes addressed in this context that makes it possible to build up a reasonably realistic expectation in the first approach. In addition, there are a few more or less tacit rules of what constitutes a good code in feedback analysis: it is easy to attach feedback to it, it describes a concrete aspect of the respondents' opinion, it is unambiguous and it is quite different from other codes. There are also conventions regarding the coding plan: codes should be of comparable size (coding a similar number of feedback elements) and leave only a few "other" pieces of feedback that do not belong to any code. Xavier Marc (2001) points out that "particular attention is paid to keeping an 'other' lower position at 5%; care is also taken to avoid codes that would correspond to only 2–3% of responses".

On the other hand, in the case of face-to-face collection, some pollsters tend to precode the responses by reformulating them in a way that tends toward uniformity of expression and highlights the classes in the coding plan that the pollster already has in mind. In this configuration, the division of labor is less clear-cut, but the analyst may not be aware of the extent to which the pollster has already rephrased what was said. A disparity often noticed at this stage is that some pollsters transcribe the answer in free indirect speech ("they are disappointed with the quality of materials used") rather than in direct speech ("I am disappointed with the quality of materials"). If several pollsters have made the collection, and some have adopted this practice, the feedback will be more heterogeneous and more difficult to analyze semiautomatically.

In terms of survey administration methods where respondents express themselves directly without transcription, in particular when they fill out the survey themselves by hand, this reformulation obviously does not take place, which means a greater authenticity for the collected information: in this context, "raw" data are an answer not reformulated by a pollster. Nevertheless, it is not because the pollster has not precoded the answers that the analysis is not likely to be reformulated, even before it has begun, on a coding plan that is too rigid and too far removed from the reality of the answers. The existence of already written material does not protect against overly top-down approaches to coding (where the analysis predefines codes and then searches for them in the text), which may come from the analyst's expectation, from the use prescribed by the way the software is designed (Bénel *et al.* 2010) or from external constraints prescribed by a customer for example. If the analyst's preconceptions can be revised, it is more difficult to modify the software that generates category leads, or to change the mind of a client who considers a category to be crucial.

The constitution of the coding plan is therefore an art, associated with know-how, which mobilizes a set of linguistic but also extra linguistic skills. In traditional surveys, the analyst is in control of both the coding plan and the way feedback data is distributed. The frictions, hesitations and possibly questionable decisions that are made during manual coding are almost never highlighted, neither in the academic world nor in polling institutes: the coding plan is given in quantitative analysis. This is a factor of opacity where the analyst's subjectivity is supposed to be compensated by their command of codification principles; in fact, this command is assumed but not tested. The use of Proxem's semantic analysis tools forces us to remove some of this opacity. On the one hand, as we have seen, the coding plan is the result of a negotiation between the client and the computational linguist and only emerges at the end of discussions that can be long and can be reactivated several months after the actual start of the project: this means that the coding plan is not delivered to the client as a given, but built with them.

On the other hand, as we will now see, the mechanization of codification makes us explicitly express the logic of codification in the form of formal or semiformal rules that will be automatically applied by the software. By using the software, the client can see in each piece of feedback which expression in each class of the coding plan is active, report errors or challenge certain activations. Compared to the manual coding done in the survey institutes, the approach adopted by Proxem appears from this point of view to be more transparent and collaborative.

4.6. The constitution of linguistic resources

The effective classification of feedback in the coding plan is not done unitarily, but through the composition of linguistic rules based on the presence or absence of certain words, their order, their nature, etc. There is therefore a systematization task that consists of identifying the lexical elements justifying that a piece of feedback is attached to a code. In the software, the text segments that activate the language rules are underlined: these are referred to as *annotations* on the text. These annotations relate to *named entities*, a term conventionally used in computational linguistics, but usually refer to specific semantic elements, namely certain proper nouns: people, places and organizations. The annotation refers to the text's lexical observables, where the named entity constitutes its wording. As a result, the underlined text segment may be different from its wording. At Proxem, annotations can be common nouns, verbs and adjectives, but also groups of words of a varied nature. Because of the annotations, the user browsing the feedback can consult not only the activated codes but also the named entities that activated these codes.

However, the coding rules applied by the software are not entirely transparent; their writing and comprehension is a technical skill that is rarely transferred to the customer. In addition, the size of the corpus may discourage the client from a detailed verification, even unitary, of the analysis, and force a distancing from the documents that can be related to the distinction between close and distant reading in literary analysis (Moretti 2000).

```
a small price    :à petit prix
small price :à petit prix
small prices    :à petit prix
announced price :devis
announced prices    :devis
at a price that defies all competition  :à des prix défiant toute concurrence
bill    :facture
bills   :facture
billing :facture
billings    :facture
budget
budgets :budget
commission
compare 0.9 :comparateur
compare price   :comparateur de prix
cost    :tarif horaire
cost per hour   :tarif horaire
costs per hour  :tarif horaire
cotation    :prix
cotations   :prix
```

Figure 4.3. *The first 20 entries of the "Price" gazetteer used for retail projects whose client is a retailer*

COMMENT ON FIGURE 4.3.– *The score determines whether the lexical observable must be detected and has redirections, activators and inhibitors. Thus, on the first line, the adjective "high" will be annotated for the notion of price if it is preceded or followed by the word "price" ; this annotation will refer to an entity named "too expensive".*

Until 2016, when new software for writing linguistic rules was gradually introduced[4], the codification rules were written in the form of entries in specialized dictionaries and gazetteers[5], which take the form of text files (Figure 4.3). An input is composed of several elements separated by tabs. The fundamental element is an expression composed of one or more words, generally reduced to its basic form, also called a lemma (infinitive for verbs, singular for nouns, etc.). When an element is written in the form of a lemma, the analysis engine will take into account all the arrowed forms of this element. Thus, if the computational linguist creates the entry "to buy" in a gazetteer, the words "bought", "buying" and "will buy" will be detected. Conversely, if she creates the entry "will buy", only this form will be analyzed. Other elements can be added to the main entry:

– a score between 0 and 1, which describes the prior probability that the expression should be recognized;

– the word's "activators" or "inhibitors" (respectively, preceded by a symbol "+" or "-") that influence the score to increase it or the decrease it;

– since 2016, the indications "left" or "right" are used to specify whether the activator or inhibitor must be on the left or right side of the entry;

– another expression to which the entry must be redirected to form a grouping.

Of all these elements, only the first expression is obligatory; the other elements are used to get around linguistic difficulties:

– ambiguity and polysemy of words or expressions;

4 More precisely, two changes have occurred with respect to this initial configuration. In the course of 2015, software was developed in-house, which made it possible to centralize the linguistic knowledge base and to modify it via internal software installed on the computational linguists' workstations, rather than managing this knowledge base with a versioning system. In March 2017, software was launched enabling not only Proxem's computational linguists, but also its clients, to create and manipulate linguistic rules, revisited with a new syntax.

5 From the noun "gazetteer", we literally mean a "directory", "nomenclature" or "index".

– the synonymy between terms;

– hyponymy and hyperonymy relationships between concepts (for example, saying that an orange is a fruit makes “orange” the hyponym of “fruit”, and, in turn, “fruit” the hyperonym of “orange”).

Furthermore, the computational linguist preparing these entries must anticipate or deactivate the natural normalization processing applied to them on a case-by-case basis: deletion of diacritics (accents, umlauts, cedillae, etc.), roots and lower case letters. It is thus possible, for example, to force the analysis engine to detect a term only if it is written in capital letters or accented. Without specification, the normalization phase increases the performance and generality of the tool at the cost of a loss of information that is significant from a linguistic point of view but considered negligible from a semantic and pragmatic point of view: the concern at least is, in order to perform the computations in a reasonable time, to “realize a reduction of data with a ‘minimal loss of meaning’” (D’Aubigny 2001). As a whole, computational linguists evaluate the optimal solution on a case-by-case basis.

It should also be noted that the writing of these entries is not done entirely from scratch for each project: a certain number of gazetteers or entries can be reused as is or after adjustment. The computational linguist can draw on a linguistic knowledge base built up collaboratively and cumulatively over the course of projects. In the area of customer experience, the use of this knowledge base can be the main source of input. In projects that are similar in terms of their linguistic and pragmatic context (the client’s business sector, length and method of data creation), the entries from one project can be reused as they are or almost as they are on another project: this is notably a resource-efficient way of proposing a demonstration of the software to a potential client on their own data, specifying that there is room for improvement in the proposed analysis. Customer experience projects thus have not only input, but also an intermediate coding plan made up of positive (so-called *Congratulations*) and negative (so-called *Problems*) points that recur from one project to another, which are then reorganized into a coding plan co-constructed by the customer and the computational linguist during the project.

Projects are not the only driving force behind the creation of gazetteers: computational linguists also rely, whenever possible, on preconstituted knowledge bases that could be imported into the formalism of gazetteers, at least in the form of a flat list. Some gazetteers, such as brand names, toponyms, color names, etc., are stable from one project to another and the expressions analyzed remain almost identical. For example, the names of French departments are stable overall. However, other formulations, other periphrases, may exist, and some may have homonyms. Thus, Cantal is a department but it is also a cheese: in a project whose pragmatic context is that of large retailers, it will be necessary to rework the *Cantal* entry in the departmental gazetteer by adding activators or inhibitors because the mention of the cheese is more likely than that of the department.

One way to feed these mostly stable gazetteers is to build bridges to the ontologies of the semantic web. Proxem has built its own ontology for internal use with Wikipedia (independently of the DBPedia project) and is also a contributor to the WordNet lexical database in French. Conversely, other techniques can be used to automatically generate gazetteers or project-specific gazetteer elements "on the go". The terminology extraction mentioned above is one of the ways of doing this. Since 2016, Proxem also integrates the word embeddings of Mikolov *et al.* (2013), a technique that enables the generation of a base of multiword expressions from a corpus and formally represented not as a "bag of words" (where the words of an expression are stored "flat", without hierarchy or structuring) but as vectors allowing algebraic addition and subtraction operations on expressions. Although based on recent technological advances using artificial neural networks, this approach is in line with the logic of distributional linguistics like Harris and Bloomfield (Sahlgren 2008) where the meaning of a word depends on its context of use, and in particular on the relations of co-occurrences that it has with other words, especially close words. Distributionalism refers to a conception of language closer to Wittgenstein than to the Vienna Circle. After textometry (Lebart and Salem 1994) and latent semantic analysis (Landauer and Dumais 1997), the distributional approach thus continues to serve as a theoretical framework (often ignored by computer scientists and statisticians) for statistical and computational approaches to language.

As far as the acquisition and constitution of linguistic resources is concerned, the epistemology that governs the work of computational linguists is therefore more of a Feyerabend "anything goes" approach, where everything that can contribute to improving the accuracy and coverage of semantic annotations is integrated, even if it has to be reworked later on to become homogeneous with the rest of the resources. The question of the epistemic status of these resources does not therefore arise at this stage, contrary to the debates that may take place among ontology designers. There is no question of constituting formal semantics, where meaning is modeled as a computation, nor a universal representation of concepts with a realistic aim, but rather of identifying a maximum of lexical elements structured in taxonomies and which may relate to concepts likely to be of interest to the client. The meaning of the observables produced by semantic analysis is rather, as in textometry, a Rastier-like interpretative semantics (Pincemin 2012), but now collaborative or social since both the computational linguist and the client are involved. Moreover, the approach is more a matter of engineering, of the actual construction of linguistic resources, than of their scientific validation.

4.7. Constituting the coding plan

In the previous two parts, we have successively described two stages presented as relatively distinct: the constitution of the coding plan and the creation of linguistic resources. In practice, there is a permanent back and forth between these two tasks. Indeed, the identification of named entities motivates the creation or development of a code, while a more conceptual work of structuring themes leads to the emergence of codes to which lexical correspondents must be found. In addition, there is an intermediate step between the detection of named entities and the supply of the coding plan. This step allows one to combine, subtract or merge named entities before transforming them into code. For example, a retailer may have several hundred stores, often identified by its customers through their geographical location. To detect these stores, computational linguists generate codes corresponding to the co-occurrence in a sentence segment of the entity named "store" and toponyms (place names). So an element of feedback like "I went to the Pontoise hypermarket to buy cantal" will activate in principle codes like *visit in store*, *Pontoise store* and *cheese*. It should be noted in passing that some codes are not systematically thematic as they are classically seen in a coding plan. In reality, several coding plans with elements of quite different nature can coexist within the same project.

Because of this iterative work, the desire to identify meaningful and linguistically valid lexical elements is not the computational linguist's only motivation. It is not a purely linguistic work aiming to account for the lexical and semantic reality of the corpus: this work is equipped as it is in lexicometry, a linguistic discipline at the service of the social sciences (Guérin-Pace 1997). The search for significant lexical elements is influenced by other motivations:

– the search for a consensus with the client who has in mind certain topics that they specifically wish to identify;

– reusing existing language resources as much as possible and in a reasonable manner;

– taking into account as many corpus elements as possible with a view to annotating each piece of feedback at least once.

Supplying the coding plan is therefore an internal and external negotiation: internal, because the computational linguist arbitrates and makes choices shaped by different injunctions. Re-using existing resources may be motivated by time constraints, by an insufficient budget allocated to the project, or by the computational linguist's personal motivation. The negotiation can also be external, with the client, who sometimes imposes a coding plan upstream of the project. The computational linguist then tests the coding plan with regard to the themes actually addressed in the feedback, and tries to convince the client to review, reformulate or delete codes that have no or little empirical counterpart in the feedback. Reformulation may be the subject of prolonged conversations. Indeed, the wording of the codes must speak for all the interlocutors, describe their content explicitly, while corresponding to a "business" vocabulary (a sociolect or a technolect, to speak linguistically) specific to the client. This sometimes lengthy negotiation is one of the elements that can lead the info-linguist to have a nominalist attitude toward the coding plan where the class only corresponds to what has been delimited as such. From the client's point of view, it is on the contrary the means to achieve a realistic position in which the classes will be able to receive meaning. While the linguistic meaning of the classes and their content is, with a few differences, common to both the computational linguist and the client, it is above all the client who can anticipate the practical issues associated with the codes, namely the problems they illustrate for the company.

Another important negotiation takes place at the group level, when the coding plan is a co-creation of the computational linguist and the client. It is often this work of regrouping and redrawing that generates the most discussion. For example, managers of customer management centers have to manage several types of delays in their daily work: telephone waiting time, e-mail response time, time to process the customer's problem, time to refund a purchase and so on. From a computational linguist's point of view, the easiest configuration to implement is to create a single *Delay* code. From the client's point of view, these different types of delays are worth distinguishing: the management of e-mails and reimbursements may belong to two completely separate departments within the company, which will not be at all interested in the returns that concern the other department. On the other hand, the processing of e-mail and telephone requests may belong to the same service, which makes it possible to group together the two corresponding notions of delays. On the one hand, the client may want to stick to the reality of the company, or simply want the coding to be as complete as possible. Conversely, the computational linguist may show that a piece of feedback such as "unbearable delays" is too imprecise to determine whether it is a telephone or e-mail contact. If the information exists, the client can then propose to enrich the data provided with the source of the contact, which will allow disambiguating the notion of delay from metadata. On the other hand, the client may decide that from the point of view of company policy, it is necessary to show that delays are an important issue. They will then ask the computational linguist to group together as much as possible the different notions of delay to go deeper into this theme in search of additional lexical elements around this notion, so as to be able to show that it is, in volume terms, the most frequently cited theme. The work of dividing and grouping codes is therefore subject to a certain arbitrariness from a purely linguistic and semantic point of view, but which is justified by the context and the function of textual analysis.

Negotiating how the coding plan is adapted and nurtured highlights the complexity of the epistemological standards at work within the same project. First of all, there are three levels of norms: those governing the identification of interesting lexical elements (the annotations), the constitution of the coding plan and the articulation between the two materialized by the way the coding plan is supplied by lexical elements.

The first step is the most consensual. It is the least accessible for the client, who relies on Proxem's tools and the skills of computational linguists to do this tedious work. From the client's point of view, it is an epistemology of trust that governs the validity of the results of this task. This trust comes in particular from the fact that the materiality of the text is perceived in a non-problematic way: it is an object whose positivity makes it possible to mechanically, objectively (for the customer) and extract relevant elements “naturally”. From the computational linguist’s point of view, the task is somewhat more problematic, even if the interest of certain lexical elements is obvious. The very fact that some elements may not be interesting is well known to the computational linguist but may come as a surprise to the client who would like “everything” taken into account and the work of the computational linguist evaluated in terms of quantity or proportion of annotated terms; for the computational linguist, on the contrary, sometimes important segments of the feedback are of limited interest from a codification point of view. Moreover, there is a distance, often unknown to the client, between what exists in the corpus and what is accessible via the syntax of linguistic rules: computational linguists know that detection can be imperfect, and in particular that the ambiguity of a term may be obvious to a human reader, but cannot, or hardly, be captured by formal rules. This difficulty stems both from a practical limitation of the tool, but also (and perhaps especially in some cases) from a theoretical limitation. It is the problematic elements that challenge the positivity of the meaning of the elements to return to a hermeneutic epistemology, where meaning emerges through interpretative reading and is no longer permanently contained in the materiality of the text. In this case, the semantic analysis engine is not capable of interpretative reading, but it does equip the computational linguists for their reading. This reconfigures the role of technical objects, which are not producers of knowledge, but support and equip the epistemic activity. Nevertheless, whether the position of computational linguists is realistic or hermeneutical has little influence on the work done, which depends more on practical (technical) modalities than on theoretical positions.

The phases of building and supplying the coding plan are more problematic. As we have seen, in the absence of an ideal coding plan to which we would approach, it needs another form of legitimization than its “natural” character. The coding plan will not have a degree of perfection but a number of epistemic virtues that will help stabilize it. These virtues include:

– its empiricity (there are indeed pieces of feedback corresponding to the codes);

– its homogeneity (the amount of feedback assigned to each code is of the same order of magnitude);

– its consistency (the codes complement each other and do not overlap);

– its completeness (all the themes discussed in the corpus are covered);

– its readability (the code wording makes it possible to understand how it is powered);

– its usefulness (it allows the client to meet their objectives).

Although the first points are valued, it is in practice the last that governs the whole. In the end, it does not matter whether the coding plan is inconsistent or not representative of the feedback, as long as it allows the client and the company to meet their objectives. Its themes must reflect intelligible indicators that allow it to measure and decide. As a result, we move from a position where the coding plan must reflect reality in order to be usable to a different one where it is valid as soon as it is usable. Validation is marked by the end of the computational linguist's intervention on the project, and not by the finalization of an ideal coding plan. Thus, while formulating their remarks to the computational linguist in realistic terms, the client is in fact, as will be discussed in more detail in Chapter 7, bringing a pragmatic epistemology, where knowledge is what enables action.

This pragmatism governs all the steps by feedback. Computational linguists do not focus their work on what they believe to be scientifically valid according to linguistic standards, but rather on what the client wants. They therefore adopt a relativistic stance, open to pluralism of interpretation and the questionable nature of the analysis. Negotiation around the redrawing and regrouping of codes accentuates this relativism: if the first coding plan they propose to the client may seem to them to have many epistemic virtues, the multiple negotiations of this first proposal lead to a final result that may seem particularly arbitrary. This arbitrariness is not something random or nonsensical, but is also not necessary.

In short, codification is an activity that is operationally handled by computational linguists, but which proceeds from a social epistemology: its norms of constitution and stabilization are distributed among distinct agents with different aims. Each agent goes through a certain number of epistemic postures, which are not stable:

– computational linguists may initially adopt a rather realistic position with regard to the detection of named entities, where the highlighting of thematic elements has an assertion status (i.e. it may be true or false), and can therefore be corrected or, in more Popperian terms, falsified. Nevertheless, the diversity of the sources of linguistic resources, as well as the encounter of edge cases that lead to software difficulty, leads to a more hermeneutic position, where meaning emerges from the reading and makes a pluralism of interpretations possible. The position in relation to the coding plan can evolve from a mixture of empiricism and coherent rationalism to a pragmatic nominalism;

– the client begins with a realistic stance regarding the codes but gradually becomes aware of their arbitrariness. The client generally remains realistic with regard to the detection of named entities, which can (and should) be corrected, which means that it fits into an epistemology where it can be good (right) or bad (wrong); correctly detected named entities have true knowledge status. On the other hand, their stance in relation to the coding plan is also evolving toward a pragmatism that governs the whole, while maintaining a certain number of epistemic virtues such as coherence or empiricity, but which do not have the status of mandatory standards.

4.8. Visibility of the language activity

The finalized coding plan is not the only element that receives some form of feedback. The negotiation work that leads to the coding plan is also materialized by intermediate objects that complement the oral or written exchanges between the computational linguist and the client. There are many Excel files circulating, some of which are relatively standardized. One of them enables centralizing the feedback made by the client, whether it is a detection error or a request for reorganization of the coding plan. The organization in columns makes it possible to find the requests but also their execution, possible remarks from the computational linguist, etc.

Nevertheless, the main graphic form is the software developed by Proxem and made available to clients (see Figure 4.4). Until 2017, this was not used to configure the semantic analysis but only to return it to the client. The advantage of the software form compared to a static support (such as a basic web page, a report, a printed document) is its integration of elements of interactivity. For this purpose, it has an interface that allows us to see as much as it allows us to do.

In concrete terms, the coding plan(s) and metadata are materialized in the form of sections called "facets" using terminology derived from search engines. Next to each code is indicated, in brackets, the number of corresponding feedback. Initially, the software was indeed designed as a faceted search engine, allowing several kinds of filters and the ability to consult the feedback corresponding to these filters. A button enables materializing the named entities detected in the feedback by underlining them. The codes listed in each facet are clickable: clicking allows filtering on the subset of the corpus corresponding to the code. The codes are also accessible by autocompletion via a search bar, which also enables a "plain text" search for words or expressions.

Since 2012, searches called "advanced" can be done by combining codes and expressions with the Boolean operators "AND", "OR" and "NOT". When a search is performed, the counts corresponding to the indicators are updated dynamically to match those in the selection.

The search features have gradually been supplemented by visualization possibilities. A "statistical" view enables visualizing the counts corresponding to a facet in the form of a bar chart or a treemap. When the feedback is dated, a tab represents the development of the volume over time in the form of a line diagram. A tagcloud can be generated on the basis of term extraction or other information extraction methods. Finally, a heatmap enables crossing two facets to visualize statistical overrepresentations.

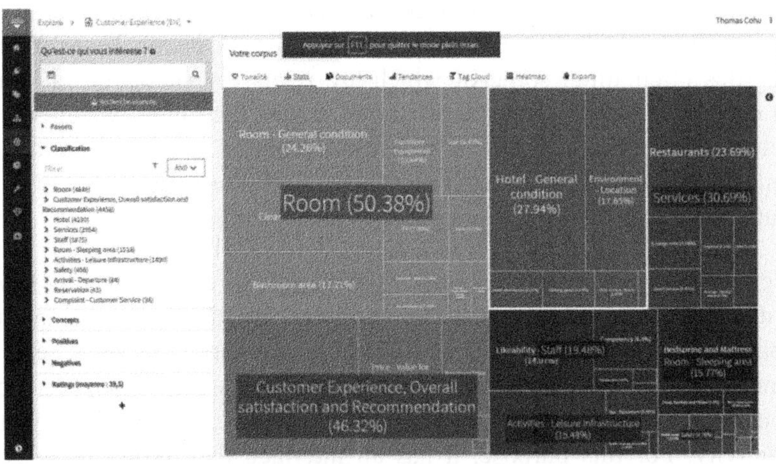

Figure 4.4. *Screenshot of the software showing a hierarchical view of the coding plan (central panel), the intermediate coding plan "Problems" (left side panel) and the metadata "Region" (right side panel). For a color version of this figure, see www.iste.co.uk/schmitt/data.zip*

Through these visualization features, based on volumes, the search tool also becomes a statistical analysis tool. It borrows interface, interaction and representation conventions from these different worlds. These features combined with the targeted uses make up the software part of the lineage of business intelligence and its tools based on the statistical exploration of business data for decision making in companies.

The software and its interface are the result of engineering and design work, which we will come back to later. Let us keep in mind for now that the software is evolving daily alongside projects carried out by Proxem. This development is based on customer feedback and analysis of their use, but also on internally identified avenues. In particular, Proxem has a "Market Research" unit that I set up and which is an intensive user of the software. Rather than showcasing/displaying the work of the computational linguists through the software, this division offers Proxem's clients study reports that reflect both linguistic and statistical analysis. Over the course of the projects, a working method has been developed to create these studies; this method has been enriched with the development of the software and has also been at the origin of new features. Concretely, the data export and visualization functions have been added under the impulse of the needs of study managers, and in coherence with the needs of Proxem's clients who use the software.

4.9. Storytelling and interpretation of the data

This method thus plays a decisive epistemological role in the intelligibility of the data reported in the study reports, as well as in client usage. Like any technical object, the software prescribes uses by making them possible; the closer it comes to an implementation of the work method of the research department, the more this method is prescribed to clients through the software, independently of any training on the tool that would explain this method. This method becomes the software's default usage model, especially for Proxem's clients who do not have a strongly predefined usage framework, for example because the project carried out with Proxem has a prospective status of experimentation for them.

This method also has a particular epistemological status: it is not purely empirical or heuristic, nor is it the pure product of a disciplinary tradition. It is partially formalized and transmitted mainly orally and by example. It draws upon scientific and technical legacies (and in particular the French tradition of textual statistics applied to the social sciences) while experimenting with what the raw material dictates as possibilities. Finally, it occupies a specific status in relation to the results presented in this book: it is largely nourished by the observation and doctoral research work presented here. While the presentation of the codification process has hitherto been based on an ethnographic approach, the explanation of the study unit's working method is a reflexive work of description and conceptualization.

The basis of this method is a quantitative approach, largely inspired by statistics for the social sciences. Indeed, the coding of feedback is a quantification process that results in assigning a numerical weight to the different codes, this weight corresponding to the amount of feedback assigned to each code. Quantity is first of all descriptive: it reports textual data in an aggregated way by indicating what the feedback is referring to and in what proportions. Instead of a linear reading of each piece of feedback, it substitutes a synthetic reading, whose graphical form will be that of data visualization.

The first visualization of a study consists of reporting the coding plan in the form of a bar chart or a treemap for two-level coding plans. As such, it is similar to the visualizations used by survey institutes to report on the distribution of responses to a closed-ended question. However, unlike a question such as the respondent's age, the coding plan is not a partition, i.e. a breakdown where each item is assigned to one category and one category only. On the one hand, several codes can be assigned to a piece of feedback and, on the other hand, some feedback has no code at all. Therefore, the quantified coding plan cannot be considered as a distribution, and should not be represented by a pie chart. First of all, as we will see in Chapter 6, this type of visualization has been severely criticized for more than 30 years (Cleveland and McGill 1985) by the community of statisticians, psychologists and designers interested in these issues (Su 2008), starting with Tufte (1997) who we have already presented. This community relies on empirical research that evaluates the readability of different types of visualization by comparing the time it takes to determine which is the largest and smallest measure on different graphs. The representation of quantitative information by angles makes comparison between measurements particularly difficult, especially when the pie chart is distorted by a 3D effect (Few 2007). Furthermore, the pie chart can only be used to represent a series of data that constitutes a partition, i.e. it can be described by a series of percentages whose sum makes 100%, which is never the case for the elements of a coding plan.

In addition, while the measurement of the age distribution within a population can be degraded by poor sampling, poor response rates and respondents lying about their age, the quantification of codes is also sensitive to coding errors. Also, even if all the feedback was classified, with a single code, the errors in this distribution would be of a different nature than errors present in answers to closed-ended questions. In this way, the codification also differs from the work of the survey institutes and suggests different standards of validity. It should also be pointed out that the error rate on codes tends to decrease with volume: the higher the error rate, the more reliable the code prioritization is because the number of correctly detectable named entities increases with volume. As a result, the quantification of the codes is part of a statistical reason where the reliability of the results converges according to the law of large numbers (Desrosières 2010); in this case, the precision of the coding increases with the volume and not with the quality of the sampling.

The quantification of codes is a way to identify regularities, a statistical standard. It has a nomological character, which reveals a form of consistency. Nevertheless, it can also serve as a basis for an analysis that will on the contrary look for anomalies, outliers and surprising elements. From this perspective, the quantified code scheme is the starting point for an exploratory analysis similar to the approach described by John Tukey and applied to data mining. The search for outliers in relation to the coding plan is done by crossing it with other angles of the analysis: temporal or geographical information, metadata, but also other coding plans. This crossover takes a known form of multivariate statistics: the contingency table, which traditionally allows us to estimate the dependency between two variables. Nevertheless, in the context of Proxem the pivot table is not used to produce a summary of information in the form of a dependency score. Conventional scores, such as the one produced by the χ^2 test, are used and considered valid for samples of the order of a thousand items or smaller volumes. On large volumes, this score, correlated with volume, ends up expressing nothing more than the sample size (Gelman and Shalizi 2013). Empirically, I found that the dependency score between the code design and another angle of analysis is always statistically significant by conventional statistical standards. This score is therefore not usable as it is: on the other hand, there is the variability of an analysis angle in relation to another, which can be captured, for example, by computing the local residue of χ^2 for each count of the contingency table. This allows the detection of outliers, leading to analyses of an idiographic nature.

Because of the inapplicability of hypothesis testing, we thus move from a nomological analysis that produces norms to an idiographic analysis that looks for singularity through variability. Statistical crossovers draw a space to be described and explored in the same way as one would a geographical space. This exploratory phase is similar to the approach developed by Marc Reinert in the framework of the Alceste textual data analysis software, which he also describes in cartographic terms:

> "Our approach is more like that of a cartographer than a gold digger. It is first of all a question of exploring an unknown world in its main reliefs, before trying to find your way there, according to your interests, according to the hazards of the terrain, to find the golden nugget of meaning." (Reinert 1990)

This perspective is thus easily comparable to multivariate statistical approaches based on the analysis of variance, and particularly to the factorial analyses of the French School of Statistics such as the correspondence analysis developed by Jean-Paul Benzécri in a perspective that is conducive to the analysis of open questions. As Michel Armatte (2008) reminds us, Benzécri's work in the 1960s:

> "centered on an inductive approach to linguistics through the analysis of word distribution tables (in line with the work of Z.S. Harris, as opposed to that of Chomsky), formed in 1962 the framework of the the invention of correspondence analysis as a method of factorial analysis for contingency tables with a χ^2 metric imposed by the principle of distributional equivalence."

It is indeed remarkable that the correspondence analysis, which will later be used for all kinds of structured categorical data, was initially imagined in an inductive linguistic perspective, strongly compatible in its origin with the approach developed by Proxem today. Alceste's methodology is also based on this. The crossovers between the coding plan (rather than the word distribution) and another variable are materialized in the software by an interactive heatmap of the deviations from independence, designed from the perspective of the studies unit, but they are also found in the form of factorial experiments in the study reports proposed by Proxem. By crossing the coding plan with all the closed questions in a survey, we obtain a Burt's table similar to the "lexical table of questions" developed by the sociologist Philippe Cibois (1990), which is based, as with Benzécri, on the distribution of vocabulary. This lexical table of questions is subjected to a correspondence factor analysis that highlights the attractions between words and sociodemographic characteristics or opinions (Figure 4.5).

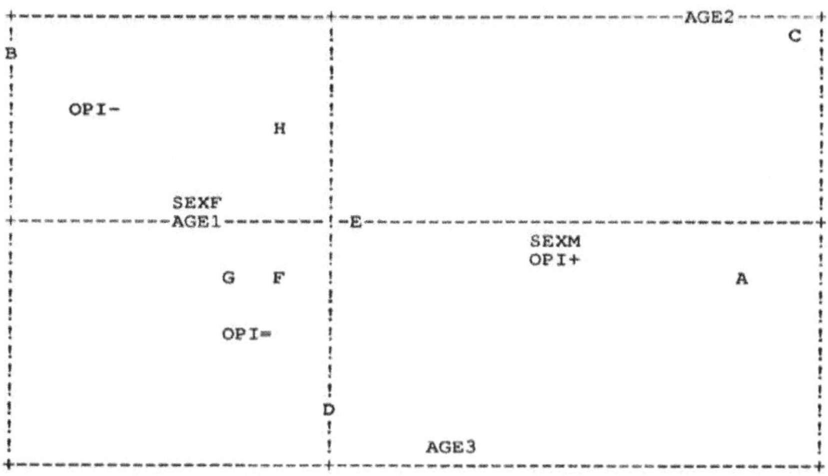

Figure 4.5. *Example of a factorial design relating vocabulary answers to an open-ended question (represented by letters A, B, C, etc.) and responses to closed-ended questions (gender, age and opinion). Adapted from Cibois (1990)*

Another way of looking at these pivots is in the mode of co-occurrence. When two axes resulting from semantic analysis (for example two coding plans), or even a coding plan with itself, are crossed, this amounts to computing the co-occurrence matrix of codes, which correspond to linguistic occurrences of terms. Linguistic co-occurrence also has a methodological history and a tradition of interpretation; it is a notion that is already loaded with meaning beyond its computational manipulability. In distributional linguistics, terms that have the same neighbors are considered similar or even synonymous. The neighborhood of a term is what determines its meaning: in François Rastier's interpretative semantics (2001, 2015), for example, the meaning of a term is conceptualized as different from its context, and the meaning of a text depends on the corpus of which it is part. As summarized by Pincemin (2012), frequent or statistically significant co-occurrences can be promoted in correlations within an interpretative path that validates their meaning:

> "What the textometric computation produces, therefore, are co-occurrents, in terms of signifiers; and what is aimed at is obtaining correlates, in terms of the signified. We pass from the former to the latter through an interpretation that recognizes the presence of a common semantic trait between the word or words serving as a starting point for the search, and the co-occurrent then qualifiable as a correlate."

This co-occurrence analysis has two characteristics: the first, inherited from the textometric tradition, is that co-occurrence does not reveal anything by itself, but must be interpreted in order to be validated and promoted in correlation (and possibly in causality) via an interpretative path. The second is that the analysis is never described as such, in the form of a text alone, a linearized writing, but is systematically accompanied by visualization: heat map, factorial experiment or graph visualization in an independent specialized software such as Gephi (Bastian *et al.* 2009). For this third option, the codes are represented by nodes and the co-occurrences by links, in line with the habits of analysis of thematic networks or lexical co-occurrences in practice for more than 20 years (Grefenstette 1994; Leydesdorff 1995).

In these three options, visualization plays the dual role of an intermediate object, heuristic, and as a form of restitution of the study; in Reichenbach's terms, it is used in a context of discovery as well as in a context of justification. As we underlined above, the pivot tables trace a space to be described: the role of these intermediate visualizations is then precisely to map this space to be explored via its representation, and to interpret it in order to bring about, always in an idiographic perspective, the relevant clues. In the form of restitution, these clues are highlighted by graphic signs that reconstruct the interpretation: circled areas (or arrows) accompanied by a commentary that provides the reader with a representation that has already been interpreted, while allowing the visualization, which is always visible, to play its role as quantitative and topological evidence.

This visual rhetoric, to which we shall return in Chapter 6, is accompanied by a narrative rhetoric, that is, of the study report itself. Consisting of PowerPoint slides, it is not a simple paratactical juxtaposition of unrelated data visualizations. It is conceived as a narrative that presents a progression, stages and coherence. The structure of this narrative has invariants from one report to another, but each study is unique in terms of its content. This narrative and argumentative character is reinforced by the systematic practice of an oral defense where the researcher defends their approach and their point of view on the data. The report thus has the dual status of reconstructing the investigation through its narrative, and of a reasoned restitution leading to a conclusion based on an argumentative mode of hypotheses. The oral defense is also a time for discussion with the client, who interrupts the narrative, asks for precisions or clarifications, completes paths, comments on hypotheses, etc. Oral commentary forsters comprehension by explaining graphic choices; it can also intervene at an additional level of commentary by passing judgment on the written comments in the report. It is the whole made up of the graphic representation of the visualizations, the narrative form and finally the time of the oral narration and dialogue, which builds the intelligibility of the data for the client, who can then decide on the validity of the knowledge produced, and in turn share the study carried out with other stakeholders. Whether it concerns the codification of the feedback itself, or the statistical analysis of the results, the meaning of the corpus does not emerge purely as a computation, but at the end of an interpretative path based on textual data, where semantic, statistical and pragmatic validations follow one another by different actors working under their own epistemic regimes.

4.10. Conclusion

We have presented two modes of computational analysis of textual data in companies and cultural sciences based on the concrete case of the company Proxem. These two modes, that of the software and that of the study, are not exclusive but complementary:

– on the one hand, *software*, as a computer tool, plays the empirical transcendental role that we highlighted in Chapter 3, and is in fact the condition for the study's material possibility;

– on the other hand, the *method* used by the latter is what guides the development and changes in the software. This constitutes the material implementation of the standards, gestures and successions of steps specific to this method.

Thus, the software does not automate the processing of textual data, but programs actions; it delimits the field of possibilities, not to the point of reducing it to a single necessary sequence, but inscribing it in a usage model designed by the method of analysis. It belongs to several methodological lines that stem from linguistics, quantitative methods in the social sciences and the encounters that have taken place between the two, including the one embodied by the French School of Statistics. The articulation between software and method is similar to that of another important tool of this history, the Alceste software developed by Reinert (1990) in the 1980s, and whose implementation in the free software Iramuteq (based on the programming language R) by Ratinaud and Déjean (2009) constitutes today a reference in the academic world for the analysis of textual content.

Compared to this methodological tradition, the approach adopted by Proxem presents a certain number of breaches. First of all, it does not explicitly claim to do so: it is the genealogical work I have done that has revealed its similarities and brought the epistemic culture of coding and statistics to the social sciences. Moreover, the nature of the data induces a certain number of strong breaches with the orthodoxy of quantitative methods in the social sciences. Indeed, the aggregation of data from multiple sources, following heterogeneous logics, abolishes the norm of representativeness, central in statistics, to replace it with the compatibility of the pragmatic contexts of the different sources, commensurable from the perspective of the client's expectations of Proxem.

Moreover, the division of labor leads to a strong disconnect between the constitution and analysis of data. For computational linguists and researchers, the data are considered in their positivity and not in their quality of representation, which is a sign of a certain reality. It is also a material object that needs to be recast in a certain technical format. Its status as a representation of reality can only be reconstructed at the end of the analysis through the interpretation rendered by visualization and narration. Prior to this restitution, data preparation phases, choices for managing missing or heterogeneous granularity data as well as the exploration and mapping phases are more reminiscent of the epistemic culture of Tukey-style exploratory data analysis and database knowledge discovery.

The global approach thus proceeds from a hybridization of the epistemic legacies of textual data analysis in social sciences and business intelligence. This hybridization also materializes in a social epistemology where the epistemic cultures of the different agents condition their respective contributions to the final result. It is nourished by these legacies, adopts some of their epistemic virtues, while being on the one hand dependent on know-how, a technique that is difficult to formalize, and on the other hand governed by a pragmatic epistemology, both in its common sense of a way of doing things that adapts to constraints without strong allegiance to general theoretical principles, and in its philosophical sense of a conception of knowledge determined by its practical consequences.

5

From Narratives to Systems: How to Shape and Share Data Analysis

In the previous chapters, we presented two components of the methodological paradigm required for knowledge production through computational analysis of big data: the ability to confer an epistemic value to big data through their evidential status, and the role of the empirical and autonomous transcendental in relation to the epistemic cultures in which it is mobilized, here the data sciences. In these two components, the idiographic and exploratory dimension returns as a leitmotiv that contradicts the widely held view of big data as a process of quantification and automation through data and computation. Our case study then highlighted that these components are indeed necessary, but not sufficient, to make the data intelligible: they are complemented by know-how that is itself guided by the pragmatic context of the epistemic project in which the data analysis takes place, and which varies according to the nature and value of the data.

More specifically, our case study presented a stabilized pragmatic context: that of a client who appoints a service provider for a codification project on the matter of customer experience. This stability allows the formation of habits that settle down to gradually constitute a method, iteratively integrated into dedicated software. In the words of Simondon (1958) talking about machines, the software is "a human gesture fixed and crystallized into working structures". This case study thus illustrates a transformation dynamic between the two configurations that a big data processing project can have, and that we present here: the *narrative configuration* and the *system configuration*. These two configurations are distinguished mainly by their form of restitution, but also by the process of data analysis that leads to this restitution. They are the two ends of the spectrum for big data analysis projects.

5.1. Two epistemic configurations

The *narrative configuration* thus follows a classic process of knowledge production: a problem is posed, empirical elements are sought to answer it and the results are delivered orally or in writing, typically a report, a conference or a scientific paper. This narrative is the output of a time-bound project, the results of which it presents in a written form that looks back at the investigation more or less linearly, but whose form of expression is linear. The narrative reconfigures the time of the inquiry and gives it this linear form.

It is therefore a narrative that achieves a temporal synthesis of the heterogeneous (Ricœur 1983), and is inscribed in a reading or diction time, distinct from the time of the event and the time of the investigation. A narrative is a way to tell stories that can mobilize the full range of rhetorical and narrative levers to gain the interest, attention, approval or trust of the reader or audience. The legitimacy of the narrative comes not so much from the evidentiary regime it can establish as from its narrative coherence and its ability to draw the reader into that coherence. The contract that is established between the narrator and the reader in the case of a work of fiction, for which the latter agrees to enter into a referential other than that of the world they know, is also established here to authorize the narrator to make manifest and intelligible what is not there, as in Ricoeur's historical narrative. The levers of crime novels lend themselves particularly well to this configuration: it is a question of reporting an investigation, which can be done by following the timeline of the investigation, but also that of "crime", or else deconstructing this linearity by first revealing all the conclusions, then revealing how the investigation made it possible to achieve it.

From the point of view of the inquiry process (and not the narrative), the empirical elements aimed at answering the problem are numerical data that are more logically collected after the formulation of the problem, even if it may happen, conversely, that obtaining them triggers the epistemic project itself. If the data are pre-existing, then the project will be in essence "what are these data about and what can I do with them?". Among Proxem's clients, for example, not all have a specific need related to one of the company's jobs. The big data phenomenon has propagated in companies a form of injunction to lead digital data analysis projects without a precise objective, initiated either by existing “innovation” departments or by job creation such as that of a “chief data officer”. The mission of these stakeholders is generally to evaluate and experiment with the tools and uses of data; therefore, data processing is for them an end in itself, which is not based on an epistemic project, such as a hypothesis to be confirmed or a phenomenon to be measured. These projects are the most difficult for Proxem because they have no criteria for success. However, they tend to become rarer as the big data phenomenon matures in companies, which manage to define data uses that are appropriate to their business.

Moreover, the narrative configuration is also present in scientific production in computer science, machine learning and in cultural sciences using digital data such as digital methods: restitution in the form of a research article remains the norm in the academic world, even if the effort to capture the reader’s attention and put them under stress is less strong there than in other contexts. In our case, these are articles that relate the computational exploitation of a dataset characterized as “big data”. Finally, this narrative configuration is also the preferred form of emerging data uses, such as data journalism, whose outcome is generally an article with data visualizations, or data storytelling, whose name explains its narrative form while serving a variety of uses, amateur, professional, academic or other. The notion of data storytelling could also refer to any form of restitution resulting from the narrative configuration.

In all cases, the narrative configuration is a matter of craftsmanship and innovation: it is a matter of retracing through the narrative a new articulation between an epistemic project and analyzed data, between hypotheses or intentions of knowledge, and a way of testing them. The epistemic project may be old, but may never have exploited the specific type of data used in this case: the challenge is then to find, through the analysis of digital footprints, knowledge produced differently in the past. Conversely, the data allow the emergence of a new epistemic project, or even a new kind of epistemic project: when a data scientist is given a dataset to analyze, there is no predefined hypothesis to confirm; he/she must imagine the knowledge that such a dataset could generate, whether or not it is the first time that the data are being studied. It is not necessary for the epistemic project or the data to be unpublished, but that the articulation between the two is.

As a result, this innovative character gives this type of configuration an almost necessarily artisanal twist, inasmuch as a novel articulation presupposes not only know-how, i.e. the ability to implement a way of doing things, but also inventiveness in the method and procedure followed, i.e. the ability to imagine new ways of doing things. It implies that there is no formal procedure stabilized prior to the epistemic project, because the development of this procedure is precisely the product of the project whose narrative accounts for this; this is why we speak of invention. Applying the methodology and standards of a specific science is not an option because the articulation at stake is in essence a methodological innovation that goes beyond existing epistemic norms; the narrative is an account of the invented solution to a novel problem. This solution consists of actions on the data, tools developed *ad hoc* or reassigned and an interpretative logic. For example, in the reports proposed by Proxem, the mobilization of the correspondence analysis developed by Benzécri integrates the mobilization of an existing technique, the interpretation of codes as factors and their effective manipulation according to the technique adopted.

The reassignment of existing tools for the solution of a given problem falls under what Gilbert Simondon defines not as inventiveness, as suggested above, but as creativity, i.e. the ability not to limit the properties of technical objects to their general use, but to derive new properties from them that allow them to play an instrumental and mediating role in the situation, which is a key element of the definition. This role consists of serving as an operational bridge between the present situation and the mental image of the desired outcome formed by the creative person in advance. As Simondon points out in *L'invention dans les techniques* (2005), creativity is thus distinguished from intelligence by its relationship to a given situation:

> "Intelligence can be presented as a general problem-solving ability, while creative intelligence is not manifested in all problems, but in those where the solution is made possible by the selection of a particular case, or by the selection of a single particularly quick and effective mediation among several possible solutions."

Creativity also differs from invention, to which he gives a particular meaning, and of which he proposes a theory in which the invention proceeds from a reasoned method consisting of several distinct phases, to which we will return later. A creative solution is indeed a new solution, but it is also a unique one: what may have worked in this particular case, in this given situation, cannot be generalized or repeated as it stands. Creativity develops its own logic, its own rationality, although it can mobilize other logics by equipping them. The narrative makes it possible to give an account of this singular rationality and to restore its meaning. As we have described it, configuration in narrative corresponds both to a form of restitution, the temporal synthesis of heterogeneity through narrative, and to a procedure of constitution, creativity based on the reassignment of familiar objects.

The second configuration of digital data processing projects is the *system* configuration. It consists of producing a nonlinear computational form, typically application software, which is the result of a software design and engineering process, and whose outcome is intended to function autonomously. It is composed of instructions, programmed elements, data and elements for interfacing with its technical milieu (the machine, the operating system, other programs, etc.) and human milieu (the developer, the user). Contrary to the narrative, this outcome is not fixed, on the one hand, because it allows user interaction and, on the other hand, because it is developed iteratively and can evolve over time. This interactive character delineates data manipulation and defines a space of possible action sequences. Indeed, the software makes it possible to process data; it is the empirical transcendental that determines which operations on the data are accessible to the user. Where the narrative configuration was based on a singular situation, the system configuration provided a usage model that was virtually compatible with an infinite number of situations, singular moments and repeatable gestures. This usage model exists in the recommendation mode: through the framework it defines, it suggests possible actions, but does not carry them out, because it is always the user who remains the agent of the interaction decisions.

Under these conceptual and general terms, system configuration actually describes a multitude of very familiar examples. All or most of the algorithms that enthral or frighten the media and their audiences, as well as part of the cultural science research community, fall within this system configuration. Facebook's news feed, Google's search engine, Amazon's product recommendation, Netflix's cultural product recommendation, advertising targeting, and so many other "algorithms" are in fact systems that integrate not only algorithmic data processing procedures but also, and perhaps above all, suggestions for action, a capacity for interaction and a logic for taking this interaction into account retroactively. These systems exist in suggestion mode because it is the user who decides what content they will comment on, which web page they will visit and which product they will choose[1]: they are all recommendation systems.

It should be stressed here that considering all systems based on big data processing as recommendation systems may seem provocative in view of the number and diversity of such systems. Thus, Yeung (2017) also shows that many systems are indeed subsumed under this definition, but she distinguishes them from a second category, automatic systems, which would not produce recommendations but decisions. Nevertheless, when we look closely at her analysis of these systems, we can see that her examples are rare and similar: automatic speed cameras, traffic light regulation, detection of debit card fraud, detection of an attempted intrusion into an information system, etc. In all cases, these are systems, or more precisely subsystems, regulation and control systems, which are not built for a user, but only for an administrator. Some of these control subsystems exist in the form of suggestions rather than automatic decisions: the system considers that fraud may occur, but does not itself trigger a sanction. Furthermore, whether or not they make an automated decision, these subsystems do not perform the system's primary function, but ensure that this function is performed as intended. Thus, the function of a credit card payment system is not to detect fraud, which is a secondary objective, but to enable user payment. These control and regulation subsystems are secondary in larger systems, which in turn produce a recommendation for a user.

To produce these suggestions, all of these recommendation systems create measures, i.e. they establish distances (or similarities) between items to be recommended, between users, and between items and users. Any suggestion is the result of a mathematical function that minimizes one or a combination of these distances. To effectively compute this minimum distance, the data scientist who programs the recommendation has at their disposal all the computational techniques from the lineage we presented in Chapter 3, and the ability to reassign these techniques to their epistemic project regardless of their original lineage.

1 It should be noted here that, as far as search engines are concerned, there are actually two decisions: the first is related to the search criteria (terms, date restriction, type of content, etc.) and the second is related to the web page visited by the user. It is on this second choice that we are focusing for the review of recommendation systems.

The recommendation as a means of presenting knowledge also raises questions about the nature of action in this particular context. Thus, one could notice that the user really has no choice, that this choice is predetermined and oriented, that the user is locked in a limited number of options. This is indeed the meaning of the notions of suggestion or recommendation: even if the user remains the agent of choice, it is not the user who formulates the different options from which they can choose. The establishment or prioritization of these different options can have serious moral consequences not only for the user's freedom but also for the influence of these programmed choices on their preferences and actions.

However, conceptually and technically, the user is presented with several options, and can select one (or more) of them. There is within the system the indivisible, atomic ability to decide between several options. This distinction, however tenuous it may be when choice is limited, is what separates a recommendation system from a decision system, where there is no human user as a decision maker. Thus, recommendation systems are autonomous in that they do not need a developer to continue to function[2]; on the other hand, they are not independent in that they belong to a larger system of relations and interactions, of a different nature, which integrates the software but also the user without whom this larger system is incomplete and inactive.

Finally, it should be noted that, because these software programs incorporate machine learning logic, the user (inter)action is the trigger for a system reaction (content is published, a product is purchased, a page is displayed, etc.), but also constitutes additional data, which is incorporated by feedback into the data processing procedures that predetermine the system's future recommendations. Three elements thus constitute the data processing activity from the user's point of view: the system proposals, the user decision and the feedback for learning. However, these three elements remain associated with the final user; they are the restitution form of the result of the data processing. Thus, just as the narrative configuration could be approached by its constitution procedure as well as by its form of restitution, the system configuration can also be approached via its results, but also via the genealogy of the system itself.

2 On the other hand, they often need system administrators, as computer software is very prone to failures.

5.2. The genesis of systems

The genealogy of a referral system leads us into that of the software industry in general. The recommendation engine will be called the feature that computes choices for the user; retroactively taking into account the user's decision and allowing them to improve their results is a subfeature of the engine. This engine is part of an ecology, i.e. a technical milieu made up of hardware, software, other engines, interfaces, programmed tasks, databases, a network, temporal and computational constraints, etc. The "recommendation engine" element can be conceptualized on a theoretical level, as a function that minimizes distances between elements. It can be broken down into elementary tasks that will be similar from one system to another, using similar techniques such as collaborative filtering algorithms. Conversely, its ecology and implementation are a singular assemblage whose modalities can hardly be generalized. In each implementation (i.e. each recommendation system that actually exists), the conceptual scheme of the recommendation engine is subject to a process of individuation and concretization in the sense of *On the Mode of Existence of Technical Objects* (Simondon 1958). It is a tailor-made answer to the problem of creating repeatability.

The mobilization of Simondon is here a bearer of intelligibility, because the implementation of a recommendation system is exactly a technical object "in which there is specific genesis proceeding from the abstract to the concrete". At the conceptual level, the recommendation engine plays the role of the scientific representation whose implementation is the passage from the abstract (a minimization function) to the concrete (a technical object inserted in its milieu). The computer scientist's obsession with optimization, which we highlighted in Chapter 3 through the notion of computational thinking, is the psychological driving force behind the process of improvement and concretization that constitutes the genesis of the technical object: it allows the object to adapt to itself (internal milieu) and to its technical milieu (external milieu). This improvement takes place in its internal milieu by improving the function of minimizing a distance, and in its external milieu by reducing friction (slowness and errors) in interactions with its technical milieu. The simpler, more straightforward, more effective the code is, the more technically advanced it is considered.

However, Simondon's involvement with digital objects cannot take place as it stands: when he wrote *On the Mode of Existence of Technical Objects*

(*METO*), Simondon was contemporary to the development of cybernetics and information machines that prefigured contemporary computing, but his examples came mainly from industrial design, particularly mechanics and electronics. The illustrations of the first part of the *METO* (the diode, the turbine, the engine, the automobile, etc.) are definitely prior to the digital era; they are industrial, manufactured objects whose substrate is material. He was more interested in their invention than in their manufacture. Their production is in mechanical engineering, where recommendation engines are in software engineering.

The specificity of software engineering compared to conventional engineering, whether civil, mechanical or chemical for example, is that the product can be continuously transformed because of its digital substrate: the design and manufacturing phases are almost not distinct. This statement is less true of embedded systems, associated with a specific physical substrate, where developers no longer have access to the software after delivering it (or with difficulty, through a massive product recall for example) but it does describe web applications particularly well. Unlike the bridge, the car and the transistor, which has to be rebuilt if you want it to be different, the software is always (almost) entirely modifiable. It should be noted here that there is a significant difference between the construction process of a bridge (single object) and that of a transistor, which is mass producible from a synchronic point of view and evolves from one generation to another from a diachronic point of view. Between the emergence of civil engineering for major public works, starting with military engineering, around the middle of the 19th Century, and the development of the chemical and electronic industries in the 20th Century (Fauré-Fremiet 2017; Rodrigues 2017), there were already two figures of the engineer who could be distinguished, but who generally belonged to the same ethos, which we will detail below. In software engineering, it is not necessary to physically modify production lines to allow an improvement to be taken into account, contrary to the traditional context where this is part of a substantial technical and financial economy. The reproducibility of the digital object is always already virtually infinite and instantaneous (although the cost is not completely zero). As a result, its genesis is different from that of physical objects; in particular, one cannot dissociate, as Simondon does, the invention and manufacturing stages.

Indeed, there is no longer a design phase and then a production phase, but rather design and implementation phases that are generally strongly intertwined, where design choices are made before and during computer programming, and an almost instantaneous production phase, which consists of publishing the code. It should be noted here that a software engineer is not only someone who writes code: apart from the tasks related to management and communication within a company (or other organization), their work is also seen as an exercise in reflection and solution finding. By design, we mean here the work of reflection which also consists of thinking about the program's structure, its architecture, the way it orders its successive operations and its integration into the technical milieu; the implementation corresponds to the actual writing of the code, which often raises new design questions as they arise, hence the strong interweaving of these two phases, which are somewhat artificially separated here. The program is less conceptually similar to the manufactured product of industrial engineering, which is concrete and reproducible, than to the production line, i.e. the element that must be able to produce the same result reliably and repeated indefinitely, according to the pattern defined by the technical object. Nevertheless, the parallel with the Simondonian concepts reaches its limit here. This is because the concretization of the technical object is done differently than by successive invention; they remain relevant, however, when thinking about the individuation of technical objects (the algorithm, the program, the engine, the system, etc.) in relation to their milieu.

The genesis of a recommendation system is roughly divided into two stages, the first of which, although it is a technical matter, rarely belongs to software engineering. Indeed, the computer sector is characterized by a permanent back and forth between craft and industry (whereas Simondonian concepts were formulated with the industrial era in mind and again become difficult to apply). The recommendation engine developed by an organization usually starts by existing with an experimental status; its realization, once the basic, initial, form is reached, where we realize that we cannot "hack" a solution that will work effectively in all cases, is first of all the responsibility of a type of team that may have various names, but falls under a "research and development" scope. This type of team produces solutions that are more complex than basic hacking, but in a more artisanal rather than industrialized form, which cannot be released for production.

Indeed, while we have so far mentioned the figure of the computer scientist, we have overlooked the complexity of the jobs and functions directly related to IT. It should be recalled here that IT is an economic sector in its own right, employing millions of people throughout the world, with a diversity of profiles that also raises real challenges for recruiters. These profiles have training of varying levels and length (self-taught, technician, engineer, PhD, etc.), different specialties (development, integration, administration, network, etc.) and varying roles within the company (software development, support, maintenance, technical project management consulting, etc.). It is also a field of research, which frequently innovates, resulting in the constant transformation of the professions that fall within this competence.

The engineer title creates additional confusion in this milieu. In France, the term is charged with a particular history, traced in particular by Porter (1995). The *grandes ecoles* of engineering, historically created to train members of the great bodies of the State, founded this figure as opposed to that of the scientist. Initially very theoretical and centered on mathematics, training as a (civil) engineer took on the meaning we give it today at the beginning of the 19th Century, notably under the impetus of the *École polytechnique* and the *École des ponts et chaussées*. In 1819, the Council of the *École polytechnique* declared as follows:

> "When we consider the development that industry in France is taking every day, and when we consider the necessary relationship of this industry with the form of government established by the Charter, we must feel that the execution of public works will tend, in a very large number of cases, to pass into the system of concession and enterprise. Our engineers must now know how to regulate and direct this movement. They must know how to evaluate the particular or general usefulness or disadvantage of this or that initiative; they must therefore have accurate and precise ideas about the elements of all this speculation, i.e. about the general interests of industry and agriculture, about the nature and influence of currencies, about loans, insurance, association funds, sinking funds, in a word about everything that can be used to assess the probable profits and costs of all enterprises: this is the set of objects that have just been added to the program." (Fourcy 1828, cited by Porter 1995)

This quotation, deliberately reproduced here in an extensive manner, reflects a turning point in engineering education that echoes the one that the *grandes écoles* are going through today (although in reality the *École polytechnique* has largely retained its predilection for abstract training, particularly in mathematics[3]). In 1819, emphasis was placed on the importance of evaluation and judgment skills, knowledge of the general context (especially economic) of a project, in short, different elements taking into account what we have called the ecology of a project. As Maria de Lurdes Rodrigues (2017) points out in an article on the engineering profession in Portugal:

> "engineers are not only technical, but also managerial and organizational – in other words, the relational, administrative and managerial dimensions of engineers' work are as important as the technical dimension. These are the people in organizations (companies, public administrations, banks, services) prepared to exercise hierarchical management functions or in teams trained to find solutions, taking into account technical and economic constraints, to problems that are not purely technical."

Moreover, the figure of the engineer is associated with a set of moral values and a form of responsibility to nature and society, which can be seen, for example, in the commitment made by Canadian engineers since the beginning of the 20th Century[4]:

> "As an engineer, I, (full name), pledge to practice Integrity and Fair Dealing, Tolerance, and Respect, and to uphold devotion to the standards and dignity of my profession, conscious always that my skill carries with it the obligation to serve humanity by making best use of the Earth's precious wealth.
>
> As an engineer, I shall participate in none but honest enterprises. When needed, my skill and knowledge shall be given without reservation for the public good. In the performance of duty, and in fidelity to my profession, I shall give the utmost."

3 As Theodore Porter (1995) outline, "If Polytechnique was a school of engineering it was no institution of nuts and bolts, or gravel and paving stones. Engineering at the Ecole Polytechnique was as abstract and mathematical as the study of roads and bridges or artillery could possibly be, and possibly even more so."

4 http://www.ironring.ca/contexte.php [Accessed March 22, 2017].

Canadian engineers belong to a professional association, just like doctors or lawyers. Their profession refers to specific skills, in particular the ability to take into account the context and the technical and non-technical constraints of an engineering project, but also to moral obligations, failure to comply with which may result in their being banned from practicing. This moral responsibility stems both from the feeling of being invested in a social and political role (Diogo 2017), and from a responsibility that is more related to the risks of construction sites and buildings, particularly in areas such as nuclear power.

On the other hand, the French *grandes écoles* now provide training courses in which computer science plays a large part, and which can be said to train computer scientists. Nevertheless, although students obtain an engineering degree at the end of their training, the fact that they train computer engineers is open to discussion[5]. Computer education in the *grandes écoles* refers essentially to a set of theoretical and technical skills related to the design and implementation of computer programs; engineering schools train good programmers in this respect. The ability to think about system architecture and ecology is seen as a later skill, which comes with experience; software design and development methods are also superficially taught at best. We would therefore like to argue that while there are developers, technicians, integrators, IT consultants, etc., there are fewer computer engineers, and more specifically software engineers, and that it is more a question, beyond the completion of the diploma, of a qualification that is achieved with experience.

In particular, "research and development" teams produce solutions which, as we said, cannot be released for production as they are, and are not software engineering work in the sense we understand it, although they do resemble the figure of the creative enthusiastic computer hacker. However, these are teams that bring together profiles with significant technical skills, above average levels of education and training prestige. It is particularly in this type of team that we find the highest proportion of PhDs, not only in

5 Including among computer scientists themselves; see, for example, "You are not a software engineer" (May 2011), http://www.chrisaitchison.com/2011/05/03/you-are-not-a-software-engineer/; "You think you're an engineer but you're not" (April 2013), http://nic.ferrier.me.uk/blog/2013_04/you-are-not-an-engineer; "Programmers: Stop Calling Yourselves Engineers" (November 2015), https://www.theatlantic.com/technology/archive/2015/11/programmers-should-not-call-themselves-engineers/414271/ [Accessed May 22, 2017].

computer science but also in physics, chemistry, economics and more broadly from highly mathematical scientific fields. What these profiles have in common is a better command of the algorithmic and machine learning techniques at work in data sciences, as well as the underlying mathematical concepts. Ideally, they have a multitude of skills (programming, communication, graphics, business knowledge), the list of which is constantly growing (see Figure 5.1) to the annoyance or amusement or interested parties. In practice, profiles with all of these skills are very rare or inaccessible to companies because of their salary requirements; data scientists most often have a good knowledge of applied mathematics and more or less basic programming skills. In addition, they are generally more proficient in programming languages that are more suited to mathematical calculation or statistical analysis, such as MATLAB and especially R, than in languages that are preferred for information systems and complex architectures such as C++, Java or C#.

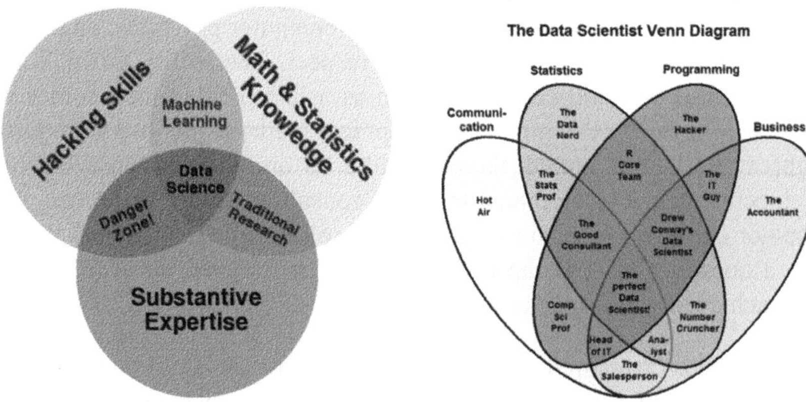

Figure 5.1. *Two visions of the ideal data scientist's skill set, the first by consultant Drew Conway,*[6] *and the second by Dr. Stephan Kolassa,*[7] *"Data Science Expert". For a color version of this figure, see www.iste.co.uk/schmitt/data.zip*

Thus, while the data scientist's contribution is necessary to the genesis of recommendation systems, it is of a specific nature, focused on the internal

6 http://drewconway.com/zia/2013/3/26/the-data-science-venn-diagram [Accessed May 23, 2017].

7 https://datascience.stackexchange.com/questions/2403/data-science-without-knowledge-of-a-specific-topic-is-it-worth-pursuing-as-a-ca [Accessed May 23, 2017].

functional scheme of the recommendation engine rather than on its integration into the system. In Simondonian terms, we will say that they are more actors of the autocorrelation of the technical object than of its mediation: they act on its improvement, so to speak *in abstracto*, independently of its technical milieu. This observation can be explained for several reasons, the first of which is the one we have developed above concerning the figure of the data scientist: taking into account the ecology of the object is rarely taught as a necessity in engineering courses, and just as rarely addressed in research projects carried out by PhD students in computer science.

It also comes from the situation in which they work. Indeed, because of their role in the company, they do not intervene on the recommendation system visible to users, but on datasets extracted from it, which are used for experimentation. Thus, it is a form of "*in vitro*" research work where data scientists can focus on the autocorrelation of the recommendation engine and mobilize the multiple families of algorithmic techniques presented in Chapter 3 in the service of the distance minimization function between elements. This configuration carries a risk associated with extracting the dataset, which may be increasingly out of sync with the new data used in production.

It is also reminiscent, in reality, of the narrative configuration, insofar as data scientists work on a specific situation, determined by the dataset, which they report to their colleagues with the result, but also with a form of oral or written report that traces their work process. To make this work, they usually start by adopting an exploratory approach, which involves data visualization, both to obtain an overview of the data, and to check the results of their computations. Moreover, their work is sometimes creative (as we have seen, characteristic of narrative configuration) and sometimes inventive: thus, like the narrative configuration analyst, they mobilize pre-existing computational techniques and combine them to form a solution that resembles more a do-it-yourself solution than an invention. Deep learning techniques in particular require many adjustments to produce convincing results. These adjustments are more a matter of trial and error than of mathematical or computational refinement; nevertheless, the quality of the results is very sensitive to these adjustments.

Conversely, while the techniques that make it possible to implement a recommendation engine do indeed constitute a form of toolbox that can be reused in various situations, the data scientist must nevertheless give shape to a solution that corresponds to a more specific problem: the problem of recommendation in general; it is not the same as proposing content, physical objects or cultural products. Every company is also characterized by a certain approach to the problem: in terms of music recommendation for example, organizations like Deezer, Spotify and last.fm have different strategies. As such, the work of the data scientist does not always consist of "amending" a solution, but in inventing one, in formulating a singular and new proposal in relation to a given problem.

This proposal then circulates outside the research and development teams, although it may have to come back to it and go back and forth. In order to be released for production and reach the hands (or eyes) of the users, it will be subject to new steps that fall within the realm of software engineering, i.e. technical design and implementation work that takes into account the project's ecology, or what Simondon would call the associated milieu. Like all engineering, it is organized around diagrams, techniques and development methods that structure its activity. The methods known as "agile" thus represent a break with industrial production methods while drawing on their innovations. These methods do not only encompass the technical development of software products, but tend to structure all technology companies whose activity is focused on software development. Thus, the "lean start-up" method presented by Ries (2011) is not so much a software development method as a management and organizational method for companies developing products based on computer technologies, which is also inspired by the organization of Japanese automobile production, particularly Toyota. Moreover, the promoters of these methods systematically tend to extend their field, from a methodological tool for team management to principles for structuring and operating the entire company, or even to a philosophy of life mixed with moral principles.

More concretely, the core of all these methods is to operate on rapid and successive cycles of development and evaluation. In the SCRUM method, the work of a team is broken down into sprints, periods that can range from a few hours to a few weeks, at the end of which the scrum master evaluates the work produced and plans further sprints based on decisions that are often taken collectively. The general orientation of the software is therefore quickly re-evaluated, without the need to define all of its content beforehand. These approaches, which make it possible to obtain outcomes and adjust objectives without waiting for the end of the complete product development, were developed in particular in response to traditional development cycles such as the V-Model, which became the standard for large IT projects in the 1980s, where evaluation was only possible at the end of the project, and itself inherited from the waterfall model resulting from civil engineering.

In addition to these methods of organizing and managing teams, there are also methods of IT development in the strict sense of the word, for example test-driven development, which consists of writing unit tests of a feature before the corresponding code. A unit test is also a program, which makes it possible to check a precise aspect of the feature by automatically verifying, through a binary test that it produces the expected result; the same feature can include several dozen unit tests, whose corresponding code can be longer than the one that implements the feature itself. These unit tests are executed by continuous integration tools that automate their execution as well as that of other tasks such as code compilation and performance testing in order to regularly check the stability of the software's features. There are also methods for structuring the software at the micro- and macrolevels; design patterns define good practices for the layout of modules, functions, classes, etc. Finally, tools and methods govern not the writing of code but its circulation: for example, version management tools such as Git allow us to contribute to several on a project and control its development over time.

All these elements of structuring software production are in the direction of developed engineering, which is both distinct from and related to classical forms of engineering. In contrast to individual experimentation or research projects, the project of creating and developing software can hardly be carried out successfully without this methodological and instrumental structuring. The figure of the software engineer matches the figure of the design engineer, highly experienced, to which the figure of the hacker is opposed.

Although there are exceptions, and we have drawn two opposing figures where they rather form a spectrum on which any developer fits, the figure of the engineer capable of industrializing and making a system robust is particularly related to the software development phase that follows the design phase of the recommendation engine, in the system configuration. In other words, when an analyst uses a programming language and its libraries rather than graphical user interface (GUI) tools, they do so in the hacking mode, writing disposable code (a script) that is intended to be used only once. This is typically the data science consultant's method, who will propose a demonstration that will work until the conclusion of the project and rarely beyond. The same applies to the data scientist in R&D departments who works, often autonomously, on the development of a learning recommendation engine. In both cases, they work on a situation defined by the data and the problem. Therefore, even if they were to adopt the methods and tools of software engineering, they cannot, by definition, intervene in the consideration of the technical milieu that becomes necessary when data processing is no longer *in vitro* but *in vivo*, or in other words, in production.

In the web software world, the production milieu is the one that is accessible to users. This is the “true” version of the software, the most definitive, the most up-to-date and the one that must not break down. This definition is valid from applications and web services, where the user connects to the software installed on that milieu, but also downloadable versions. This production milieu contrasts with other milieus for internal or semi-internal use, such as test, acceptance, integration and validation milieus. The integration phase of the recommendation engine into its system aims both to anticipate the interactions between the engine and the other components of the system, and to prepare it for its transition to production.

One of the major concerns of software engineering with respect to the contributions of data sciences is that of scale or scalability. The program that works in a known, specific and controlled situation is in a fragile configuration if it is deployed for thousands of users, for an indefinite period of time, on a different milieu. A good part of the technologies marketed with the label “big data” are thus used to respond to the problem of carrying out a common computational operation, such as sorting or aggregation, but on several servers, and the particularities of which are unknown at the time of development. Without necessarily switching to a distributed architecture, it may be necessary, for example, to rewrite the recommendation engine code in another programming language, which is more efficient in terms of program execution times. Furthermore, a computation will be able to run on the data sample used by the data scientist to develop their engine, but not on the production data. They are likely to make good suggestions, but after a delay that is unacceptable to a user. Most recommendation systems are only acceptable if their suggestions are virtually instantaneous: you can’t imagine having to wait several hours or even minutes before being able to view your Facebook feed or the movies suggested by Netflix. The software’s time is therefore also subject to engineering: some computations will be simplified to be executed “on the go”, when the user clicks on a button or enters a request; others will be decorrelated from the time of use, generally executed at night, sometimes on other servers, through programmed tasks that in turn belong to systems for planning and distribution of the computation load. Music recommendation services thus offer several types of suggestions: daily or weekly suggestions, whose content is computed in a different time from the listening time, and "on the go" suggestions that can also be based on the result of longer computations.

In order to become a recommendation system in the strict sense of the word, the engine goes through a series of steps, following a reasoned method that is reminiscent of Simondon's conceptualization of the invention. The prototyping stage by a data scientist is similar to the process of data analysis in the narrative configuration, while the arrival of the prototype in the hands of software development engineers prepares for it to be repeated in a multitude of situations that must be anticipated. These two phases of internal and external adaptation of the technical object are necessary for its effective operation. This repeatability is implemented by moving into production, where the system becomes effectively accessible to users. For them, the system is an instrument with which they can interact, in particular by choosing from suggestions proposed by the system.

5.3. Conclusion

From the recommendation algorithm, derived from a technique or an aggregate of techniques presented in a scientific journal, effective on a specific *in vitro* situation, to the recommendation feature integrated in its system, there is an increase in complexity which is specific not to data sciences, but to software engineering, where the weight of the algorithm is counterbalanced by the multiplicity of technical and human components of the system, and their interactions. Faced with this complexity, software engineering makes it possible to develop not the infallibility of systems, i.e. their ability to prevent accidents, but their robustness, i.e. the ability to function despite the accident, to incorporate it and to ignore it. It makes the system no longer a response to the singular situation defined by the data and the problem, but a category of situations that can correspond virtually to an infinite number of real-life situations. The computational techniques of data sciences play a necessary role in this, because without them functionality does not exist, but far from sufficient in the project ecology constituted by the industrialization of functionality in the system.

The system configuration thus differs from the narrative configuration by the form of restitution it proposes, as we have seen, as well as by its method of constitution, which extends far beyond the field of action of data sciences. Nevertheless, the genesis of these systems almost always passes through a more artisanal phase that is more akin to the narrative configuration, and inherits the role it gives to creativity: we can say that the system configuration integrates the other form. In practice, there are continuous circulations between these two configurations, as well as between the epistemic values, procedures and methods they mobilize. Just as the opposition between the do-it-yourselfer and the engineer represents the two ends of a spectrum, which are moreover far from reflecting all the complexity of the developer's job, the opposition between the two configurations provides two concepts put under tension that make it possible to characterize concrete situations.

Thus, the way in which the software implements the data analysis method at Proxem is not a matter of integrating one configuration into the other, but of transitioning from narrative mode to system mode. In this transition, we go from a singular situation to a multitude of situations from which we can extract, by commensuration, the common elements, which can then be industrialized in the software. Furthermore, the space occupied by the recommendation engine takes up different places from one example to another. At Proxem, several forms of recommendation are at work, both to identify potentially relevant lexical observables (annotation suggestions), to assemble them (grouping suggestions) and to browse them (search engine, autocomplete and search results); none of them, however, constitutes the heart of the system. In the case of Google, it is the opposite: the software is nothing more than a system that produces web content suggestions, and around which are articulated ancillary functions.

Beyond the differences that we have highlighted between the different configurations that big data processing processes follow, similar patterns remain between them, relating both to the computational mechanics of the results produced and to the interpretative space proposed by their materialization. The space of possible actions drawn by the interface echoes the manipulability of the data visualizations in order to improve them. The mechanics of data processing is a mechanics that has some slack; this slack is not a defect but a necessary moment that leaves room for human intervention that creates significance. The interface, the visualization, makes this intervention possible and easy. In each case, there is something that is given mechanically by the computation, but which must still be transformed to make sense and allow action, which must be the object of judgments and manipulations that are alternately the responsibility of the user's idiosyncrasies and the analyst's expertise. Only in this way does infra-conceptual knowledge take shape, acquires its meaning and become action. We will now look more specifically at the role played by data visualization in building this knowledge.

6

The Art of Data Visualization

As noted above, data visualization plays a critical role in both understanding data, i.e. in the analyst's interpretation of the results of the computations made on the data, and in conveying that understanding. As a result, the graphical representation is both a *source of intelligibility* for the analyst and a *rhetorical lever* to communicate and convince a recipient. Graphical representation is not the hallmark of big data, and it is by no means a recent invention. As we have amply seen through its role in the exploratory data analysis that emerged in the 1960s, particularly with John Tukey, it predates him by a long way. The cultural sciences, and especially geography, have developed an art of visual materialization that predates the development of computer science, and *a fortiori* its massification; its uses go far beyond the context of scientific practice. Nevertheless, the density of data and the complexity of the instruments increase the need for visual mediation to understand the results of the processing. This need for mediation takes on specific forms in the context of big data, while at the same time remobilizing or restoring meaning to graphic forms that have more or less fallen into disuse.

6.1. Graphic semiology

In its principle, the service rendered can be described simply: visualization simplifies and summarizes what cannot be embraced with a single glance, be it the "physical" eye or the "mind's" eye and its intellectual apprehension of information. As we saw in Chapter 3, it is particularly valuable in John Tukey's opinion as a mediation of exploring the data itself, made tangible when comparing the data (assuming that they can be represented textually) by examining their visual representation.

Thus, to assess a relationship between two variables for example, I can try to look at the data themselves. In their book *Doing Data Science* (2014), Rachel Schutt and Cathy O'Neil give the example of behavioral data on any social network, which records, among other things, the time spent on the site by a user and the number of friends to which they are connected. Looking at the first values taken by these variables with the naked eye (see Table 6.1), it is difficult to get an idea of their relationship, although one can have an intuition about it.

7	276
3	43
4	82
6	136
10	417
9	269

Table 6.1. *First lines of a behavioral dataset recorded on a social network, representing the variables "time passed on the website" and the user's "number of friends". The relationship between the variables is not easily readable*

Note that the table is a graphic representation, which in Goody's work (1979) materializes a conceptual category, a structure of thought distinct from linear reading. Nevertheless, while this representation plays a structuring role, whereby each element derives its meaning from its content but also from its position, it does not perform content aggregation. Conversely, if we graphically represent no longer the first lines but the whole dataset with a data visualization like a point cloud (see Figure 6.1), we achieve a spatial synthesis of the heterogeneity that reveals the dependency relationship between the variables we had intuited: the number of friends increases with the time spent on the site. If we reproduce the exercise not on one user, but on a sample or all the users of the social network, we will be able to bring about a regularity, a norm relating to these variables and in relation to which we can explore variations. Through its synthesis function, visualization plays a role similar to statistical modeling in the natural sciences, a role of simplified representation of the object that becomes intelligible and manipulable through it.

First of all, it should be noted that data visualization is a form of graphical representation that has a mechanical character: unlike a drawing, an illustration or a diagram, it produces a precise result from the chosen form and the data are represented. In this sense, its production is not subject to interpretative work: two people trying to represent the same data, for example a male/female distribution in the form of a pie chart, will obtain the same angle values to represent the circular sectors corresponding to the number of men and women; there is only a formula to transform the corresponding quantitative values into areas, given the form and content of the visualization. Because of this necessary character, visualization can be *generated like a computation* by a machine (or more precisely, a software or a programming language with a graphics engine).

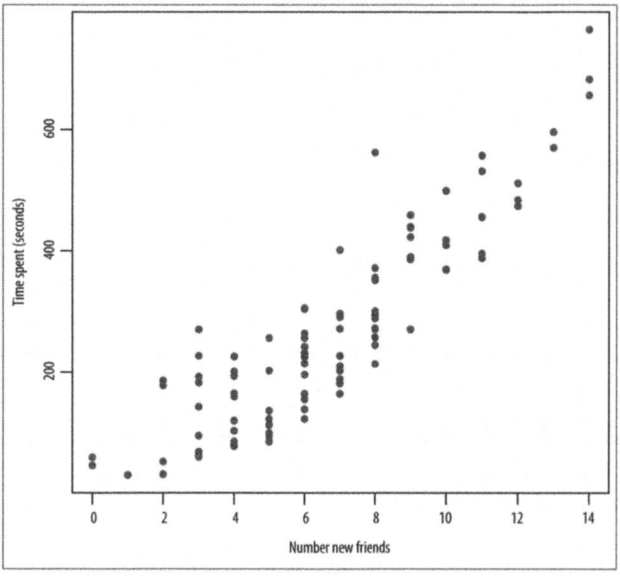

Figure 6.1. *Scatter plot representing the variables "time spent on the website" and a user's "number of friends". The positive correlation between the variables (when one increases, the other also increases) is easily readable*

Historically, the emergence of visualization software has greatly facilitated and spread the use of data visualization. Bertin (1970) thus emphasizes that unlike other semiotic forms such as figurative (or not) images, which can be subject to a multitude of interpretations relating to aesthetics, history, culture, etc., data visualization (which he calls "graphics"[1]) is monosemic. The meaning of graphic signs is deduced mechanically as in mathematical language. Nevertheless, contrary to this language that supposes a linear reading, inscribed in a monodimensional temporal duration,[2] "graphics" is inscribed in the space formed by the two dimensions of the plane and the chromatic variation, which gives it a three-dimensional character. In addition, it is a matter of immediate perception, whereas perception is only a preliminary to reading in the case of linear language. In the visualization of data, space takes on a representational status where it is not only self-descriptive: positions, distances and colors become a "complete, independent 'system of signs', with its own laws, i.e. its 'semiology'" (Bertin 1970).

Bertin defines eight *visual variables* for any data visualization:

– the horizontal and vertical position of the element;

– its shape (rectangle, square, triangle, freeform, etc.);

– its orientation;

– its size;

– its "hue" (i.e. its color in relation to a palette comprising, for example, red, yellow and blue);

– its "color" (more precisely, the intensity of its color, almost-white red, dark red, etc.);

– its "grain" (i.e. in the case of coloring the surface by line patterns (hatching), the thickness of these stripes, or in the case of coloring by dot patterns, the size of these dots).

Any data visualization, whether it is a diagram, a map or a graph representing a network, can be fully described according to these variables. The meaning of these variables is partly *conventional*: for example, on a map, rivers are represented by blue lines, population densities by circles of varying size or surfaces of varying color intensity, etc. The significance of

1 Unlike Jack Goody, for whom the list and the table are graphic forms, "graphics" for Bertin refers only to the visualization of data.

2 Bertin's assertion is moreover questionable, insofar as the reading of complex mathematical formulas is not purely linear: in practice, one evaluates in turn its general form, its various elements, between which one navigates until one is able to make a syntactic reading of the formula as a whole.

these variables is partly conventional. Nevertheless, nothing prevents the geographer from depicting rivers in red and seas in green. From the graphical semiology point of view, these choices are valid as long as they are applied in a coherent way, and explained, for example, by a legend.

While these choices are valid, they are not necessarily desirable. Indeed, although the meaning of the graphical elements proceeds from deduction and not from interpretation, the analyst has a certain freedom in the execution, and must make a certain number of choices. Visualization software tends to orient these choices by proposing "default" parameters, which are then adjusted instead of having to define everything beforehand. On the other hand, drawing by hand, or using a graphics editor, will force the graphic designer to anticipate all these choices (or at least a first version of these choices) before implementing them, while depriving them of the largely automated nature of generating data visualization by software. Even under these conditions, the default settings are not always, if ever, the best from a semiological as well as an aesthetic point of view.

This freedom in the execution of the visualization concerns both the type of visualization chosen, the visual variables and the explanatory elements chosen (titles, keys, etc.). The digital medium also adds a dimension of interactivity, whereby the user can filter, select, zoom in or out, etc. A distribution can be represented by a bar chart or circular diagram; the development of a quantity over time can be represented by a line or a histogram. Maps are generated from a specific projection of the globe, such as the equirectangular projection or the Mercator projection, which transforms the surface of the globe into a plane. Cartograms are types of maps where the geographical space is distorted according to the quantities associated with a variable, for example a map of Europe where the surface area of countries increases with their population. All these variations within the same visualization category constitute the analyst's *space of freedom* when visualizing data.

This space of freedom is in practice where the *art of data visualization* emerges. It is an art in the full sense of the word because it requires technical know-how while also being appreciated under aesthetic criteria. Based on mechanically established meanings, the analyst has a margin of maneuver within which they can obscure or on the contrary make clear the meaning that emerges from the visualization. In this space of freedom, certain practices are considered good or bad: for example, truncating an axis to attenuate a difference between several bars of a histogram is seen as a dishonest choice; the use of shadows, distortions and 3D effects is considered harmful. In general, lengths are preferable to surfaces, because the translation of a quantity into length is linear, while its translation into surface is at least exponential. The visualization conventions mentioned above are also part of the elements that facilitate reading. Rivers represented in blue usually do not need a caption to be immediately understandable, while another color can create perplexity. The fact that a suitable geographer will immediately recognize them not by their color, but by their shape and position on the map, does not justify the unmotivated and unjustified adoption of unconventional choices.

In the fields of human–machine interfaces and ergonomics, which are concerned with data visualization and are derived in particular from cognitive sciences, visualization can be evaluated on a measurable *readability criterion*. The intelligibility of data visualizations has been the subject of work for some 40 years, shortly following the appearance of computer-based data visualization. The peculiarity of this work is that it does not focus on understanding visualizations from a cognitive but from a perceptual point of view, distinguishing between thought and vision[3].

Thus, Cleveland and McGill (1985) study "elementary graphic perception" or "preattentive vision" rather than cognition:

> "Visual decoding as we define it for elementary graphical-perception tasks is what Julesz calls preattentive vision (6): the instantaneous perception of the visual field that comes without apparent mental effort. We also perform cognitive tasks such as reading scale information, but much of the power of graphs – and what distinguishes them from tables – comes from the ability of our preattentive visual system to detect geometric patterns and assess magnitudes. We have examined preattentive processes rather than cognition."

The measuring devices are those of experimental psychology: a sample of individuals is subjected to an experimental situation according to which they must perform certain tasks and answer certain questions. For example,

3 As a result, this work is part of a theoretical framework where vision is not a cognitive task, or not exclusively, which is moreover subject to debate, especially when one is in an enactivist framework.

individuals are placed in front of a diagram and asked to answer questions such as: "what is the largest measurement?", "is element A larger than element B?", "is element B the same size as element A?", or "what is the ratio of element A to element B?". Their response time to questions and their error rate are measured, which can then be used to quantitatively compare different types of visualizations or different variants of the same visualization. This type of work highlights the reading difficulties linked in particular to pie charts and graphs with a 3D effect (Stevens 1981; Marr 1982) and already mentioned in Chapters 3 and 4.

This work focuses more specifically on the effect of size variations, form and position. The other visual variables are also angles for improving the readability of the graph. Sufficient contrast between colors is recommended for all visual creation work. On this point, the W3C, the web standardization body, bases its recommendations on work in ophthalmology concerning legibility for the visually impaired[4]. It is a question of paying attention to contrasts:

– between shades (purple opposite to its complementary color, yellow, will be more contrasted than a purple opposite to a neighboring color such as red);

– in terms of saturation (a bright purple versus a grayish purple);

– and in terms of brightness (a dark purple, almost black, compared to a light purple, almost white).

Furthermore, the use of distinguishable colors according to the different forms of color blindness is part of good data visualization practices.

Finally, another axis of readability is the establishment of a *graphic economy* that eliminates unnecessary visual elements. Edward Tufte, whom we have also quoted several times, thus proposes in *The Visual Display of Quantitative Information* (2008) a dogmatic approach to this economy, in which it is absolutely necessary to maximize the quantity of ink (or non-transparent pixels) presenting quantitative information. In his words: "Graphical excellence is that which gives to the viewer the greatest number of ideas in the shortest time with the least ink in the smallest space".

4 https://www.w3.org/TR/UNDERSTANDING-WCAG20/visual-audio-contrast7.html [Accessed November 16, 2017].

Ideally, each drop of ink (or each pixel) used for visualization should be used to represent a quantity, so that nothing can be erased without losing information: the *data-ink ratio* should be optimized. What remains is chartjunk that has to be disposed of. It also happens that the graphical variables are so poorly exploited that the reader is forced to read the labels displaying the numerical values of the data series. Under these conditions, visualization is useless, since the reader performs the same mental operations as in front of one or more lists of numbers, and returns to a linear reading.

The challenge of data visualization is precisely to avoid, or reduce as much as possible, this need to return to linear reading, by making possible a nonlinear spatial and chromatic reading. To illustrate this requirement for *graphical excellence*, Tufte takes several examples of visualization from the press or books and revises them to demonstrate his instructions. Figures 6.2 and 6.3 illustrate his revision of the representation of the New York State budget between 1966 and 1977.

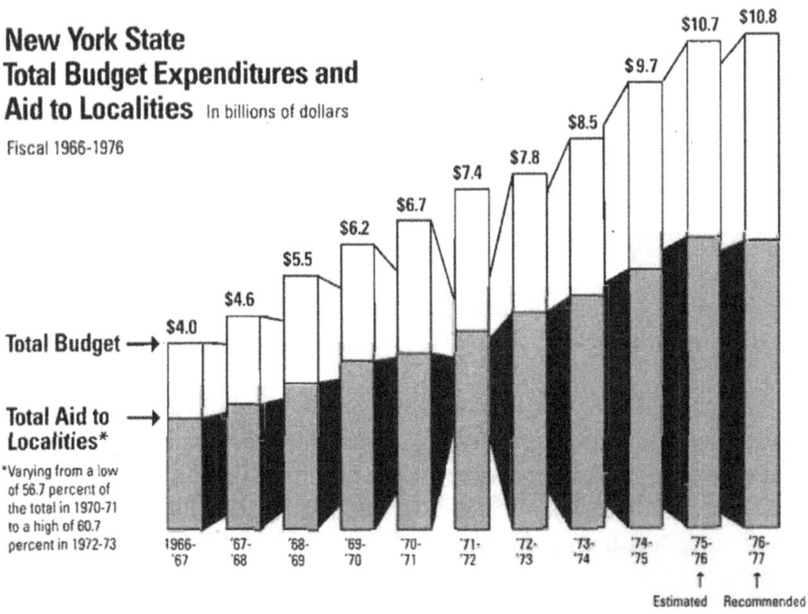

Figure 6.2. *Graph taken from the New York Times, February 1, 1976, presented by Edward Tufte (2008) as a dishonest example of data visualization designed to suggest that the budget for 1977 is higher than in all previous years*

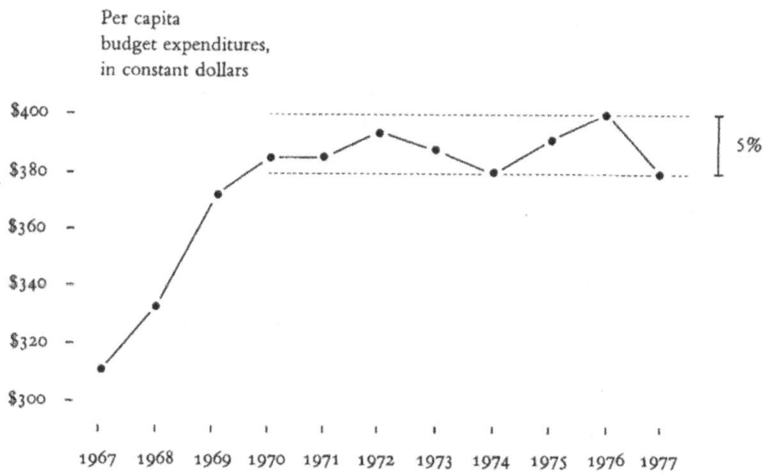

Figure 6.3. *The same graph as Figure 6.2, redrawn by Tufte according to his guidelines*

COMMENT ON FIGURE 6.3.– *Many elements have been removed including shading, borders, annotations and some scales. The indicated values have also been changed. In addition, the population of the State of New York has risen and the dollar has experienced substantial inflation in the range represented. As a result, a different measure is used to show the change in the budget taking these factors into account: per capita expenditure in constant dollars. The ratio devoted to local aid, which expresses another idea, was eliminated; finally, an annotation shows that the variable expressed decreased by 5% between 1976 and 1977, contrary to what the original graph suggested.*

The criteria of legibility and the data/ink ratio are criteria of general application, whatever the idea expressed by a graph. They constitute standards or recommendations for an efficient graphic semiology. Nevertheless, as can be seen from the example in Figure 6.3, the question of how one shows information quickly leads to a need to revise what is shown. Thus, in the Tufte revision, the variable itself changes: it is no longer the budget in absolute terms, but the expenditure per capita (to neutralize the impact of population increase) and in constant dollars (to neutralize the influence of inflation). Without this modification, the numerical values displayed actually represent different information, population growth and inflation; the modification allows us to refocus the visualization on the expression of a single idea. The need for highlighting leads to rework on the statistical elements materialized by data visualization, and to mobilize knowledge of the field and external information. Thus, in this case, additional data were used to calculate the new variable:

– qualitative knowledge, such as the fact that the government budget is correlated with the size of the population, and the concept of inflation;

– quantitative knowledge, i.e. the demographics of the state of New York between 1967 and 1977, and the measurement of inflation over the same period.

Finally, an additional skill is required of an arithmetic nature: the ability to compute a new variable by combining the initial dataset and the added quantitative knowledge in the right way.

In the exploratory phase as well as in the preparation of the restitution, the improvement of the visualization makes it possible to give a better idea. For the analyst in the exploratory phase, it is a matter of discerning with increasing acuity the information that emerges, i.e. separating it from the other information materialized by the visualization, and from the statistical noise that can appear; thus, there is a progressive discovery or confirmation of an idea as it is separated from the multitude of information present in the data. In the restitution phase, the idea must be highlighted in the least ambiguous way possible to prevent any confusion: whatever the reading conditions, knowledge and culture of the reader, visualization must have the same meaning for all the readers it is aimed at. This remark is important because, while it is desirable for a visualization to be universal, it can also be constituted for a specific restitution context: for example, a map drawn for a convention of geographers will not fit into the same conventions of representation as a map intended for a press article and for general public distribution, for example.

It is always possible to avoid confusion in interpretation by also writing down the idea one wishes to express through visualization. Nevertheless, the writing "in good English" of the idea to be expressed does not replace visualization, assuming it is equivalent to it. Indeed, visualization also plays an evidential role: writing that the budget did not increase in 1977, or that it decreased by 5% compared to 1976 (two textual formulations of the same idea), is not the same thing as showing it with a data visualization that presents a quantitative justification of the information. For the substitution to be complete on a simple visualization such as a curve of temporal evolution, it would in fact be necessary to explain all the numerical values, their differences in absolute value and in percentage, which are as much information visually accessible without being explained.

Even if this textual explanation is not of great interest, it can still be envisaged in the case of a simple visualization such as a trend curve. The most common visualizations have a level of equivalent simplicity; they are almost all constructed around three elements: the bar, the curve and the circle. A circular diagram can also be redrawn like a pie chart or a line chart, such as a histogram[5]. Visualizations based on these three elements can generally be described textually with little difficulty; this is far from being the case for most other types of visualizations.

Indeed, the academic world likes the point as a basic element, which is spatialized according to two coordinates representing two variables, as in Figure 6.1 proposed by Rachel Schutt and Cathy O'Neil. A scatter plot is much more complex to describe textually. This visualization shows:

– the location of each point;

– its distance from others points;

– the general shape of the scatter plot (is it a line, a circle, several shapes?);

– the density of the scatter plot (are the points fixed around a line?);

– the outlying points (far from the general form).

Because the scatter plot easily materializes several tens or hundreds of elements, a textual description would become infinitely long. This remark also applies to maps, of which the textual translation would be interminable and unintelligible. In these examples, the complexity of the textual

5 Note here that a bar chart is not the same as a histogram: the former represents the quantities associated with the values taken by a qualitative variable (e.g. quantities associated with "women" and "men") while the latter represents a discretized continuous variable (e.g. age, broken down into slices). The convention for distinguishing them, apart from their meaning, is to space the bars in the case of the bar chart and not for the histogram.

description makes it possible to account for the amount of information materialized in visualization such as the scatter plot or the map.

However, the context of big data favors these richer representations, especially in the exploratory phase. Correspondence analysis factorial design, graph visualization and co-occurrence matrices are all elements that are not so much used to represent an idea as to search for interesting ideas, or to materialize a set of ideas. This type of visualization is assessed and evaluated under specific criteria, distinct from the standards explained by Bertin or Tufte.

6.2. Data cartography

We propose to understand these as richer and more complex visualization cartographies, i.e. systematic and exhaustive representations of a specific object, which give a global and synthetic view of this object while allowing us to search for more precise ideas:

– on the one hand, a cartography has a *systematic* aspect due to the fact that it unrolls all the possible combinations, generally between two or more variables characterizing the object: thus, it constitutes a global representation of the object. Naturally, the combinatorics relate to the statistical representation available and not to the object itself, which is therefore not exhausted by its statistical or visual representation;

– on the other hand, this global representation constitutes a space that can be browsed for *clues*. The type of expression one has is not a global or synthetic one, but an analytical expression that breaks down space into areas that are likely to materialize an interesting idea.

Thus, a heatmap (Figure 6.4) is a type of cartography that exhausts the combinatorics between two variables while materializing two quantitative measures: the volume associated with each combination and an over-representation score that expresses a relationship between two elements. A correspondence analysis systematically explores, in a simplified manner, the relationships between several variables. A graph visualization materializes and spatializes the set of weighted relationships between elements. Overall, these cartographys are based on three types of information: measurements or quantities, relationships (especially for graph visualization) and coordinates (for maps).

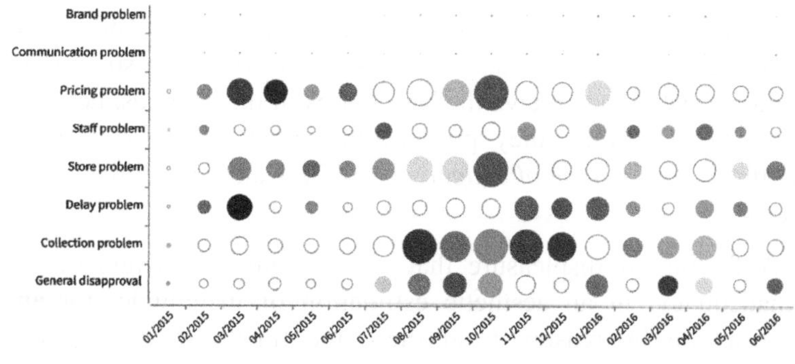

Figure 6.4. *Heatmap made with Proxem's software, representing the types of problems identified in a set of customer feedback concerning ready-to-wear brands, crossed with the evolution of volume over time. For a color version of this figure, see www.iste.co.uk/schmitt/data.zip*

COMMENT ON FIGURE 6.4.– *The size of the circles represents the volume of feedback corresponding to each combination, while the intensity of the color represents an overrepresentation score. Several areas draw our attention, such as problems with the March 2015 deadline, problems with collection between August and December 2015 and general dissatisfaction in March 2016.*

The semiology of maps is distinct from that of the simpler visualizations analyzed by Tufte: they do not serve to represent a specific idea but a *representational space*, whose properties are well within the realm of graphic semiology (positions, colors and shapes have a programmed meaning), and in which the interpretation gives rise to various potentially interesting ideas. As a result, the notions of graphic excellence advanced by Tufte do not apply, or only partially, to this type of visualization, especially when they are intermediate work objects. The meaning of a map is rarely self-evident and needs to be elaborated progressively through the exploration of the map space. The first version of a map, generated with the default settings of the software, allows the analyst to verify that the generated representation is indeed the one that was sought, but not yet draw a meaning from it. The abundance of points represented usually creates a feeling of disorientation.

The hermeneutic effort can indeed be disturbed by an aesthetic overload. In an article on data visualization in the context of big data, McCosker and Wilken (2014) compare the disorientation experienced when faced with visualization with the experience of the mathematical *sublime*, as discussed by Immanuel Kant, himself inspired by the sublime in the work of Edmund Burke. Burke is interested in large objects, those which are so large that the imagination, unable to perceive the boundaries of these things, believes them to be infinite; therefore, they produce the same effects as if they were actually there[6]. In *Critique of Judgment* (1987), Kant defines the sense of the sublime as:

> "A feeling of displeasure that arises from the imagination's inadequacy, in an aesthetic estimation of magnitude, for an estimation by reason, is at the same time also a pleasure, aroused by the fact that this very judgment, namely, that even the greatest power of sensibility is inadequate, is [itself] in harmony with rational ideas, insofar as striving toward them is still a law for us."

In other words, the sublime evokes a simultaneous feeling of pleasure and displeasure. The feeling of displeasure comes from the inability of the imagination (that is, here, the ability to apprehend a perception) to give a reason for the perceived greatness. The feeling of pleasure comes from the fact that by being made sensitive, this inability of the imagination reveals how small these sensitive magnitudes, however great they may be, are in comparison to the ideas of reason, to which we must aspire, like Kant; this aspiration is the source of the feeling of pleasure.

The perception of a large quantity of objects, or large spaces, reveals our inability to understand them synthetically, as a unit: the aesthetic hold of the object takes precedence over its epistemic understanding. We successively perceive each element without being able to make a meaningful summary of it. In these terms, a map-like visualization can thus create a sense of the sublime: the quantity of elementary elements and the graphic variation on these elements is a magnitude that perception cannot understand as a unit. Nevertheless, contrary to what McCosker and Wilken suggest, not all visualizations of data generated from big data provoke this feeling: the graphical overview of large volumes produced by a bar chart or a line chart allows one, on the contrary, to synthetically understand all the data represented and to bring them back to the frontiers of both sensitive perception and

6 "Some large objects are so continued to any indefinite number, that the imagination meets no check [and thus, by] not being able to perceive the bounds of many things, they seem to be infinite, and they produce the same effects as if they were really so" (Burke, taken from McCosker and Wilken (2014)).

intellectual understanding. The problem posed by map-type visualizations is that instead of eliminating the disorientation caused by the abundance of data, this "deluge" that used to come back as a leitmotiv in big data discourse, they reproduce this abundance, which leads the analyst to work within it to recompose meaning.

Thus, where simple visualization is the result of a process that aims to highlight something almost factual, which leaves no room for interpretation, cartography refers us to the index paradigm and the exploitation of leads, clues, in a space that is now graphical and no longer merely statistical, in which it is a question of finding one's bearings and orientation. This type of visualization is not the result of an exploration, but what is used to explore (tool), and what there is to explore (object). It is not a question of understanding a map in its totality, without which we come up against an aesthetic feeling of sublimity that prevents epistemic activity, but of looking *inside* the cartography space, in search of clues.

This type of visualization thus belongs resolutely to the exploratory phase. It can only be envisaged as a form of restitution after *adjustment work* to facilitate interpretation at the time of restitution. This *refinement* is in itself a form of exploration that involves the meaning of data, the cartography technique and visual rendering. It brings back, contrary to the initial map, Tufte's search for graphic excellence: this refinement will reduce the quantity or visibility of graphic elements that are not used to express an idea. It also aims to remove, or at least diminish, the sense of sublimity associated with the initial map, in order to reduce its aesthetic dimension to a hermeneutic and rhetorical function: hermeneutic, because it is easier to interpret sice it is undertaken on an aesthetically pleasing object, and rhetorical, because its aesthetic character seduces the observer before having to convince them. The modalities of this adjustment or improvement phase depend on the visualization mode:

– in Proxem's heatmaps, it is a matter of determining and adjusting the categories represented, the order in which the values appear, the over-representation score used, but also the length/width ratio of the visualization or the size of the labels from the perspective of readability;

– in the case of correspondence factorial analysis, the work consists of evaluating the different axes represented, masking certain points, cropping interesting portions of the factorial plane, but also avoiding the superimposition of labels, adjusting colors, etc.;

– in the case of graph visualization, software such as Gephi is almost entirely dedicated to the creation of the visual representation, with two phases: one that places the nodes in space, defining which variables govern the size and color of the nodes, and a second, more cosmetic phase where thicknesses, borders, typography, etc., are adjusted.

These phases of adjustment, or even trial and error, are emblematic of exploratory data analysis in the sense that they allow us to become familiar with the data, to gradually identify one or more interpretations, and to prepare a form of restitution. In this way, a map can become a form of restitution provided that it is worked on according to a certain interpretation. It is a technical work that also seeks to remove the sublime character of a map, so as to reduce the aesthetic dimension of visualization to a rhetorical function in the service of its intelligibility. This interpretation can be materialized in several ways (which are not mutually exclusive):

– directly in the visualization, erasing or masking elements that generate noise in relation to the desired reading;

– overloading the view with other graphic elements (arrows, circled or highlighted areas) that draw the viewer's attention to a particular area of visualization;

– by textual explanation via titles, labels and legends, which can be combined with the two previous points.

An example combining these three points would be, in the case of graph visualization, to gray out all the nodes of the graph except those to which one wants to draw attention (direct transformation of the visualization), to point to the area concerned with an arrow and to place a comment at the end of the arrow. In this way, a map retains its ability to demonstrate as much as it contextualizes the element put forward and allows it to be placed in its entirety, while facilitating reading and comprehension.

This adjustment phase is specific to the exploratory context, but it is also the one that prepares the form of restitution. In Reichenbach's terms, it is an instrument for discovery but also for justification. By making the interpretation explicit through textual and graphical elements, the analyst prepares the visualization to be shared with others. In the case of a narrative configuration in particular, data visualization is an integral part of the narrative. This is particularly true of the "data storytelling" that explicitly aims to give the greatest possible space to visualization, to the detriment of a textual narrative. In this type of format, if we consider that the narrative is the overall form, the visualization is both its content, the parts of a whole, and a specific, visual form, nested within the general "narrative" form.

It should be noted here that data visualization occupies a place quite distinct from that of illustration in works of fiction. It is not a question of reproducing or illustrating what is already presented in the story, but of substituting what could have been a portion of the text. As we have seen, the narrative effectiveness and readability of data visualization is superior to textual restitution in the context of computational data analysis. The textual elements that overload visualizations are not autonomous narrative elements per se, but interpretive aids that complement the visualization and clarify its meaning, in the same way that a footnote can clarify a developed idea. Data visualization also does not have the same status in data storytelling as in a scientific publication. For the latter, we can see that the text thread is not interrupted to let the visualization temporarily replace it: the proposed graphics are next to the text, indicated by cross-references. The information expressed in the graph is repeated in the article thread, and often in the legend. The visual narrative does not replace the textual narrative, but complements it, notably by playing an evidentiary role.

6.3. Representation as evidence

Indeed, data visualization is not drawn freely according to an intention or an idea that one would like to represent, but a result first generated by a program and then transformed. This *initially generative* character makes it appear as the mechanical consequence of the data, whose epistemic properties it inherits. As such, it is not only used to effectively express an idea, but also to justify it. The epistemic value of the data, which was attributed to them at the time of their constitution or aggregation, and which was maintained after their computational manipulation, is carried over into their visualization because of this mechanical character. It is because these data are not "natural", purely empirical, but theoretically loaded that this theoretical load can propagate through the various manipulations they undergo.

In the case of Proxem, for example, the value attributed to the data is above all an *epistemic contract* with the client: the data to be processed are considered to always have, prior to their processing, a certain validity and a certain capacity to represent the object that one wants to study. Thus, the burden of proving data validity is not on Proxem, but with the agents who have compiled the dataset. In the case of digital methods, it is the analyst who, in order to constitute the data, defines an *acquisition logic* motivated by an epistemic project. As we saw in Chapter 2, it is motivated both by an aim of representing social phenomena, by an empirical and experimental state of mind operating in the trial-and-error mode, and by a critical vision of this approach that can be seen as a *justification by self-falsification*. Indeed, if, by trying to invalidate their corpus constitution logic, the analyst does not succeed, this failure appears as an element of validation of the approach. Such falsification may also reveal limitations that are determinations of the scope of the data, the possible area of knowledge they are likely to cover.

The theoretically charged gesture of constituting the dataset is a starting point that confers an epistemic potential to these data. This potential is realized through the manipulation of the data and in particular its graphic processing. During these different stages, the epistemic value of the data is mechanically transferred from one stage to another, while being subject to epistemic control by the interpretative posture. As such, data processing involves several forms of objectivity: mechanical objectivity and judgment.

As Daston and Galison (2007) have shown, there are several forms of objectivity, which are historically constituted. Objectivity appears not so much as an intrinsic property of scientific knowledge as an ethos with which the researcher identifies in the practice of science. Among these forms of objectivity, we will select two that correspond to the ways in which knowledge is constructed and justified in data sciences:

– mechanical objectivity is an ethos based on erasing the individual's subjectivity, their ego, and their stylistic idiosyncrasies by substituting the human craftsman with an instrument "without will". In this sense, photography was perceived, at the time of its invention, as more objective than painting, because it was considered capable of representing nature as it is, unlike an artist who will imbue their style, their affects, their faults, etc.;

– objectivity as an active effort based on the trained judgment by a willing subject, necessary to produce a faithful representation of the object. It is this form that is at work when the experienced physician is able, by dint of practice, to detect a pathology by examining an X-ray. It involves notions of intuition and interpretation that contradict or complement the mechanical nature of the image produced.

In Daston and Galison's general description, these two forms of objectivity do not characterize the observables themselves but the epistemic activity and position in relation to the observables. In our terms, we will say that they do not concern the data themselves but the operations carried out on them. It is not the data that are objective, but the processing. Objectivity then appears not as a regime of knowledge validity, where knowledge is valid because it is perceived as objective, but as a condition for preserving that validity. Objective processing *preserves* the epistemic value of data. As such, objectivity is constructed in two stages:

– computational processing, including data mining and machine learning techniques, and also the initial generation of data visualizations, are mechanical processes that automatically preserve the epistemic value of data;

– the interpretation and refinement of the maps, but also the preparation, formatting and cleaning of the data, as well as the configuration of the algorithms used, are steps that require intervening over and above the mechanical processing by virtue of trained judgment.

Data preparation is a good example of a step illustrating the fact that mechanical objectivity alone is not enough: depending on the initial format of data, not reworking them would be a source of noise, aberrant results, or even make their computational exploitation impossible. It is therefore necessary to involve a judgment by means of which a number of choices are made in order to make the data usable. The same judgment is found in the refinement of a map, which makes it possible to move from an unintelligible visualization, disturbed by the disorientation of the sublime, to visualization that makes interpretation possible. The objectivity of the trained judgment therefore not only preserves the epistemic value of data but also *reveals* it. It results from data hermeneutics that requires the mobilization of external knowledge from the cultural sciences, but also the mastery of the semiotics corresponding to the visualization technique used. For example, the language of graph visualization is not the same as that of correspondence factor analysis. They are based on sets of graphic signs that have a programmed meaning, plus the contextual interpretation of that meaning. For example, geometric proximity is interpreted, in factorial correspondence analysis, as a similarity between elements: this is its programmed meaning. This geometric proximity is then interpreted according to the elements represented: it can be political, musical, historical, geographical, conceptual, etc.. The interpreter's work consists precisely of contextualizing this programmed meaning to determine where it is relevant, but also where it is accidental due to a bias or statistical aberration.

Revealing the epistemic value of data therefore entails both giving meaning to certain signs and discarding others. If this value must be revealed, it is because it is not unambiguous or obvious. Indeed, on the one hand, it takes the art of judgment to identify the elements of meaning, and, on the other hand, these data must be manipulated, maneuvered, for their meaning to appear. The adjustments and improvements made in the context of graph visualization are not actions that distort raw data to make it lie, but on the contrary a set of gestures that give shape to the data so that it becomes intelligible. As can be seen in Figure 6.5, a "raw" graph without this adjustment work is completely unreadable. The same graph (right), reworked, spatialized and colored, suggests elements of meaning without even knowing what is represented. In Daston and Galison's work, the trained judgment is not considered as a subjective point of view that would pervert an objective image and would transform the raw data into distorted data. On the contrary, it is the source of the representation's objectivity, which gives it its true meaning. Similarly, in data visualization, as in all phases of data science interpretation, this judgment is what makes the data readable. The difference with Daston and Galison's analysis of the trained judgment is that it is also a *trained manipulation*, an art of wisely transforming the representation so that it becomes readable and reveals its meaning.

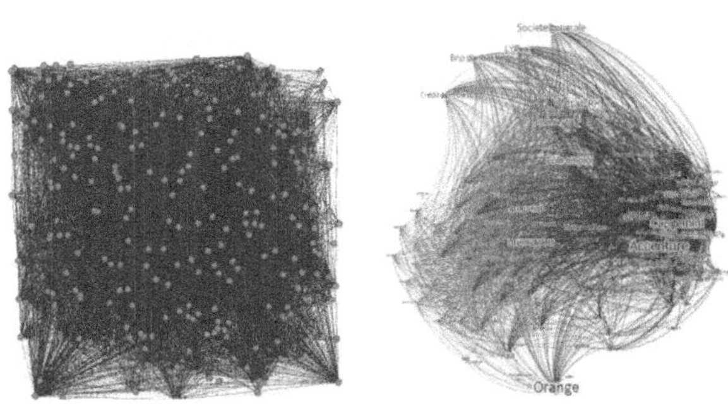

a) b)

Figure 6.5. *The same graph represented twice: a) without adjustment or spatialization, as it appears when the file is loaded into the Gephi software; b) after the work of "trained manipulation" including coloring, spatialization, filtering, formatting, etc. The "raw" graph is illegible while the reworked graph suggests interpretations. For a color version of this figure, see www.iste.co.uk/schmitt/data.zip*

A visual representation such as a map can therefore only play its role as evidence because it is the result of both mechanical procedures that preserve the epistemic value of the source data and an interpretation stabilized by a trained judgment. These successive operations of manipulation, which are objective because they are mechanical or sound, preserve or reveal an epistemic value that must itself be justified by a falsifiable discourse describing the logic of data acquisition. In the narrative configuration, this discourse is the narrative itself, which describes this logic of acquisition while retracing the stages of data transformation, whose value is preserved or revealed by these stages. The narrative remobilizes the exploitative role of data visualization, through which the analyst constitutes the interpretation of the data, while exploiting the visualization's demonstration ability. Visualization is successful because it is able to (re)present objectively constituted meanings on legitimately constituted data in a legible manner, as long as this objectification and legitimation can also be made explicit by the narrative.

While reinvoking previous steps, we have thus shown how data visualization and its integration into the narrative configuration present, complement and bring evidential value to the results of computational data construction and analysis. Visualization demonstrates while the narrative justifies the assertions made by the visual elements, while recontextualizing them in the pragmatic context of the recipient of the narrative.

These modalities of knowledge validation, which are specific to narrative configuration, are not found, or at least hardly, in the system configuration, although it also mobilizes a visual language. Contrary to the configuration in narrative, this language, even this grammar, is not that of data visualization, but that of the interface as it is conceptualized and designed by the work of the designer.

6.4. The visual language of design in system configuration

The figure of the designer is at least as difficult to describe as that of the engineer, with the additional obstacle that it is a figure whose institutionalization is more recent, starting around the 1970s (Petit and Deldicque 2017), and in relation to which we therefore have less historical perspective. This institutionalization is that of industrial design, whose role is to design manufactured products; as such, this figure can be said to embody part of the engineer's tasks in the context of industrial engineering, and to emerge from it. Today, design covers a multitude of issues more specifically dealt with by information design, interaction design, interface design, experience design, etc. Given an object to be produced, design will be considered as (1) the analysis of the actions that the object must make possible and (2) the production of an outcome (schematic, model, prototype) that proceeds from both aesthetic and functional research, materializing the shape of the object. This aesthetic dimension is central; French design first uses the term "*esthétique industrielle*" ("industrial aesthetics"; Petit 2017). It also takes into account ergonomic research, i.e. a study of the usual gestures, but this is not systematic insofar as the work of ergonomists is only possible if there is already a product, or similar products, whose uses can be empirically analyzed. Ergonomic work is only carried out if there are measurable elements (comfort, legibility, etc.) within which there is room for maneuver. In the absence of an already existing product (for example, in the context of designing a product with a disruptive innovation), the designer cannot analyze their users' habits and must anticipate the possible uses through their imagination and their analysis of the problem.

In the context of industrial design, this involves analyzing other existing models, uses, the contexts in which the object is used and the technical and economic milieu before proposing a new object by describing or manufacturing it. To take a relatively recent example, the award-winning Dyson vacuum cleaners (Figure 6.6) use a number of technological innovations (cyclonic separation, bagless, particulate filter) and have a unique appearance that combines aesthetic appeal and functional efficiency. The shape of a Dyson vacuum cleaner is difficult to describe in comparison to other vacuum cleaners, but it can be understood from its operating diagram, which it formally embodies.

Figure 6.6. *Photo of a Dyson vacuum cleaner (Dyson DC52 Allergy Pro model, source: Dyson)*

In the digital context, design is first associated with what is visible on the screen: the graphical user interface. It is thus assimilated to a work of graphic creation (or modification), which consists of making aesthetic an already existing interface created by the developers. The use of a designer often consists, in software development, of commissioning a graphic mock-up once the software or feature is developed. This trend is widely denounced by designers who refuse to be considered as interface decorators, and claim a place, or even a central role, in design work. Stéphane Vial (2016), lecturer in design, writes as follows: "It is necessary to go beyond the superficial and tenacious point of view which would involve believing that the design would only bring a visual/formal embellishment or a functional improvement which would simply bring 'a plus' to the project".

Within the framework of interface design, it is true that the designer's job is to develop the readability and usability of a graphic interface and to make it aesthetically pleasing, so as to make it pleasant to use. However, it does not boil down to that. The role of human–machine interfaces, in general, is to enable "communication between the human and computer components of a system" (Thierry 2013); a graphical user interface is an interface that fulfills this function with visual elements. While aesthetics, legibility and usability are criteria that favor communication, the central question remains the content of this communication, which is determined before it is displayed on the screen.

We therefore agree with the point of view supported by the designers and the refusal to restrict the design to a problem of adjustment that would occur at the end of the process. More specifically, we consider design in our context as a function not embodied by a single person, but distributed in a software development team. It thus goes far beyond the function of embellishment that is lent to it. This function indeed consists of thinking the graphic interface, but also what it materializes: it is a work of conception of the invisible as well as the visible, which is not reduced to interface design. In the context of the system configuration and recommendation engines, the design is the epitome of concerns related to what we have called project ecology. It is a question of analyzing users' expectations, their reactions to what is recommended to them, but also of creating, sometimes *ex nihilo*, new forms of recommendation. This creation is the engineer's responsibility, or even the data scientist's, as well as the designer's responsibility, because it is a question of both technically designing a recommendation engine but also of integrating the uses and ambition of the recommendation. In this conception, the articulation with the technical aspects is not only made from the point of view of the integration of the technical constraints but, at least ideally, in a dialogue between the design proposal and the technical possibilities: it can certainly be a question of integrating these constraints as they are, but also of sending the object back to the technological research side, to find technical solutions to a constraint this time posed by the ambition of the product.

As such, design refers both to the work of designing the recommendation itself (product design) and the way it will be made visible to the user (interface, experience and interaction design). Recommendation and its representation maintain a relationship of co-determination in which each influences the other. Indeed, the interface must reflect what the recommendation engine produces and highlight the different features of the software. However, on the other hand, the interface can be decisive in the definition or evolution of these features insofar as a feature that is difficult to materialize or misunderstood by the user will in principle have to be transformed. A software feature is not only determined by what is deemed relevant or effective by the software development teams, but also by design considerations, analysis of user behavior, and in particular their reaction to the feature provided by the interface.

Therefore, it remains true that a graphic interface can be evaluated on aesthetic or readability criteria, but it must above all be what gives access to the features and makes their use possible, or in other words, that "makes visible" and "enables action", to use the title of Benjamin Thierry's thesis on the invention of graphic interactivity and the concept of the user in computer science. To achieve this, any graphical interface is built around two key concepts: display, which materializes elements of the system, and interactivity, which allows you to act on these elements. Using software means successively consulting display elements and manipulating interactive elements according to an order or a method determined by intent. In the context of recommendation systems, the two essential elements are therefore the display of suggestions (of products, content, films, etc.) and the possibility of choosing one (or more) of them, usually by clicking on them. As such, an interface such as the Netflix interface[7] (Figure 6.7) combines multiple recommendation areas, which we detail here:

7 Here we present the web interface. The application for tablet and smartphone has some variations that we will not detail here.

– a large dynamic showcase (personalized according to the user, country, catalogue entries, Netflix editorial strategy, etc.) of a particular video, which can be a film, a series, a documentary, etc.;

– a list of recommendations, suggesting that you resume playing a video or browse through several lists from suggestions;

– a search feature (truncated in Figure 6.7) that will in practice suggest videos related to the search terms, either titles containing the terms or parts of the terms, or similar terms, etc., i.e., other suggestions from videos;

– a notification area (also truncated in Figure 6.7) for new catalogue entries, but in the form of personalized suggestions for the user.

Figure 6.7. *Screenshots of two variants of the Netflix homepage presented in "The Netflix Recommender System: Algorithms, Business Value, and Innovation" (2015), an article by Carlos Gomez-Uribe and Neil Hunt, both from Netflix*

COMMENT ON FIGURE 6.7.– *The first emphasis varies (*The Others *in the first screenshot,* The Universe: Collection *in the second). The first list of recommendations is, on the one hand, a list of "thriller movies" and, on the other hand, the "top picks" for the user. The following lists of recommendations are also different.*

Apart from the account management features, and some static navigation elements, the interface is almost entirely made up of recommendation display areas, ranked through the space they occupy on the screen and through the order in which they appear. This display order reflects the order calculated by the recommendation engine in the form of a score invisible on the screen. The element of interactivity is almost always the same: a "play" button either already visible or appearing when clicking on a given video. Display and interactivity are focused on consulting recommendations and choosing one.

Like so many other interfaces, Netflix's interface is made up of two types of elements, possibly superimposed: display elements, which allow the user to see and control, and interactive elements, which allow the user to trigger an action. Seeing and acting are the two facets of Netflix as a product, i.e. as the sum of the uses made possible by the application. The definition and design of what this product is emerges jointly from the development and evolution of its technical features and from what is materialized to the user by the interface. The product is not one or the other but what emerges from the sum and interactions between the two.

We find here the status of computer science as an empirical transcendental delimiting a space of possibility. In Chapter 3, we saw that computer science delimits for the data scientist the space of computability, i.e. a space of computational possibility. In the same way, in Chapter 5, the software programmed a set of possible and repeatable actions that constitute the space within which the user can evolve. More precisely, we can now say that it is the product composed of the software's features (based on data science), and its interface, that determines the possible uses (without ever absolutely anticipating them all) and materializes their result. The interface elements allowing interactivity are like suggestions for possible action. They determine what the user can do, but never what they will actually do. It is a fact well known to all those who embody the figure of the designer that the uses of an existing product almost systematically go beyond the anticipated use model and that products are diverted, recontextualized and assigned to other uses than those intended. Because actual usage cannot be anticipated, the tracking of user actions is a necessary task in order to understand these usages, their discrepancy with anticipated usage, the types of usage and users, and thus develop the product.

The latter always only suggests uses, without imposing or programming them, from which it follows that we can now generalize the notion of recommendation software addressed in the system configuration to any software interface. Recommending means proposing different choices (possibly in a hierarchy) that already constitute a selection from the whole range of possible choices: if I tell a friend about movies to see, that I recommend, I do not list all the films I have seen. By broadening the notion of recommendation, not only to content recommendation based on computational analysis of digital data, but also to recommendation in general, a software product is what recommends actions and makes them possible, among an infinite number of actions that could have been developed as features and materialized. In this sense, any software product is a recommendation for action system, even if the only proposal for action would be to activate the product.

The difference between data science-based recommendation products, as discussed in the system configuration, and software products is their *generative nature*. In classical software, the elements of interactivity are mostly static. It is relatively easy to anticipate the state of the interface at a given time as long as one has the information associated with the user (their settings and the history of their actions). In the case of a recommendation engine, on the contrary, it is difficult to know what the interface will show except by actually consulting it. The only way to reconstruct what will be displayed is to replay the computation that produces the recommendation. It is necessary to be able to manipulate the engine and to have all the information that is taken into account in it. It is not possible to anticipate the result: the actual calculation is necessary. Even a software developer working on the product, with access to the code and the production servers, will not be able to determine the result of the computation other than by reconstructing the recommendation generation process. The simplest way to reconstruct this generation is to consult the interface, which is virtually singular by the sum of the parameters according to which it is generated. Thus, while our presentation of system configuration had many similarities with software development activity in general, software products based on data sciences differ from it in that they incorporate a research and development phase (the internal Simondonian concretization step that leads to the development of the recommendation engine), the result of which is materialized in the product interface in the form of suggestions of results designed in such a way that they cannot be anticipated. The interfaces of software products based on data science materialize information that cannot be anticipated, and can only be determined by replaying the process that produces it (or equivalent processes).

By its ability to show this information, the interface plays a role in recommendation software products similar to that of data visualization in narrative configuration. Indeed, like visualization, it materializes elements of meaning but does not carry in itself an interpretation of their meaning: it is the system composed of the interface and the user that is capable of producing such meaning. The interfaces of consumer software products are generally offered without explanation or user manuals; the user is the only one who learns how to use it and must understand what is presented to them on their own. The presence of an explanation for the recommendations themselves is still far from systematic, and this explanation is generally quite elliptical. The publications of my Facebook contacts and my Google search results are given to me as they are. Conversely, I can see on Amazon that certain products are recommended to me because other people visiting the same page that I have visited purchased these products; Netflix says that they recommend either a certain kind of video (thrillers, auteur films, etc.), recent releases or other types of recommendations. The recommendation specialists with whom we spoke agree that providing an explanation of the recommendations significantly improves the user's trigger for action: the recommendation is more readable and easier to understand. These explanations therefore play a similar role to the textual elements (labels, titles, annotations, etc.) added to data visualizations for playback. Like visualization, the interface that presents suggestions (and possible explanations) is a computationally generated visual form, presenting conventional semiotic elements, but also an addition of unexplained meaning that appears only through interpretation, and therefore exists only in anticipation of a user.

6.5. Materialization and interpretation of recommendations

The recommendations generated by software products are generated over a time period that is distinct from the design and development time (and occasionally from the consulting time); unlike the narrative configuration, there is no analyst who personally defends and justifies the results of their work. As noted, explanations for the proposed elements are sometimes available, but these explanations themselves are generated by a calculation: virtually, an analyst who wants to justify a list of recommendations would also have to justify the explanation generated with them. As a result, explanations such as those proposed by Netflix leave a lot of room for interpretation and possible justifications, or even, as we will outline, a questioning of the explanations and recommendations they accompany.

So when Netflix tells me, for example, that one of the movie lists it recommends to me is a list of historical movies, it does not tell me why it is recommending that genre or how those movies have been categorized as such. In an abductive mode, the user must formulate explanatory hypotheses to understand this choice of recommendation: I can assume that it is suggesting historical movies because the last movie I saw was one, because I have seen several in the last 30 days, or because it is the kind of movie I have watched the most since I created an account. In the absence of a justification for this categorization, I can imagine all sorts of explanations. Furthermore, the historical classification of the recommended movies is also not explained to me: was it done manually by a film specialist or by genre? Is this a consensus of many specialists? Is this a category provided by the director or by movie theaters? Is this the label manually added to an automatic grouping of movies with similarities generated by an algorithm? What were the factors of this grouping? While the category "historical film" may appear as a natural and obvious category, the upsurge of edge cases or disagreements calls into question an initially naturalistic position.

Thus, in Figure 6.8, the first film in a list of recommendations labeled "historical films" is the documentary broadcast in May 2017 on Emmanuel Macron's presidential campaign. In terms of audiovisual genre and the historical period covered, the regime of historicity and the mixing of documentary and historical film are widely debatable: it can easily be contested whether they are identical categories, or appreciated by the same people, but they can also be found to have similar characteristics. In any case, the appearance of this edge case denaturalizes a category that might otherwise have appeared homogeneous.

Figure 6.8. *Screenshot of the Netflix interface showing part of the list of recommended "historical films". The first proposal is not a historical film but a documentary (*Emmanuel Macron, les coulisses d'une victoire*) on a contemporary subject*

Through an example of a malfunction, we see how the meaning of recommendations is not given by the interface, but constructed by the user's interpretation. The proposed groupings do not correspond to institutionalized genres as to emerging categories that need to be given meaning and which are all potential solutions to the analysis of audiovisual content. At a meta-level, these recommendations also constitute suggestions for the typology of such content. In contrast to categories such as the cinematographic genre, which are categories explicitly defined and conceptualized by experts, with more or less fine identification criteria, institutionalized in the mix of film genres and the set of references to different genres have become a common phenomenon in audiovisual creation; the emerging recommendation categories are defined only by example. By adding a cinematographic genre indication to these recommendation lists, Netflix attempts to link its emerging categories, made up by example, to existing categories, or in other words, to return the particular back to the general: the interface offers not only recommendations for audiovisual content, but also suggestions for linking this content to more general categories. It replays and materializes the classic problem of supervised classification, which attempts to link the diverse nature of the data (rather than the diverse nature of the experience) to known concepts through computation.

By considering the concept of a film genre as a form of knowledge about the object, we propose to describe these emerging categories as *tacit and infra-conceptual knowledge* that can become effective knowledge through the user's interpretation. Instead of abductive reasoning, through which the user formulates an explanatory hypothesis for the recommendations made to them, in order to understand the elements of the interface before making their choice, one can indeed apply inductive reasoning to these emerging categories in order to conceptualize them and bring them to a higher level of generality. This work naturally requires expertise that is not simply that of the user, but of a specialist in the field who will be able to mobilize external knowledge and conceptual or narrative diagrams. In this virtual situation, which detracts from the intended use of recommendation systems, but which would allow the epistemology of cultural sciences to be reintegrated into system configurations, we are in reality close to the analyst's work in the narrative configuration: from visually materialized elements, the interpreter elaborates possible meanings that acquire a systematicity through a work of justification and self-falsification of the proposed categories, restituted no longer in the form of an interface, but in the form of a narrative.

There are thus multiple possible circulations between the narrative and system configurations, including in their respective modes of data visualization. One can also see the interface as a spatialized narrative, which would achieve not a temporal synthesis, but a spatial one, of the heterogeneous, in Ricoeur's terms, and would leave room for play in the narrative mechanics to include the reader in its construction. Whatever the configuration, data visualization plays a semiotic role that is also heuristic, enabling the production of knowledge, of rhetoric, facilitating its explicitation and explanation. Because of its initially generative nature, it also plays an evidential role through an empirical foundation, in which it demonstrates the data, i.e. elements of representation of reality. It preserves and reveals the meaning of the data, constructed by the analyst's computation and choices, highlighting an interpretation whose validity comes from the recipient of the analysis and its epistemic context.

7

Knowledge and Decision

In the preceding chapters, we have seen how knowledge emerges, whatever the configuration, from a combination of preservation and revelation actions, from data to which an epistemic value is attributed. Data transformations go through a large number of non-linguistic and infraconceptual stages, belonging to computation and then visualization. The result of these transformations is only put into language at the end of the process, in order to make sense of it. On the one hand, computational processing *preserves* this value, while the analyst's choices, and the interpretations they formulate, *reveal* the meaning of the data. Thus, these activities ground the knowledge derived from the data in two ways: they legitimize it, by providing evidence, but more importantly, they turn something unintelligible into a statement. In terms of analytical philosophy, they are said to be both truth-bearers and truth-makers (Armstrong 1993).

Indeed, for the knowledge derived from the data to be valid, it must first be knowledge, i.e., assertions that can be falsified and to which a degree of belief is given. Visualization is a knowledge carrier or truth-bearer that sets out the terms in which we formulate valid or invalid knowledge; interpretation is a falsifiable assertion formulated from this visualization, i.e. hypothetical knowledge. As such, visualization plays a role similar to that of the model in science: "According to the semantic view, scientific knowledge is embodied in models, which make statements true, but are not themselves true or false" (Perini 2012).

In other words, visualization is the structure in which knowledge is materialized; it is an assertion that can be true or false. Moreover, it is precisely the judgment made about the visualization (i.e. its interpretation) that can be validated or falsified and constitutes an assertion, while the visualization poses the terms in which this assertion is made.

Nevertheless, visualization is also a source of knowledge or a truth maker in that, as we saw earlier, it evidences what it represents. It is therefore not only a question of formulating hypothetical knowledge, the truth value of which is unknown, but of justifying this knowledge and supporting this truth value by means of data visualization.

However, our borrowing from analytical philosophy with the notions of truth-bearers and truth-makers, is placed in a rather realist conception where knowledge draws its truth regime from its correspondence with reality. However, this realist stance does not fit well with the status we have given, through the various preceding chapters, to data and its processing. The epistemic value of data is constructed in its constitutive gesture of selection; the processing is evaluated from the perspective of objectivity as preservation and revelation of this value. This epistemic value was never posed as a correspondence to reality, which could never be anything other than supposed from the analyst's point of view. It is precisely the characteristic of the analyst's position to make of the data what is (or what is given), the world to be explored independently of its possible correspondence to the real world. Data can occasionally be posed as a correspondence to reality, but above all it is always an indication of it, which must be manipulated and interpreted in order to be reconnected to the event that generated it and to make sense.

As a result, the realistic position, which was by default that of the mythology of big data, cannot be supported when we take into account their modalities and their regime of knowledge constitution. In view of the remarks already made on the status of the knowledge produced, we propose to assess it through the prism of an approach that is not realistic, but rather pragmatic, which tightly articulates the notions of knowledge and action.

7.1. Big data, a pragmatic epistemology?

If we take into account the context in which they are used, the purpose of data sciences is not to to seek and describe truth. If the results of computational processing can occasionally be seen as truthful, it is not for this purpose that they are realized: the very production of knowledge is instrumental, in the service of something else. As a result, they can be analyzed and interpreted in a realist framework, but also, as we shall now see, in an instrumentalist framework. If the two interpretations coexist, each providing an understanding of the nature of the knowledge produced, we will see that the instrumentalist interpretation governs the realistic interpretation. Although truthfulness itself has a role in the validation of knowledge and especially in the trust placed in it, it is the instrumental character of knowledge derived from data in general (and not from knowledge equipped to produce other knowledge, as found in instrumentalist epistemologies) that characterizes data sciences in relation to other scientific practices. Grounded in a corporate or business setup, they are in fact articulated with the purpose of the company: its survival and growth. The knowledge produced by a company is, in principle, produced for only one of these purposes. This articulation between knowledge and the company's purpose is achieved through the notion of decision, and more precisely through the ability of knowledge from massive data processing to improve decision making. The purpose of such processing would thus be to make data-driven decisions. In an article that attempts to clarify the links between data science and decision making, Foster Provost and Tom Fawcett (2013) write:

> "Data science involves principles, processes, and techniques for understanding phenomena via the (automated) analysis of data. For the perspective of this article, the ultimate goal of data science is improving decision making, as this generally is of paramount interest to business. [...] Data-driven decision making (DDD) refers to the practice of basing decisions on the analysis of data rather than purely on intuition."

The promise of data science here is not so much to produce new knowledge, but to enable companies to act more rationally, basing their decisions empirically and not on intuition alone. Below, they point out that this empiricism has practical consequences, which justify the use of such an approach:

> "The benefits of data-driven decision making have been demonstrated conclusively. Economist Erik Brynjolfsson and his colleagues from MIT and Penn's Wharton School recently conducted a study of how DDD affects firm performance. They developed a measure of DDD that rates firms as to how strongly they use data to make decisions across the company. They show

> statistically that the more data-driven a firm is, the more productive it is – even controlling for a wide range of possible confounding factors."

In these terms, data-driven empiricism is motivated by the practical consequences it has on the survival and growth of the firm through the improvement of its performance: data are analyzed in order to work toward an end. The intrinsic epistemic value of the results produced is incidental, or at least of interest only in so far as these results lead to a beneficial decision for the company. This is anti-realism, not in the sense that it rejects a realistic interpretation of these results, but in the sense that it is indifferent to its realistic nature.

One could go so far as to say that the validity of the results is determined not on scientific criteria, but precisely in terms of the benefits that these results can bring. The epistemology of data sciences would then be a form of pragmatism, i.e. a theory of knowledge based on Peirce's pragmatist maxim (1878): "Consider what effects, that might conceivably have practical bearings, we conceive the object of our conception to have. Then, our conception of these effects is the whole of our conception of the object".

Critics of Peirce's work (Tiercelin 1993; Hookway 2013) have pointed out how little Peirce makes explicit the process for determining these practical consequences. Nevertheless, this quote can be supplemented by explaining the general state of mind of Peircean pragmatism, which consists of rejecting metaphysical statements and looking at knowledge in terms of what it actually means, in relation to problems that actually arise. In these terms, knowledge is validated not from a metaphysical framework, but with regard to a situation that it may or may not resolve. Thus, we understand that not only is knowledge what makes action possible, but knowledge is knowledge only because it makes action possible.

In these terms, data science is a specific form of pragmatism, where knowledge from big data processing is only known because it facilitates a decision in a company and that decision will somehow be translated into action. It appears to be a more restricted form of pragmatism, articulated to the notion of decision making and not to that of action in general. Indeed, decision making is a form of action, but knowledge production is also a form of action: the notion of action is broader than the notion of decision making, which makes the epistemology of data sciences more restrictive than pragmatism in its conception of knowledge. It would not only be a pragmatism in the ordinary sense, i.e. a form of "common sense" that would foster what can be easily implemented rather than theoretical and philosophical work, nor a linguistic pragmatism as we have seen at work in the codification of customer feedback, but a theory of knowledge governed by the concept of action, related to philosophical pragmatism, all the more strongly articulated to the concept of action as it would be an operationalized, not purely conceptual, practical philosophy.

Nevertheless, the hypothesis of a pragmatic interpretation needs to be discussed. At first glance, it assumes that there is an almost mechanical link between knowledge and action. However, if the concept of decision that articulates them is, as we shall see, central to the data processing processes, it is understood in a very specific sense, and it is not certain that it proposes a mechanical articulation, and therefore that the knowledge produced is indeed pragmatic in the sense that Peirce understands it.

So we need to start by looking specifically at the concept of decision in general and in the context of big data. In its general sense, a decision is the result of a process that involves the evaluation of one or more possible choices (deliberation) and the selection of a choice. Deliberation is a discursive action, individual or collective, which allows a judgment to be made. Deliberation and selection are mental processes that have no mechanical consequences: deciding to buy an apartment will not make me a homeowner. These mental processes also reflect the state of my beliefs at a given time: I will choose one of the possibilities because it will seem more desirable to me in view of my knowledge and moral standards at that time. A decision can be seen as an action (of the mind) that will lead to other actions. Nevertheless, the relationship between a decision and an action can be far-reaching: I can decide something and never carry out my decision. When a business leader presents a strategy, they set out a set of decisions that will have to be rewritten and broken down many times before they can be implemented. *A posteriori*, one can evaluate the actions associated with this implementation and their adequacy to the initial decision; in this way, it can happen that one believes that a decision is being implemented, but in reality the translation of this decision into action is erroneous. In this situation, there is indeed an action that has been carried out, but which does not correspond to the implementation of the decision in question. Thus, regardless of the fact that deciding is an activity in itself, a mental operation, the fact that an action is the practical consequence of a decision is not obvious, and can be assessed *after* the fact to ensure this.

This decision concept that serves to link knowledge and action is a key notion in data science, which, as we have seen, is intended to initiate evidence-based decision-making. In its polysemy, it goes through all the processes of massive data processing. So, if we retrace these different stages:

– the *gesture of constituting the data* is a decision, apparently arbitrary;

– *theoretical computer science*, and any subsequent computation, answers the problem of Hilbert's decision to pose a problem as an alternative between several choices to be decided upon. Theoretical computer science is then the art of designing an effective procedure to decide between these different options, and thus solve the problem by making deliberation a computational procedure;

– analysts and developers are constantly making decisions and *design choices* about the right way to clean, analyze and visualize data;

– the user of the system configuration decides from the *recommendations* made;

– as we have just seen, the results of this processing are intended to lead to better *decision making*.

Through these different points, different conceptions of the decision emerge, which we will detail before delving deeper into the one that could materialize the connection between knowledge and action.

– First of all, the decisions made by determining the computation are made by non-human agents: to say that an algorithm and the program that implements it "decides" the content that will be proposed to me via a recommendation system can be seen as an abuse of language. At a minimum, it should be stressed that algorithmic decisions and human decision-making have a distinct ontological status. Program decisions are not those that allow the company to accomplish its purpose, but interim determinations that allow a specific user, the decision-maker, to be offered several options. The algorithm indeed plays the role of a mechanical procedure in order to solve a problem posed as a decision problem: this procedure allows us to decide by computation the choices that will be submitted to the user. As a result, recommendation systems can be seen as decision support systems (and not decision systems) that are pre-selected from the full range of possible choices. The logic and configurations of this preselection are determined by a computation that is itself the result of a multitude of design and implementation choices by the analyst or developer. This pre-selection is a support to the deliberation phase that precedes the selection of a choice but the computation itself is not a form of deliberation. This stage will be referred to as determinations rather than computational decisions.

– The analyst's or developer's epistemic decisions are, for their part, seemingly arbitrary choices in the domain of the non-necessary, governed by a certain logic (of acquisition, of transformation), which have direct consequences on the knowledge produced. These are decisions in the primary sense that we have proposed: mental operations that result in the selection of a choice among several possible options. These choices are made by virtue of an ability to produce judgments and manipulations that preserve or reveal the data's epistemic virtues. Without these choices, the data remain unintelligible: decision making is a key step in the production of knowledge through the processing of big data.

– At the end of the transformation chain, this knowledge is mobilized by users to facilitate a decision. In the system configuration, the recommendation offers different options while the software makes it possible to select one of these options. However, this recommendation scheme, which consists of preselecting options, also exists in the narrative configuration. Indeed, the narrative's consumers expect that the narrative will not only present the conclusions of the investigation, but recommendations for action will flow from these conclusions: the type of knowledge expected is not a summary that accounts for the data, but proposals for action informed by this summary.

This relationship between conclusion and recommendation is an important point in the claim for a possible pragmatist epistemology to articulate a relationship between knowledge and action. Data processing is based on decisions by both human and non-human agents, but it is this recommendation stage that presents an articulation between the knowledge produced (not the generation of knowledge) and the action mediated by the decision. We will examine it in more detail.

As mentioned earlier, the narrative configuration can take the form of a study report presented to a client. This was particularly the case for the services offered by Proxem. However, on several occasions, I observed, in producing and presenting reports of this type, that Proxem's clients may have been disappointed by the study report produced, which was judged "useless", not very "meaningful". The findings were not challenged (i.e., it was not their epistemic validity that was in question) but the client did not see how or why they could use them. In pragmatic terms, it could be said that these conclusions were not knowledge inasmuch as they did not allow the client to draw practical consequences, decisions for action.

As a result of this feedback, the reports produced and referred to were redrafted in order to reformulate the summary into proposals for action, for example by transforming a conclusion such as:

> "Service interruptions are a major source of customer dissatisfaction".

In the proposal:

> (implied, "we recommend to you") "Propose a gesture of goodwill in case of service interruption".

The reports thus updated became a narrative that was still based on data visualization, but whose conclusion took up the narrative elements produced throughout the narrative and reformulated them into proposals for action.

It should be pointed out here that the introduction of elements of recommendation in an analytical report may be surprising with regard to the standards of scientific publications, but remains quite ordinary in the professional world. In the consulting business, proposals for action are called recommendations (or even *recos*); this is a stable term to describe the contribution of consulting firms, whose role is not so much to provide expertise as to propose actions on the basis of that expertise. The expectations of Proxem's clients with regard to the study reports produced were therefore more the responsibility of the consulting firm than of the research institute, whose role is initially to carry out a survey and summarize it[1]. As a result, a report ending with recommendations is systematically perceived as more useful.

1 Increasingly, research institutes are also subject to the injunction to produce recommendations. This injunction is accompanied by a restructuring of the market in which

This usefulness, which reflects an instrumentalist conception of knowledge where its validity does not (or not only) depend on its truth value, is often expressed through a recurrent term in the universe of data-driven decisions: the notion of *actionability*. The term describes what can be acted upon, on the basis of which action can be taken. Knowledge is actionable when an action that flows from that knowledge can be easily identified. Activating actionable knowledge is implementing it. In a pragmatic framework, knowledge is by definition actionable: it is only knowledge if it can have practical effects, consequences relating to action. By requiring that the narratives end with recommendations rather than summative conclusions that are descriptive of the intelligibility of the data, the recipients of these narratives place the knowledge produced by the analysts within a pragmatic framework. As the actions to be produced are those of these recipients, only they can effectively attest to their actionability: the analyst can imagine and anticipate possibilities of action corresponding to what has emerged from the data, but it is the decision-making recipient who can determine whether a given piece of knowledge should be followed by action.

Between recommendation and action, there is thus a third term that links them, and which does not belong to the analyst's field of action: it is the field of decision in its meaning. Like other previous stages, it in turn mobilizes, as we shall see, a capacity for interpretation and judgment supplemented by external knowledge.

7.2. Toward gradual validity of knowledge

Throughout the data processing process, it is as if the potential knowledge contained in the data was materialized. Interpretation and computation generate assertions that are neither made up *ex nihilo* (they come from the data), nor directly manifest in the "raw" data, i.e. the data that has not yet been manipulated. The decisions made by the analyst or developer, and the computational "decisions" of the programs are the driving forces of this knowledge updating process. Nevertheless, this updating process is incomplete without a validation step, which makes the knowledge effective, validating it as knowledge. However, in a pragmatic framework, what validates this knowledge is the fact that it is possible to make use of it,

---

these research institutes are increasingly integrated into large groups of communications consultancies. The different entities of the group are thus able to produce the analysis but also the recommendation, as well as to implement it in an operational manner.

to act on the basis of this knowledge. The epistemic agent able to determine whether an action is possible is the recipient of the narrative (or the user of the system): without them, knowledge is always only potential, because it is their ability to act that is at stake to make knowledge effective.

Following this logic, one may then wonder whether pragmatic knowledge is in fact knowledge (a) when it is admitted that it can give rise to an action, (b) when it can give rise to a decision to act or (c) when the action has actually been implemented. In a system configuration, these three possibilities can be very close together or even indistinguishable: the choice is always already possible and operational, programmed through the interface, accessible with a click. The only part that is not provided by the system is the essential atomicity of the user's decision and the possible deliberation that may precede it. This decision is not only a mental process; it is almost mechanically repeated with a click that instantly operationalizes it and triggers the implementation of the corresponding action. Again in the Netflix example, when I click on one of the recommended movies, I am operationalizing my decision to watch it, which triggers my viewing. Strictly speaking, the system does not make a decision (except in the sense (1) of computational determination), but supports all the material conditions of possibility of the decision, so that the operationalization of the user's mental processes can be instantaneous. It thus preserves the user's decision making capacity, whose role is however reduced to this small portion. The infraconceptual knowledge produced by the recommendation is still updatable using the interface, i.e. actionable and activated by viewing.

On the other hand, in the narrative configuration, the articulation between (still potential) knowledge, and action, is more distant. A narrative that is passed on may not be followed by a decision. It can be understood both as a truthful narrative aimed at the truth, and as a pragmatic narrative aimed at action. In the event (c) that it is the implementation of actions decided on the basis of the recommendations arising from the conclusions of the data analysis that validates and gives consequence to these conclusions, there is a high probability that the knowledge arising from a narrative configuration will never be updated and will remain only possible knowables, like the data themselves before analysis. Whatever the analyst has produced, the recipient may never make a decision on the basis of this information or implement any decision they may have made.

In addition, recommendations could be assessed not on whether or not the decision maker has implemented an action (which would confirm factually the actionability of the recommendations) but on the consequences for the undertaking of that action. For example, in the example cited above, where the analyst suggests proposing a gesture of goodwill to customers who have experienced a service interruption, this practice could be too costly, damaging the company's profitability in the economic equation between the expense corresponding to the sum of these business gestures and the benefits of improved customer satisfaction. In this hypothesis, knowledge would not be evaluated by its actionability, but by the economic consequences of its activation. It should also be noted that this suggestion cannot be activated as such: before doing so, it is necessary to determine precisely the nature and amount of this commercial gesture, and the characteristics of the interruption, including its duration, whether it is total or partial, etc. The decision maker may also incorporate other criteria, such as the value of the customer estimated by an internal score: the company will be more inclined to compensate a loyal customer, who represents an above-average revenue, who is likely to change supplier, etc. The decision maker will also be able to integrate other criteria, such as the value of the customer estimated by an internal score: the company will be more inclined to compensate a loyal customer, who represents an above-average turnover, who is likely to change supplier, etc. In this way, the actionability of the recommendation is no longer the analyst's sole responsibility, but it also becomes the decision maker's responsibility, who must formalize the procedures for its activation. Ideally, this formalization also integrates the economic consequences of these modalities through an economic forecast that enables validating that this activation is viable for the company. All the elements produced constitute an action plan, which makes the decision explicit so that it can be effectively implemented. This action plan contains practical knowledge, which refers not to a representation of the world, but to norms of action.

The validity of the knowledge produced is therefore a responsibility distributed between the analyst and the decision maker who receives the narrative[2], in a context where the "accounting" of knowledge has an epistemic as well as an economic meaning. The action plan complements the

2 It should be noted, however, that the sponsor of the study is not necessarily a decision maker, that it is not always clear who is the decision maker on an issue, or even whether such a decision maker exists within the company. A company's daily life is also made up of these "holes" in the decision making process that hinder the implementation of concrete actions.

analyst's recommendation to build actionable knowledge. We can speak of a social epistemology, i.e. a configuration in which the production of knowledge does not result from a singular individual, but from a set of agents that contribute, in the same or different ways, to the production of knowledge. These agents collaborate successively and/or simultaneously to achieve the final result. The autonomous narrative is only one part of the whole, which constitutes an actionable knowable, and therefore also involves the decision-maker.

As a result, the company is not a passive recipient of the knowledge produced by its provider. Through the decision maker (or people working with or for the decision maker), it is engaged in the production process of knowledge. This is at least the configuration required to achieve effectively actionable knowledge. In practice, this social epistemology is not necessarily obvious to either the client or the provider. Traditionally, the person commissioning a study does not see themselves as an operational resource: their role is to express their expectations to the service provider, who takes on the task of fulfilling them in return for a fee. Likewise, the provider does not consider themselves responsible for the economic consequences of activating recommendations. The social epistemology of the data sciences producing actionable knowledge thus reconfigures the nature of the knowledge produced (in relation to a research institute, for example, which would produce conclusions without recommendation) but also the organizational modalities of this production. In this sense, the production of actionable knowledge is transformative of the modes of organization and operation: to succeed, the production process must have operational consequences on the company for which it takes place. Thus, not only must the knowledge produced have practical consequences in order to be validated pragmatically, but the constitution process itself must have similar consequences.

Nevertheless, these production and validation methods remain both new for companies and difficult to implement. A validation of knowledge that would take the form of a binary judgment, positive or negative, based on the economic consequences of the actions proposed by these consequences, could only rarely be carried out, and would most often end in invalidating the work carried out. Moreover, the pragmatic texts do not, to our knowledge, allow us to make a distinction between the different hypotheses for validating knowledge that we have formulated, from the possibility of action to the evaluation of economic consequences, via the translation of the decision into an action plan, and its effective implementation: all these hypotheses describe knowledge that has practical consequences. We therefore propose to reject the use of a binary judgment criterion based on the economic consequences of the implementation of the suggested decision to adopt a system of gradual validation of knowledge. In this system, knowledge is not "useful" or "useless" in a binary and exclusive way, but has a degree of validity that can be estimated by the analyst and the sponsor. Such an estimate examines, for example, the following criteria:

– the conclusion is presented as a proposal for action;

– the proposal for action is explicit, precise and well defined;

– the proposed action mobilizes external knowledge that is not derived from the processing of data;

– the proposed action is in line with the company's strategy;

– the proposed action can be translated into an action plan;

– the action plan is implemented;

– the implementation of the plan is successful from an economic point of view.

Thus, we can return to our initial example that used the following conclusion:

> "The service interruptions are a major source of customer dissatisfaction".

Several proposals for action can be made, starting with the proposal to ensure that there are no service interruptions. However, knowledge of the customer's industry (in this case an Internet service provider) indicates that it is not possible to guarantee a complete absence of service interruption (i.e. an Internet outage), and that reducing such interruptions will be very costly, requiring a major overhaul of the network infrastructure, involving external stakeholders who will also have to be convinced of the value of such a revision. As a result, proposing a gesture of goodwill is a solution that immediately appears to be less costly. On the other hand, it requires the development of a precise casuistry describing which gesture of goodwill should be proposed according to the interruption encountered by the customer, its scope, duration, etc. It also presupposes being able to verify that there is indeed an interruption, beyond the claim made by the customer, or to opt for the payment of a discount on the sole testimony of the customer, without a verification that may also have an implementation cost. It also involves an action plan detailing how customer relationship managers who handle complaints can do this, and how to train them on the new policy. Finally, the evaluation of this gesture of goodwill policy must itself be detailed through the development of evaluation criteria and an implementation plan for the measurement of these criteria. In short, a proposal for action brings with it an infinite number of "detailed" implementation steps necessary for the proposal for action to become effective and to be economically validated.

In the face of this complexity, the system of graduated validity is designed to determine not whether the proposal is valid, but how valid it is, or in other words, how far the sponsor may have gone in their implementation and validation. Although it is not based on a realistic position, it proceeds from norms similar to confirmationist epistemologies such as Carnap's norm, where knowledge is validated by degree. The knowledge produced comes from a theory that has a Carnap-style confirmationist structure, but pragmatic norms, in that the degree of validity of the knowledge is primarily a degree of actionability, or in other words, of "pragmaticity", of the knowledge produced.

We have thus seen that in the system configuration, the knowledge produced by the recommendation engine was always already practical knowledge, which was not intended to describe reality, but which was knowledge in the sense that it enabled an action decision (although it is always possible to rewrite it as infraconceptual knowledge that can be reduced to theoretical concepts by an agent who is not the intended user of the system). On the narrative side, this relationship between knowledge and decision was less obvious: by examining the different practical consequences that a recommendation can have, we proposed a system of gradual knowledge validation based on the degree of actionability, i.e. pragmatism, of the knowledge produced. Nevertheless, we still have to examine a point that is not covered by the way we have examined the articulation between knowledge and decision in narrative and system configurations: intermediate configurations that exploit the conclusions of a narrative configuration or the uses of systems to produce a specific form of system, the dashboard.

7.3. Deciding, knowing and measuring

The different configurations for producing knowledge from big data generate actions that can in turn be measured. Data sciences not only generate knowledge that can have practical consequences but also assess those consequences. In companies, the iconic embodiment of this measurement and monitoring activity is the *dashboard.*

A dashboard is the representation of one or more key performance indicators (KPIs) defined according to the objectives of an action plan. The dashboard aggregates these indicators in a single place. It is not necessarily linked to a precise form or a computational support, but it reaches an additional level of concretization as a technical object, taking the form not of a billboard or a digital document circulating between decision makers, but of software dedicated to this use. In our example of the introduction of business actions in the event of service disruption, the objective to be measured through an indicator would be the reduction of dissatisfaction related to these problems. The associated performance indicator would be the evolution (over time) of satisfaction after the implementation of gestures of goodwill. A more detailed indicator would capture satisfaction only for customers affected by these service interruptions. As the very notion of satisfaction is not in itself measurable, it must be converted into an indicator to find its place in a dashboard. The Net Promoter Score (NPS) method that we presented in Chapter 4 is in this perspective nothing more than a method of converting a fuzzy notion (satisfaction) into a quantitative indicator that can vary from one population to another and as a function of time.

However reductive this conversion may be, it has significant similarities with scientific practice. The conversion of a phenomenon into a measurement refers to the work of modeling reality that the researcher carries out. Every model is a reductive conversion of reality, because its epistemic function is precisely to reduce the various complexes of reality to a manipulable and measurable object. A cell model says nothing about the variability of possible cells and the exact arrangement of its parts, accidents and developments. Nevertheless, it is, from an instrumentalist perspective, sufficient for the experiments in which it is mobilized. The major dividing line between the scientific model and the performance indicator is not their reductionism, but rather their mode of validation.

Indeed, a scientific model must in principle be validated before being used. We saw in particular in Chapter 3 how computer simulation can have a role in the computational deduction of the model's consequences in order to evaluate its correspondence with reality. Experimental devices that rely on a model also make it possible to test it: it is this relationship of experimental evidence that the simulation tries to reproduce in some cases. Experimentation is both what is opposable to the model posed in a hypothetical way, and what then mobilizes the validated model to increase the knowledge of reality.

On the other hand, the conversion of satisfaction into an indicator proposed by the NPS method is, to our knowledge, based mainly on an authority argument. Consulting firms that assist companies in implementing this method highlight the number and diversity of their past experiences as well as the standard character that the method is gradually acquiring: the arguments are based on the abundance of other companies that have implemented this method and the normative status that this abundance confers on it. In particular, they highlight examples of economically successful companies, suggesting a correlation between this success and the implementation of the NPS method, which is implicitly envisaged as a cause and effect relationship. Thus, if there is justification for the modeling from which the indicator results, it is again not by correspondence with reality but via the practical consequences of the indicator's implementation. Moreover, like the scientific modeling activity, the work of designing indicators is not in itself infallible; an indicator may only have the appearance of a correspondence with reality, and be a form without content. There are good and bad indicators, just as there are good and bad models, in relation to a given context or purpose.

Despite this difference, however, in the justification, in relation to scientific knowledge, a performance indicator refers to a more traditional notion of knowledge than the one used in the recommendation. A performance indicator takes the form of a measure that tells you something about something else. It therefore appears in a regime of correspondence to reality whereby a satisfaction indicator is based on data that have a status of measurement as customer satisfaction, and not satisfaction as an abstract notion describing only the data. Through this indicator, the data are retroactively charged with an epistemic responsibility of describing reality.

As such, performance indicators based on the exploitation of the practical consequences of the recommendations, resulting from the processing of big data, refer to older practices for monitoring business activity. The notion of performance indicators goes back to benchmarking practices stemming from managerial and organizational innovations developed from the 1920s in the United States and Japan (Bruno and Didier 2013). Based on the theories of work monitoring and quality management, these practices aim to put into competition different ways of working within the company or from one company to another. This competition is based on the definition of elements of comparability, the indicators and aims which identify the "best practices" observable within or outside the company, and made commensurable through the indicators that evaluate them.

Benchmarking makes it possible to put the company's services and employees in competition with each other. Augmented by the mobilization of the traces of the company's activity and of its customers, this benchmarking can be automated by aggregating and visualizing the data that feeds these performance indicators. In data representation, visualizations play a descriptive and evidentiary role similar to that which they occupy in narrative configurations. The graphics of a narrative and a dashboard can be identical in form and content. One graphic will show the change in satisfaction, another will show the number of complaints handled, a third will show the main reasons for complaint, etc. Again in the example of managing service interruptions, customer satisfaction following the processing of their claim can be measured by keeping track of the account manager who handled the claim. By aggregating these measures, the dashboard not only provides an understanding of the driving forces of improved customer satisfaction, but also nominally identifies those account managers whose actions result in a lower than average[3] level of satisfaction. Generally speaking, it is the company's overall performance that should be improved by improving the performance of individuals on average, and not by specifically targeting those individuals deemed to be underperforming.

Benchmarking as a technique based on a correspondence to the reality of the indicators remains at the service of practical purposes. The epistemic

3 This form of benchmarking enables an individualized control of the professional activity. To our knowledge, however, this form of individual surveillance is not practiced, at least among Proxem's clients, with the exception of one project that made it possible to track down the perpetrator of illegal practices.

responsibility of describing the reality that the indicators possess is to be set against their role as instruments for evaluating the economic consequences of action plans implemented (or not) on the basis of recommendations resulting from the processing of the company's activity traces. While the recommendations help decision makers to define action plans, the indicators retrospectively evaluate these recommendations by measuring the consequences of the actions implemented on the basis of these recommendations. Moreover, this process is not only linear, from the recommendation to the dashboard: the dashboard can also suggest adjustments to the action plan or even a new strategy, which also makes it a source of recommendations.

Dashboards can exist both as a result of projects corresponding to a narrative configuration, and as part of the design of recommendation systems. In the first case, the findings of the narrative, by highlighting the main lessons that can be drawn from the data, contribute directly to the definition of performance indicators. The narrative identifies the key points while the dashboard allows us to follow their development over time. The dashboard can also be seen as a spatialized and dynamic narrative scheme, with which one interacts to identify relationships between variables, and whose meaning and "outcome" is constructed by the user through these interactions. This scheme based on a spatial synthesis is therefore similar to a system as described above.

On the system configuration side, strictly speaking, most software based on significant data processing integrates user activity monitoring features, which serves both to retroactively enrich the recommendation, but also, and to this end, to track and better understand user behaviors. Analysis of this behavior is not done by browsing raw usage logs, but through aggregated views in dashboards. In our exchanges with algorithmic recommendation specialists, measuring the quality of recommendations through performance indicators based on the measurement of user behavior with respect to these recommendations is part of everyday life. These user behaviors are first analyzed in order to derive performance indicators as in a narrative configuration, and then integrated into a dashboard that allows us to visualize their development. A dashboard is therefore an object that is compatible with multiple situations, be it big data processing in a narrative or system configuration, or other ways of feeding performance indicators within the company.

It should be stressed that the decisions taken in companies do not systematically proceed from recommendations resulting from the analysis of the traces of their activity, and not all of them are evaluated through performance indicators. Firms that rely on the same data to improve their decision making and control of their business remain rare, as these practices are not necessary from a business operating perspective: the precedence of benchmarking practices over data science attests to the unnecessary nature of the latter, without which the former may also exist. Nevertheless, some companies are adopting these new practices, because they refer to the concrete issues of management and monitoring of companies, and they can bring an improvement in the realization of these issues. From this point of view, recommendations from data science have a dual role of *legitimizing* the action plans implemented by decision makers against empirical norms that reject intuitive action decisions based on individual intuition, and a role of *partial production* (in the form of suggestion) of the decisions that give rise to these action plans. This structure is found in the system configuration where the recommendation self-justifies the decision it proposes and makes it feasible for the user. For their part, dashboards also have a dual function: (1) to monitor, by measuring the company's activity, the decisions governing that activity, and (2) to iteratively generate new decisions that make it possible to adjust or redirect the action plans that govern, at least in theory, the activity of companies.

In summary, within the pragmatist framework, data sciences generate and measure practical consequences using pragmatic knowledge. This knowledge is evaluated in terms of its practical consequences, produced by a set of individual or collective decisions and computational determinations. At the same time, this knowledge consists in proposals for action, i.e. potential decisions updated by the implementation of corresponding action plans.

Conclusion

At the end of this investigation into the discourses and practices of big data analysis, we have uncovered a methodological paradigm in which future projects for the exploitation of digital footprints can be inscribed. This paradigm governs how an epistemic value is assigned to data, but also how to construct and manipulate corpora, how to interpret the results of the computation, how to render the investigation in such a way as to make it intelligible to a reader or user and how to determine the validity of the knowledge produced. It highlights the crucial nature of the notion of decision that governs the entire process and the link between knowledge and action. Two components are also essential to the integration of this paradigm: the role of *craftsmanship* in the constitution of data, their preparation, cleaning and analysis, and that of the *rhetoric* of image and narrative, which is crucial to bringing about and making intelligible the meaning of the data. For this, several key concepts are proposed:

– the distinction between data and footprint makes the latter always an intermediate and indirect sign of the targeted reality, whose meaning is to be constructed in the situation by extracting a corpus. The *epistemic value* of the numerical footprint is the result of a construction within an *evidential paradigm*;

– the distinction between *field-based* and *corpus-based disciplines* refines for a second time the integration of these practices in the cultural sciences. It allows us to specify an access to reality, which is done by substituting a statistical representativeness of the data with a corpus *constitution logic*, the narrative of which makes sense. This logic of constitution, which makes it possible to decide what is to be included or excluded, is the result of an *epistemic project* that takes shape progressively in the course of the *investigation*, and does not pre-exist the data as research hypotheses would do in the context of classical data analysis;

– this epistemic constitution of the corpus is coupled with a *technical constitution*, within which the digital footprint is always already *manipulable* because of its computer material, and must be cleaned and formatted in a work guided by this epistemic project, and which already belongs to the data analysis phase. Information technology thus plays the role of an *empirical transcendental* that determines *a posteriori*, in an effective way, the conditions for the possibility of knowledge to be produced;

– data analysis is part of an *exploratory paradigm*, which, unlike its confirmatory counterpart, seeks to demonstrate and justify the data themselves, which constitute for the analyst the reality to be known. It mobilizes the toolbox of *data sciences* considered as an aggregate of techniques coming from different lines, and able to circulate between analysis projects because they are detached from their theoretical integration through the suppression of the precedence of modeling over computation;

– in the absence of this modeling stage, the computational manipulation performed by data sciences is necessary but not sufficient to give the corpus rationality and make meanings emerge. It is through the interpretation and *visualization of data* that the results of the computation are made intelligible, while at the same time taking on the evidential role of these results;

– these results can be restituted in two forms. The first is a *narrative* that achieves a summary of the heterogeneous elements and whose narration makes it possible to give reason for the investigation. This narrative is made up of visual components enhanced by textual contextualizations that materialize knowledge and stabilize its interpretation;

– the second form is the system, centered on the principle of the recommendation-based software which divides the data analysis into an investigative work and an industrialization work which makes this investigation repeatable;

– whatever the form of restitution, the analysis of digital footprints promotes a rational empiricism that bases its access to reality in the footprint itself and mobilizes computation, visualization and narrative as a justification of its reasoning. At each stage, the exercise of *self-refutation* tests the rationality of the investigation, and grounds it through reason when attempts at self-refutation are unsuccessful;

– at each moment, this investigation is the result of human *decisions*, choices of conceptualization and design, in the face of which the computation never has a definitive character, but only serves as a material and aid to the production of knowledge from footprints;

– finally, this rational empiricism is mobilized in a rhetoric of scientificity that facilitates trust in the knowledge produced, but does not constitute its validity regime: it is ultimately the *actionability* of knowledge, i.e. its capacity to suggest action decisions relevant to the investigation's recipient, that determines its validity from the consequences of the actions it suggests.

The methodological paradigm thus defined makes possible computational cultural sciences that mobilize both the epistemic culture of the cultural sciences, technical know-how in data sciences and a specific methodological approach based on exploration and visualization. These computational cultural sciences have here again a largely hypothetical status, with partial and localized operationalizations. In particular, the conceptual apparatus of the cultural sciences is still largely underexploited due to the institutional integration of the practices analyzed. These practices are played out far from the cultural sciences, in companies, in computer research or even by amateur or self-taught analysts.

From this point of view, it seems to us that there is both concern and hope for the future of this methodological paradigm.

First, the exploitation of digital footprints by research and the digital industry is characterized by an undermobilization of the conceptual apparatus of the cultural sciences, generally unknown and/or ignored by computational practitioners and replaced by rudimentary concepts derived from common sense, which are increasingly problematic from an epistemological and ethical point of view. The naturalization of cultural science objects such as crime (Wu and Zhang 2016) or sexual orientation (Wang and Kosinski 2017) amounts to a return to phrenology and a summary negation of the results of cultural science as a whole. These works have a performative character by which they feed the technological dystopias from which they draw inspiration, and ignore the ethical and social responsibility that must permeate research in terms of humanity and society.

There is thus a certain urgency, not only to invalidate this work, but also to revalue the conceptual apparatus of the cultural sciences and its capacity to question the consequences of their research activity; in short, there is a growing need to show that another way is possible.

Second, the cultural sciences and the digital industry have no need to go to war. The capacities offered by computation are to be seen as an opportunity for our knowledge of the human fact, and must be able to function under a regime of complementarity rather than opposition. The path of interdisciplinarity between fundamentally different epistemic cultures is by no means simple or quick, and requires a readiness to make a whole that will be more than the sum of its parts, by mourning the methodological and theoretical purity of each of them. At both the collective and individual levels, it requires a compromise between heterogeneous world views that are too often seen as incompatible. It requires being a bit philosophical, accepting to unlearn what we know and how we know it. Nevertheless, as we have illustrated with our case study, such an alliance is possible, and both sides stand to gain, not only in terms of the volume and validity of the knowledge they can derive from it, but also in terms of their own self-understanding.

This book advocates for hybridization, promoting hope over anxiety. Ecumenically, it is not about joining a camp, not even establishing one, but drawing complementary components and reporting on what each had to contribute. Formally, its contribution is a general approach to articulating these components. In its continuity, the exploration and understanding of the conditions of possibility of this hybridization, through the proposed approach as well as through other means, is the research program we are now looking toward.

References

Adam, M. (2004). Why worry about theory-dependence? Circularity, minimal empiricality and reliability. *International Studies in the Philosophy of Science*, 18(2/3), 117–132.

Agrawal, R. and Srikant, R. (1994). Fast algorithms for mining association rules. *Proceedings of the 20th International Conference on Very Large Data Bases*, VLDB, 1215, 487–499.

Amossé, T. (2013). La nomenclature socio-professionnelle: une histoire revisitée. *Annales. Histoire, Sciences sociales*, 4, 1039–1075.

Anderson, C. (2008). *The end of theory: The data deluge makes the scientific method obsolete.* [Online]. Available at: http://archive.wired.com/science/discoveries/magazine/16-07/pb_theory [Accessed 11 May 2014].

Andler, D. (2011). Le naturalisme est-il l'horizon scientifique des sciences sociales? In *Les sciences humaines sont-elles des sciences?*, Martin, T. (ed.). Vuibert, Paris, 15–34.

Andrade, N. (2010). Technology and metaphors: From cyberspace to ambient intelligence. *Observatorio (OBS)*, 4, 121–146.

Anscombe, F.J. (1973). Graphs in statistical analysis. *The American Statistician*, 27(1), 441–475.

Armatte, M. (2008). Histoire et Préhistoire de l'Analyse des données par J.-P. Benzecri: un cas de généalogie rétrospective. *Electronic Journal for History of Probability and Statistics*, 4, 1–24.

Armstrong, D.M. (1993). A world of states of affairs. *Philosophical Perspectives*, 7, 429–440.

Asur, S. and Huberman, B.A. (2010). *Predicting the future with social media.* [Online]. Available at: https://arxiv.org/pdf/1003.5699.pdf [Accessed 29 March 2020].

Bachimont, B. (1996). Herméneutique matérielle et artéfacture. Des machines qui pensent aux machines qui donnent à penser. PhD Thesis, École Polytechnique, Palaiseau.

Bachimont, B. (2010a). La présence de l'archive: réinventer et justifier. *Intellectica*, 54, 281–309.

Bachimont, B. (2010b). Le numérique comme support de la connaissance: entre matérialisation et interprétation. In *Ressources vives. Le travail documentaire des professeurs en mathématiques*, Gueudet, G. and Trouche, L. (eds). Presses universitaires de Rennes, Rennes, 1–12.

Bachimont, B. (2010c). Le *sens de la technique: le numérique et le calcul.* Encre Marine, Paris.

Barabási, A.-L. (1999). Emergence of scaling in random networks. *Science*, 286(5439), 509–512.

Barabási, A.-L. (2013). Network science. *Philosophical Transactions of the Royal Society A: Mathematical, Physical and Engineering Sciences*, 371(1987), 20120375–20120375.

Barberousse, A. and Imbert, C. (2013). Le tournant computationnel et l'innovation théorique. In *Précis de philosophie de la physique*, Le Bihan, S. (ed.). Vuibert, Paris, 1–26.

Barberousse, A. and Imbert, C. (2014). Recurring models and sensitivity to computational constraints. *Monist*, 97(3), 259–279.

Barbin, É. and Lamarche, J.-P. (2004). *Histoires de probabilités et de statistiques.* Ellipses, Paris.

Barlow, J.P. (1996). A declaration of the independence of cyberspace. *Humanist*, 56(3), 18–19.

Bastian, M., Heymann, S., and Jacomy, M. (2009). Gephi: An open source software for exploring and manipulating networks. *Third International AAAI Conference on Weblogs and Social Media*, San Jose, CA, 361–362.

Beaud, J.-P. and Prévost, J.-G. (2000). *L'ère du chiffre. Systèmes statistiques et traditions nationales.* Presses de l'Université du Québec, Quebec.

Bénel, A. (2013). Quelle interdisciplinarité pour les "humanités numériques"? *Les cahiers du numérique*, 1, 1–23.

Bénel, A., Lejeune, C., and Zhou, C. (2010). Éloge de l'hétérogénéité des structures d'analyse de textes. *Document numérique*, 13(2), 41–56.

Berners-Lee, T., Hall, W., Hendler, J.A., O'Hara, K.O., Shadbolt, N., and Weitzner, D.J. (2006). A framework for web science. *Foundations and Trends® in Web Science*, 1(1), 1–130.

Berry, D.M. (2012). *Understanding Digital Humanities*. Palgrave Macmillan, London.

Bertin, J. (1970). La graphique. *Communications*, 15, 169–185.

Bollen, J., Mao, H., and Zeng, X. (2011). Twitter mood predicts the stock market. *Journal of Computational Science*, 2(1), 1–8.

Bowker, G.C. and Star, S.L. (1999). *Sorting things out. Classification and its consequences*. MIT Press, Cambridge.

Boyer-Kassem, T. (2014). Layers of models in computer simulations. *International Studies in the Philosophy of Science*, 28(4), 417–436.

Breiman, L., Cox, D., and Breiman, L. (2001). Comment-statistical modeling: The two cultures. *Statistical Science*, 16(3), 199–231.

Brooks, L.L. and Owen, R. (2008). *Answering the Ultimate Question: How Net Promoter Can Transform Your Business*. John Wiley & Sons, New York.

Brugger, N. (2012). Historical network analysis of the web. *Social Science Computer Review*, 31(3), 306–321.

Bruno, I. and Didier, E. (2013). *Benchmarking: l'État sous pression statistique*. Zones, Paris.

Burdick, A., Drucker, J., Lunenfeld, P., Presner, T., and Schnapp, J. (2012). *Digital Humanities*. MIT Press, Cambridge.

Cailliau, F. and Poudat, C. (2008). Caractérisation lexicale des contributions clients agents dans un corpus de conversations téléphoniques retranscrites. *JADT 2008: 9e Journées internationales d'Analyse statistique des données textuelles*, Lyon, 267–275.

Calude, C.S. and Longo, G. (2015). The deluge of spurious correlations in big data. [Online]. Report. Available at: https://www.di.ens.fr/users/longo/files/BigData-Calude-LongoAug21.pdf [Accessed 29 March 2020].

Cardon, D. (2013). Dans l'esprit du PageRank. *Réseaux*, 177(1), 63.

Casilli, A. (2012). Comment les usages numériques transforment-ils les sciences sociales? In *Read/Write Book 2. Une introduction aux humanités numériques*, Mounier, P. (ed.). OpenEdition Press, Marseille, 1–9.

Caveng, R. (2012). La production des enquêtes quantitatives. *Revue d'anthropologie des connaissances*, 6(1), 65.

Chalmers, A. (2003). The theory-dependence of the use of instruments in science. *Philosophy of Science*, 70(3), 493–509.

Champin, P.-A., Mille, A., and Prié, Y. (2013). Vers des traces numériques comme objets informatiques de premier niveau: une approche par les traces modélisées. *Intellectica*, 59(1), 1–33.

Chateauraynaud, F. (2003). *Prospéro: une technologie littéraire pour les sciences humaines*. CNRS, Paris.

Chaumartin, F.-R. (2012). Antelope, une plate-forme de TAL permettant d'extraire les sens du texte. PhD Thesis, Paris Diderot University, Paris.

Cibois, P. (1990). Éclairer le vocabulaire des questions ouvertes par les questions fermées: le tableau lexical des questions. *Bulletin of Sociological Methodology*, 26(1), 12–21.

Cioffi-Revilla, C. (2014). *Introduction to Computational Social Science*. Springer, Berlin.

Cleveland, W.S. and McGill, R. (1985). Graphical perception and graphical methods for analyzing scientific data. *Science*, 229(4716), 828–833.

Couper, M.P. (2000). Web surveys: A review of issues and approaches. *Public Opinion Quarterly*, 64(4), 464–494.

D'Aubigny, G. (2001). Le traitement des questions ouvertes dans les enquêtes et sondages: Introduction. *Journal de la société statistique de Paris*, 142(4), 1–5.

Dacos, M. and Mounier, P. (2014). Humanités numériques: état des lieux et positionnement de la recherche française dans le contexte international. Report, Institut français, Paris.

Daston, L.J. and Galison, P.L. (2007). *Objectivity*. MIT Press, Cambridge.

Deerwester, S., Dumais, S.T., Furnas, G.W., Landauer, T.K., and Harshman, R. (1990). Indexing by latent semantic analysis. *Journal of the American Society for Information Science*, 41(6), 391–407.

Desrosières, A. (2010). *La politique des grands nombres. Histoire de la raison statistique*. La Découverte, Paris.

Diakopoulos, N. (2015). Algorithmic accountability. *Digital Journalism*, February 1–18.

Diogo, M.P. (2017). "To be or not to be" la construction d'une identité civile pour les ingénieurs militaires portugais. *Quaderns d'Història de l'Enginyeria*, 15, 243–256.

Dodds, P.S., Clark, E.M., Desu, S., Frank, M.R., Reagan, A.J., Williams, J.R., Mitchell, L., Harris, K.D., Kloumann, I.M., Bagrow, J.P., Megerdoomian, K., McMahon, M.T., Tivnan, B.F., and Danforth, C.M. (2015). Human language reveals a universal positivity bias. *Proceedings of the National Academy of Sciences*, 112(8), 2389–2394.

Domingos, P. (2015). *The Master Algorithm: How the Quest for the Ultimate Learning Machine Will Remake Our World.* Basic Books, New York.

Doueihi, M. (2008). *La grande conversion numérique.* Le Seuil, Paris.

Duhem, P. (1906). *La théorie physique. Son objet et sa structure.* Chevalier et Rivière, Paris.

Dupré, J. (2002). *Human Nature and the Limits of Science.* Oxford University Press, Oxford.

Fauré-Fremiet, E. (2017). Les origines de l'Académie des sciences de Paris (1840–1945). *Quaderns d'Història de l'Enginyeria*, 15, 20–31.

Fayyad, U., Piatetsky-Shapiro, G., and Smyth, P. (1996). From data mining to knowledge discovery in databases. *AI magazine*, 17(3), 37–54.

Few, S. (2007). Save the pies for dessert. *Visual Business Intelligence Newsletter*, August.

Fielding, N.G. and Lee, R.M. (1997). Applications of computer software in the sociological analysis of qualitative data. *Bulletin de Méthodologie sociologique*, 57(1), 3–24.

Fouetillou, G. (2007). Le Web et le traité constitutionnel européen. *Réseaux*, 144(5), 279–304.

Franklin, A. (1994). How to avoid the experimenters' regress. *Studies in History and Philosophy of Science*, 25(3), 463–491.

Frawley, W.J., Piatetsky-Shapiro, G., and Matheus, C.J. (1992). Knowledge discovery in databases: An overview. *AI Magazine*, 13(3), 57–70.

Frippiat, D. and Marquis, N. (2010). Les enquêtes par Internet en sciences sociales: un état des lieux. *Population*, 65(2), 309–338.

Fukushima, K. (1980). Neocognitron: A self-organizing neural network model for a mechanism of pattern recognition unaffected by shift in position. *Biological Cybernetics*, 36(4), 193–202.

Gelman, A. and Shalizi, C.R. (2013). Philosophy and the practice of Bayesian statistics. *The British Journal of Mathematical and Statistical Psychology*, 66(1), 8–38.

Georges, F. (2009). Représentation de soi et identité numérique. *Réseaux*, 154(2), 165.

Ginzburg, C. (1980). Signes, traces, pistes. *Le Débat*, 6, 3–44.

Golumbia, D. (2009). *The Cultural Logic of Computation*. Harvard University Press, Cambridge.

Gomez-Uribe, C.A. and Hunt, N. (2015). The Netflix recommender system: Algorithms, business value, and innovation. *ACM Transactions on Management Information Systems*, 6(4), 1–19.

Goody, J. (1979). *La raison graphique: la domestication de la pensée sauvage*. Éditions de Minuit, Paris.

Graham, M. (2013). Geography/Internet: Ethereal alternate dimensions of cyberspace or grounded augmented realities? *Geographical Journal*, 179(2), 177–182.

Grefenstette, G. (1994). *Corpus-derived first, second, and third-order word affinities*. [Online]. Available at: http://citeseerx.ist.psu.edu/viewdoc/download?doi=10.1.1.452.3712&rep=rep1&type=pdf [Accessed 29 March 2020].

Grossberg, S. (1988). Nonlinear neural networks: Principles, mechanisms, and architectures. *Neural Networks*, 1(1), 17–61.

Guérin-Pace, F. (1997). La statistique textuelle. Un outil exploratoire en sciences sociales. *Population*, 52(4), 865–887.

Guichard, É. (2013). L'internet et les épistémologies des SHS. *Sciences/Lettres*, 2 [Online]. Available at: https://journals.openedition.org/rsl/389 [Accessed 29 March 2020].

Hacking, I. (1981). Est-ce qu'on voit à travers un microscope? In *Philosophie des sciences – Tome 2: Naturalismes et réalismes*, Laugier, S., Wagner, P. (eds). Vrin, Paris, 305–322.

Hacking, I. (2002). *L'émergence de la probabilité*. Le Seuil, Paris.

Heidelberger, M. (2003). Theory-ladenness and scientific instruments in experimentation. In *The Philosophy of Scientific Experimentation*, Radder, H. (ed.). University of Pittsburgh Press, Pittsburgh, 138–151.

Hey, T., Tansley, S., and Tolle, K. (2009). *The Fourth Paradigm*. Microsoft Research, Redmond.

Hookway, C. (2013). Pragmatism. In *The Stanford Encyclopedia of Philosophy (Summer 2016 Edition)*, Zalta, E.N. (ed.). Stanford University, Palo Alto [Online]. https://plato.stanford.edu/entries/pragmatism/ [Accessed 29 March 2020].

Hornik, K., Stinchcombe, M., and White, H. (1989). Multilayer feedforward networks are universal approximators. *Neural Networks*, 2(5), 359–366.

Humphreys, P. (2004). *Extending Ourselves. Computational Science, Empiricism and Scientific Method.* Oxford University Press, Oxford.

Israel-Jost, V. (2016). Computer image processing: An epistemological aid in scientific investigation. *Perspectives on Science*, 24(6), 669–965.

Jebeile, J. (2013). Explication et compréhension dans les sciences empiriques. PhD Thesis, Pantheon-Sorbonne University, Paris.

Jebeile, J. (2016). Les simulations sont-elles des expériences numériques? *Dialogue-Canadian Philosophical Review*, 55(1), 59–86.

Jouison-Laffitte, E. (2009). La recherche action: oubliée de la recherche dans le domaine de l'entrepreneuriat. *Revue de l'Entrepreneuriat*, 8(1), 1.

Jurgenson, N. (2012). When atoms meet bits: Social media, the mobile web and augmented revolution. *Future Internet*, 4(1), 83–91.

Kant, E. (1995). *Critique de la faculté de juger*. Aubier, Paris.

Kitchin, R. (2014). *The data revolution: Big data, open data, data infrastructures and their consequences.* [Online]. Available at: http://www.uk.sagepub.com/books/Book242780?subject=F00&fs=1 [Accessed 19 August 2014].

Kitchin, R. and McArdle, G. (2016). What makes big data, big data? Exploring the ontological characteristics of 26 datasets. *Big Data & Society*, 3(1), 1–10.

Krämer, S. (2012). Qu'est-ce donc qu'une trace, et quelle est sa fonction épistémologique? État des lieux. *Trivium. Revue franco-allemande de sciences humaines et sociales*, 10 [Online]. https://journals.openedition.org/trivium/4171 [Accessed 29 March 2020].

Kwak, H., Lee, C., Park, H., and Moon S. (2010). *What is Twitter: A Social Network or a News Media?* ACM Press, New York.

Lagoze, C. (2014). Big data, data integrity, and the fracturing of the control zone. *Big Data & Society*, 1(2) [Online]. https://journals.sagepub.com/doi/10.1177/2053951714558281 [Accessed 29 March 2020].

Lallich-Boidin, G. (2001). Données linguistiques et traitement des questions ouvertes. *Journal de la Société française de statistique*, 4, 29–36.

Lanciani, A.A. (2011). *Analyse phénoménologique du concept de probabilité.* Hermann, Paris.

Landauer, T.K. and Dumais, S.T. (1997). A solution to Plato's problem: The latent semantic analysis theory of acquisition, induction, and representation of knowledge. *Psychological Review*, 1(2), 211–240.

Lassègue, J. (1996). La méthode expérimentale, la modélisation informatique et l'intelligence artificielle. *Intellectica*, 22(1), 21–65.

Lebart, L. and Salem, A. (1994). *Statistique textuelle*. Dunod, Paris.

LeCun, Y. (2014). *Deep learning. Week 1: Intro to deep learning.* [Online]. Available at: http://cilvr.cs.nyu.edu/lib/exe/fetch.php?media=deeplearning:dl-intro.pdf [Accessed 29 March 2020].

Leonelli, S. (2014). What difference does quantity make? On the epistemology of big data in biology. *Big Data & Society*, 1(1) [Online]. https://journals.sagepub.com/doi/10.1177/2053951714534395 [Accessed 29 March 2020].

Leonelli, S. (2016). *Data-Centric Biology: A Philosophical Study*. University of Chicago Press, Chicago.

Lewin, K. (1952). *Field Theory in Social Science*. Harper & Row, New York.

Leydesdorff, L. (1995). *The Challenge of Scientometrics. The Development, Measurement and Self-organization of Scientific Communications*. DSWO Press, Leiden.

Loeve, S. (2009). Le concept de technologie à l'échelle des molécules-machines. PhD Thesis, Paris Nanterre University, Paris.

Loosveldt, G. and Sonck, N. (2008). An evaluation of the weighting procedures for an online access panel survey. *Survey Research Methods*, 2(2), 93–105.

MacQueen, J. (1967). Some methods for classification and analysis of multivariate observations. *Proceedings of the Fifth Berkeley Symposium on Mathematical Statistics and Probability*, 1(233), 281–297.

Mäki, U. (2013). Scientific imperialism: Difficulties in definition, identification, and assessment. *International Studies in the Philosophy of Science*, 27(3), 325–339.

Manovich, L. (2007). *Cultural analytics: Analysis and visualization of large cultural data sets.* [Online]. Available at: http://scholar.google.com/scholar?hl=en&btnG=Search&q=intitle:Cultural+analytics:#2 [Accessed 24 December 2012].

Marc, X. (2001). Les modalités de recueil des réponses libres en institut de sondage: le rôle de l'enquêteur, les consignes et les procédures de contrôle, les perspectives d'amélioration. *Journal de la Société française de statistique*, 142(4), 21–28.

Marr, D. (1982). *Vision: A Computational Investigation into The Human Representation and Processing of Visual Information*. MIT Press, Cambridge.

Mayer-Schönberger, V. and Cukier, K. (2013). *Big Data: A Revolution that Will Transform How We Live, Work, and Think*. Eamon Dolan/Houghton Mifflin Harcourt, New York.

Mayo, D.G. and Cox, D. (2009). New perspectives on (some old) problems of frequentist statistics. *Error and Inference*, 49, 247–330.

McCosker, A. and Wilken, R. (2014). Rethinking "big data" as visual knowledge: The sublime and the diagrammatic in data visualisation. *Visual Studies*, 29(2), 155–164.

McCulloch, W.S. and Pitts, W. (1943). A logical calculus of the ideas immanent in nervous activity. *The Bulletin of Mathematical Biophysics*, 5(4), 115–133.

Merzeau, L. (2013a). L'intelligence des traces. *Intellectica*, 59(1), 1–22.

Merzeau, L. (2013b). Traces numériques et recrutement: du symptôme au cheminement. In *Traces numériques: de la production à l'interprétation*, Galinon-Mélénec, B., Zlitni, S. (eds). CNRS, Paris, 35–53.

Metaxas, P.T. (2012). Why is the shape of the web a bowtie? *WWW 2012, WebScience Track*, April.

Metropolis, N. and Ulam, S. (1949). The Monte Carlo method. *Journal of the American Statistical Association*, 44(247), 335–341.

Mikolov, T., Chen, K., Corrado, G., and Dean, J. (2013). Distributed representations of words and phrases and their compositionality. In *Advances in Neural Information Processing Systems 26*, Burges, C.J.C., Bottou, L., Welling, M., Ghahramani, Z., Weinberger, K.Q. (eds). Curran Associates, New York, 3111–3119.

Monnin, A. (2012). Les ressources, ces ombres récalcitrantes. [Online]. *SociologieS*. Available at: https://journals.openedition.org/sociologies/4334.

Moretti, F. (2000). Conjectures on world literature. *New Left Review*, 1, 54–68.

Mounier, P. (2015). Une "utopie politique" pour les humanités numériques? *Socio*, 4, 97–112.

Musso, P. (2010). Le Web: nouveau territoire et vieux concepts. *Annales des Mines – Réalités industrielles*, 4, 75–83.

Mussou, C. (2012). Et le Web devint archive: enjeux et défis. *Le Temps des médias*, 19(2), 259–266.

O'Hara, K. and Hall, W. (2012). Web science. In *The Oxford Handbook of Internet Studies*, Dutton, W. (ed.). Oxford University Press, Oxford.

Pak, A and Paroubek, P. (2010). Twitter as a corpus for sentiment analysis and opinion mining. *LREC*, 10, 1320–1326.

Pégny, M. (2012). Les deux formes de la thèse de Church-Turing et l'épistémologie du calcul. *Philosophia Scientiæ*, 1(3), 39–67.

Pégny, M. (2013). Sur les limites empiriques du calcul. Calculabilité, complexité et physique. PhD Thesis, Pantheon-Sorbonne University, Paris.

Peirce, C.S. (1878). How to make our ideas clear. *Popular Science Monthly*, 12, 286–302.

Perini, L. (2012). Truth-bearers or Truth-makers? *Spontaneous Generations: A Journal for the History and Philosophy of Science*, 6(1), 142–147.

Petit, V. (2017). Perspectives sur le design. Métier, enseignement, recherche. *Cahiers COSTECH*, 1 [Online]. http://www.costech.utc.fr/CahiersCOSTECH/spip.php?article26.

Petit, V. and Deldicque, T. (2017). La recherche en design avant la "recherche en design". *Cahiers COSTECH*, 1(1) [Online]. http://www.costech.utc.fr/CahiersCOSTECH/spip.php?article25 [Accessed 29 March 2020].

Pincemin, B. (2012). Sémantique interprétative et textométrie. *Texto! Textes et Cultures*, 17(3), 1–21.

Popper, K.R. (1963). *Conjuctures and Refutations: The Growth of Scientific Knowledge*. Routledge and Kegan Paul, Abingdon-on-Thames.

Porter, T.M. (1995). *Trust in Numbers*. Princeton University Press, Princeton.

Porter, T.M. (2003). Statistics and statistical methods. In *The Cambridge History of Science*, Porter, T.M., Ross, D. (eds). Cambridge University Press, Cambridge, 238–250.

Provost, F. and Fawcett, T. (2013). Data science and its relationship to big data and data driven decision making. *Big Data*, 1(1), 51–59.

Rajaraman, A., Ullman, J., David, J.D., Leskovec, J., and Rajaraman, A. (2011). *Mining of Massive Datasets*. Cambridge University Press, Cambridge.

Rastier, F. (2001). *Arts et sciences du texte*. PUF, Paris.

Rastier, F. (2015). Sémantique de corpus – Questions d'épistémologie et de méthodologie. *Texto ! Textes et Cultures*, 20(1), 1–11.

Ratinaud, P. and Déjean, S. (2009). IRaMuTeQ: implémentation de la méthode ALCESTE d'analyse de texte dans un logiciel libre. *MASHS*, June.

Reichfeld, F. and Markey, R. (2011). *The Ultimate Question 2.0 (Revised and Expanded Edition): How Net Promoter Companies Thrive in a Customer-Driven World*. Harvard Business Review Press, Cambridge.

Reinert, M. (1990). ALCESTE – Une méthodologie d'analyse des données textuelles et une application: Aurélia de Gérard de Nerval. *Bulletin de Méthodologie sociologique*, 26(1), 24–54.

Rickert, H. (1997). *Science de la culture et science de la nature* suivi de *Théorie de la définition*. Gallimard, Paris.

Ricœur, P. (1983). *Temps et récit 1*. Le Seuil, Paris.

Ries, E. (2011). *The Lean Startup: How Today's Entrepreneurs Use Continuous Innovation to Create Radically Successful Businesses*. Currency, New South Wales.

Robinson, V.M.J. (1993). Current controversies in action research. *Public Administration Quarterly*, 17(3), 263–290.

Rodrigues, M. (De Lurdes) (2017). La profession d'ingénieur au Portugal. *Quaderns d'Història de l'Enginyeria*, 15, 271–286.

Rogers, R. (2008). Post-demographic machines. In *Walled Garden*, Dekker, A., Wolfsberger, A. (eds). Virtueel Platform, Amsterdam, 29–39.

Rogers, R. (2009). The end of the virtual: Digital methods. Inaugural Speech, Chair of New Media & Digital Culture. University of Amsterdam, Amsterdam.

Rogers, R. (2010). Internet research: The question of method – A keynote address from the YouTube and the 2008 election cycle in the United States conference. *Journal of Information Technology & Politics*, 7(2/3), 241–260.

Rogers, R. (2013). *Digital Methods*. MIT Press, Cambridge.

Rosenblatt, F. (1958). The perceptron: A probabilistic model for information storage and organization in the brain. *Psychological review*, 65(6), 386–408.

Rumelhart, D.E., Hinton, G.E., and Williams, R.J. (1985). Learning internal representations by error propagation. In *Parallel Distributed Processing: Explorations in the Microstructure of Cognition. Vol. 1: Foundation*, Rumelhart, D.E., McClelland, J.L. (eds). MIT Press, Cambridge, MA.

Sahlgren, M. (2008). The distributional hypothesis. *Italian Journal of Linguistics*, 20(1), 33–54.

Savage, M. and Burrows, R. (2007). The coming crisis of empirical sociology. *Sociology*, 41(5), 885–899.

Schindler, S. (2013). Theory-laden experimentation. *Studies in History and Philosophy of Science Part A*, 44(1), 89.

Schmitt, É. (2015). La structuration disciplinaire et thématique des humanités numériques. *10e colloque ISKO France 2015*. European Doctoral College, Strasbourg, November.

Schonlau, M., Zapert, K., Simon, L.P., Sanstad, K.H., Marcus, S.M., Adams, J., Spranca, M., Kan, H., Turner, R., and Berry, S.H. (2004). A comparison between responses from a propensity-weighted web survey and an identical RDD survey. *Social Science Computer Review*, 22(1), 128–138.

Schurmans, M.-N. (2011). Expliquer, interpréter, comprendre: le paysage épistémologique des sciences sociales. *Carnets des sciences de l'éducation*, Geneva.

Schutt, R. and O'Neil, C. (2014). *Doing Data Science*. O'Reilly, Sebastopol.

Serres, A. (2002). Quelle(s) problématique(s) de la trace? [Online]. Available at: https://archivesic.ccsd.cnrs.fr/sic_00001397/document [Accessed 29 March 2020].

Shadbolt, N., Hall, W., Hendler, J.A., and Dutton, W.H. (2013). Web science: A new frontier. *Philosophical Transactions of the Royal Society A: Mathematical, Physical and Engineering Sciences*, 371(1987) [Online]. https://royalsocietypublishing.org/doi/full/10.1098/rsta.2012.0512 [Accessed 29 March 2020].

Shinn, T. and Ragouet, P. (2000). Formes de division du travail scientifique et convergence intellectuelle. La recherche technico-instrumentale. *Revue française de sociologie*, 41(3), 447–473.

Simondon, G. (2017). *On the Mode of Existence of Technical Objects*. Univocal, Minneapolis.

Simondon, G. (2005). *L'invention dans les techniques. Cours et conférences*. Le Seuil, Paris.

Snow, C.P. (1959). Two Cultures. *Science*, 130(3373), 419–419.

Spanos, A. and Mayo, D.G. (2015). Error statistical modeling and inference: Where methodology meets ontology. *Synthese*, 192(11), 3533–3555.

Stevens, K.A. (1981). The visual interpretation of surface contours. *Artificial Intelligence*, 17(1-3), 47–73.

Su, Y.-S. (2008). It's easy to produce chartjunk using Microsoft® Excel 2007 but hard to make good graphs. *Computational Statistics & Data Analysis*, 52(10), 4594–4601.

Tiercelin, C. (1993). *C.S. Peirce et le Pragmatisme*. PUF, Paris.

Tufte, E.R. (1997). *Visual Explanations*. Graphics Press, Cheshire.

Tufte, E.R. (2008). *The Visual Display of Quantitative Information*. Graphics Press, Cheshire.

Tukey, J.W. (1977). *Exploratory Data Analysis*. Addison-Wesley, Reading.

Turing, A.M. (1950). Computing machinery and intelligence. *Mind*, 59(236), 433–460.

Vandendorpe, C. (1999). *Du papyrus à l'hypertexte*. La Découverte, Paris.

Vapnik, V.N. (1998). *Statistical Learning Theory*. John Wiley & Sons, New York.

Varenne, F. (2007). *Du modèle à la simulation informatique*. Vrin, Paris.

Varenne, F. and Silberstein, M. (2013). *Épistémologies et pratiques de la modélisation et de la simulation*. Éditions matériologiques, Paris.

Vial, S. (2016). Le tournant design des humanités numériques. *Revue française des sciences de l'information et de la communication*, 8 [Online]. https://journals.openedition.org/rfsic/1828 [Accessed 29 March 2020].

Wang, Y. and Kosinski, M. (2017). Deep neural networks are more accurate than humans at detecting sexual orientation from facial images. *Journal of Personality and Social Psychology (JPSP)*, 114(2), 1–47.

Wigner, E.P. (1960). The unreasonable effectiveness of mathematics in the natural sciences. *Communications on Pure and Applied Mathematics*, 13(1), 1–14.

Windelband, W. (2000). Histoire et sciences de la nature. Discours prononcé au Rectorat de Strasbourg. *Les Études philosophiques*, 1, 1–16.

Wing, J.M. (2006). Computational thinking. *Communications of the ACM*, 49(3), 33.

Witte, J.C. (2009). Introduction to the special issue on web surveys. *Sociological Methods & Research*, 37(3), 283–290.

Wu, X. and Zhang, X. (2016). Responses to critiques on machine learning of criminality perceptions. [Online]. Available at: http://arxiv.org/abs/1611.04135 [Accessed 29 March 2020].

Wu, X., Kumar, V., Ross, Q.J., Ghosh, J., Yang, Q., Motoda, H., McLachlan, G.J., Ng, A., Liu, B., Yu, P.S., Zhou, Z.-H., Steinbach, M., Hand, D.J., and Steinberg, D. (2008). Top 10 algorithms in data mining. *Knowledge and Information Systems*, 14(1), 1–37.

Yakout, M., Berti-Équille, L., and Elmagarmid, A.K. (2013). Don't be SCAREd: Use SCalable Automatic REpairing with maximal likelihood and bounded changes. *Proceedings of the 2013 International Conference on Management of data – SIGMOD'13*. 553, 553–564.

Yeung, K. (2017). Algorithmic regulation: A critical interrogation. *Regulation and Governance*, 1–39 12(4), 505–523.

Zhao, Y. (2012). R and data mining: Examples and case studies. [Online]. Available at: http://www.rdatamining.com [Accessed 29 March 2020].

Index

G, I, J

L, M, N

P, R, S

T, V, W

Other titles from

iSTE

in

Information Systems, Web and Pervasive Computing

2020

CLIQUET Gérard, with the collaboration of BARAY Jérôme
Location-Based Marketing: Geomarketing and Geolocation

DE FRÉMINVILLE Marie
Cybersecurity and Decision Makers: Data Security and Digital Trust

GEORGE Éric
Digitalization of Society and Socio-political Issues 2: Digital, Information and Research

SEDKAOUI Soraya, KHELFAOUI Mounia
Sharing Economy and Big Data Analytics

2019

ALBAN Daniel, EYNAUD Philippe, MALAURENT Julien, RICHET Jean-Loup, VITARI Claudio
Information Systems Management: Governance, Urbanization and Alignment

AUGEY Dominique, with the collaboration of ALCARAZ Marina
Digital Information Ecosystems: Smart Press

BATTON-HUBERT Mireille, DESJARDIN Eric, PINET François
Geographic Data Imperfection 1: From Theory to Applications

BRIQUET-DUHAZÉ Sophie, TURCOTTE Catherine
From Reading-Writing Research to Practice

BROCHARD Luigi, KAMATH Vinod, CORBALAN Julita, HOLLAND Scott, MITTELBACH Walter, OTT Michael
Energy-Efficient Computing and Data Centers

CHAMOUX Jean-Pierre
The Digital Era 2: Political Economy Revisited

COCHARD Gérard-Michel
Introduction to Stochastic Processes and Simulation

DUONG Véronique
SEO Management: Methods and Techniques to Achieve Success

GAUCHEREL Cédric, GOUYON Pierre-Henri, DESSALLES Jean-Louis
Information, The Hidden Side of Life

GEORGE Éric
Digitalization of Society and Socio-political Issues 1: Digital, Communication and Culture

GHLALA Riadh
Analytic SQL in SQL Server 2014/2016

JANIER Mathilde, SAINT-DIZIER Patrick
Argument Mining: Linguistic Foundations

SOURIS Marc
Epidemiology and Geography: Principles, Methods and Tools of Spatial Analysis

TOUNSI Wiem
Cyber-Vigilance and Digital Trust: Cyber Security in the Era of Cloud Computing and IoT

2018

ARDUIN Pierre-Emmanuel
Insider Threats
(Advances in Information Systems Set – Volume 10)

CARMÈS Maryse
Digital Organizations Manufacturing: Scripts, Performativity and Semiopolitics
(Intellectual Technologies Set – Volume 5)

CARRÉ Dominique, VIDAL Geneviève
Hyperconnectivity: Economical, Social and Environmental Challenges
(Computing and Connected Society Set – Volume 3)

CHAMOUX Jean-Pierre
The Digital Era 1: Big Data Stakes

DOUAY Nicolas
Urban Planning in the Digital Age
(Intellectual Technologies Set – Volume 6)

FABRE Renaud, BENSOUSSAN Alain
The Digital Factory for Knowledge: Production and Validation of Scientific Results

GAUDIN Thierry, LACROIX Dominique, MAUREL Marie-Christine, POMEROL Jean-Charles
Life Sciences, Information Sciences

GAYARD Laurent
Darknet: Geopolitics and Uses
(Computing and Connected Society Set – Volume 2)

IAFRATE Fernando
Artificial Intelligence and Big Data: The Birth of a New Intelligence
(Advances in Information Systems Set – Volume 8)

LE DEUFF Olivier
Digital Humanities: History and Development
(Intellectual Technologies Set – Volume 4)

MANDRAN Nadine
Traceable Human Experiment Design Research: Theoretical Model and Practical Guide
(Advances in Information Systems Set – Volume 9)

PIVERT Olivier
NoSQL Data Models: Trends and Challenges

ROCHET Claude
Smart Cities: Reality or Fiction

SAUVAGNARGUES Sophie
Decision-making in Crisis Situations: Research and Innovation for Optimal Training

SEDKAOUI Soraya
Data Analytics and Big Data

SZONIECKY Samuel
Ecosystems Knowledge: Modeling and Analysis Method for Information and Communication
(Digital Tools and Uses Set – Volume 6)

2017

BOUHAÏ Nasreddine, SALEH Imad
Internet of Things: Evolutions and Innovations
(Digital Tools and Uses Set – Volume 4)

DUONG Véronique
Baidu SEO: Challenges and Intricacies of Marketing in China

LESAS Anne-Marie, MIRANDA Serge
The Art and Science of NFC Programming
(Intellectual Technologies Set – Volume 3)

LIEM André
Prospective Ergonomics
(Human-Machine Interaction Set – Volume 4)

MARSAULT Xavier
Eco-generative Design for Early Stages of Architecture
(Architecture and Computer Science Set – Volume 1)

REYES-GARCIA Everardo
The Image-Interface: Graphical Supports for Visual Information
(Digital Tools and Uses Set – Volume 3)

REYES-GARCIA Everardo, BOUHAÏ Nasreddine
Designing Interactive Hypermedia Systems
(Digital Tools and Uses Set – Volume 2)

SAÏD Karim, BAHRI KORBI Fadia
Asymmetric Alliances and Information Systems:Issues and Prospects
(Advances in Information Systems Set – Volume 7)

SZONIECKY Samuel, BOUHAÏ Nasreddine
Collective Intelligence and Digital Archives: Towards Knowledge Ecosystems
(Digital Tools and Uses Set – Volume 1)

2016

BEN CHOUIKHA Mona
Organizational Design for Knowledge Management

BERTOLO David
Interactions on Digital Tablets in the Context of 3D Geometry Learning
(Human-Machine Interaction Set – Volume 2)

BOUVARD Patricia, SUZANNE Hervé
Collective Intelligence Development in Business

EL FALLAH SEGHROUCHNI Amal, ISHIKAWA Fuyuki, HÉRAULT Laurent, TOKUDA Hideyuki
Enablers for Smart Cities

FABRE Renaud, in collaboration with MESSERSCHMIDT-MARIET Quentin, HOLVOET Margot
New Challenges for Knowledge

GAUDIELLO Ilaria, ZIBETTI Elisabetta
Learning Robotics, with Robotics, by Robotics
(Human-Machine Interaction Set – Volume 3)

HENROTIN Joseph
The Art of War in the Network Age
(Intellectual Technologies Set – Volume 1)

KITAJIMA Munéo
Memory and Action Selection in Human–Machine Interaction
(Human–Machine Interaction Set – Volume 1)

LAGRAÑA Fernando
E-mail and Behavioral Changes: Uses and Misuses of Electronic Communications

LEIGNEL Jean-Louis, UNGARO Thierry, STAAR Adrien
Digital Transformation
(Advances in Information Systems Set – Volume 6)

NOYER Jean-Max
Transformation of Collective Intelligences
(Intellectual Technologies Set – Volume 2)

VENTRE Daniel
Information Warfare – 2nd edition

VITALIS André
The Uncertain Digital Revolution
(Computing and Connected Society Set – Volume 1)

2015

ARDUIN Pierre-Emmanuel, GRUNDSTEIN Michel, ROSENTHAL-SABROUX Camille
Information and Knowledge System
(Advances in Information Systems Set – Volume 2)

BÉRANGER Jérôme
Medical Information Systems Ethics

BRONNER Gérald
Belief and Misbelief Asymmetry on the Internet

IAFRATE Fernando
From Big Data to Smart Data
(Advances in Information Systems Set – Volume 1)

KRICHEN Saoussen, BEN JOUIDA Sihem
Supply Chain Management and its Applications in Computer Science

NEGRE Elsa
Information and Recommender Systems
(Advances in Information Systems Set – Volume 4)

POMEROL Jean-Charles, EPELBOIN Yves, THOURY Claire
MOOCs

SALLES Maryse
Decision-Making and the Information System
(Advances in Information Systems Set – Volume 3)

SAMARA Tarek
ERP and Information Systems: Integration or Disintegration
(Advances in Information Systems Set – Volume 5)

2014

DINET Jérôme
Information Retrieval in Digital Environments

HÉNO Raphaële, CHANDELIER Laure
3D Modeling of Buildings: Outstanding Sites

KEMBELLEC Gérald, CHARTRON Ghislaine, SALEH Imad
Recommender Systems

MATHIAN Hélène, SANDERS Lena
Spatio-temporal Approaches: Geographic Objects and Change Process

PLANTIN Jean-Christophe
Participatory Mapping

VENTRE Daniel
Chinese Cybersecurity and Defense

2013

BERNIK Igor
Cybercrime and Cyberwarfare

CAPET Philippe, DELAVALLADE Thomas
Information Evaluation

LEBRATY Jean-Fabrice, LOBRE-LEBRATY Katia
Crowdsourcing: One Step Beyond

SALLABERRY Christian
Geographical Information Retrieval in Textual Corpora

2012

BUCHER Bénédicte, LE BER Florence
Innovative Software Development in GIS

GAUSSIER Eric, YVON François
Textual Information Access

STOCKINGER Peter
Audiovisual Archives: Digital Text and Discourse Analysis

VENTRE Daniel
Cyber Conflict

2011

BANOS Arnaud, THÉVENIN Thomas
Geographical Information and Urban Transport Systems

DAUPHINÉ André
Fractal Geography

LEMBERGER Pirmin, MOREL Mederic
Managing Complexity of Information Systems

STOCKINGER Peter
Introduction to Audiovisual Archives

STOCKINGER Peter
Digital Audiovisual Archives

VENTRE Daniel
Cyberwar and Information Warfare

2010

BONNET Pierre
Enterprise Data Governance

BRUNET Roger
Sustainable Geography

CARREGA Pierre
Geographical Information and Climatology

CAUVIN Colette, ESCOBAR Francisco, SERRADJ Aziz
Thematic Cartography – 3-volume series
Thematic Cartography and Transformations – Volume 1
Cartography and the Impact of the Quantitative Revolution – Volume 2
New Approaches in Thematic Cartography – Volume 3

LANGLOIS Patrice
Simulation of Complex Systems in GIS

MATHIS Philippe
Graphs and Networks – 2nd edition

THERIAULT Marius, DES ROSIERS François
Modeling Urban Dynamics

2009

BONNET Pierre, DETAVERNIER Jean-Michel, VAUQUIER Dominique
Sustainable IT Architecture: the Progressive Way of Overhauling Information Systems with SOA

PAPY Fabrice
Information Science

RIVARD François, ABOU HARB Georges, MERET Philippe
The Transverse Information System

ROCHE Stéphane, CARON Claude
Organizational Facets of GIS

2008

BRUGNOT Gérard
Spatial Management of Risks

FINKE Gerd
Operations Research and Networks

GUERMOND Yves
Modeling Process in Geography

KANEVSKI Michael
Advanced Mapping of Environmental Data

MANOUVRIER Bernard, LAURENT Ménard
Application Integration: EAI, B2B, BPM and SOA

PAPY Fabrice
Digital Libraries

2007

DOBESCH Hartwig, DUMOLARD Pierre, DYRAS Izabela
Spatial Interpolation for Climate Data

SANDERS Lena
Models in Spatial Analysis

2006

CLIQUET Gérard
Geomarketing

CORNIOU Jean-Pierre
Looking Back and Going Forward in IT

DEVILLERS Rodolphe, JEANSOULIN Robert
Fundamentals of Spatial Data Quality

Printed and bound by CPI Group (UK) Ltd, Croydon, CR0 4YY

15/09/2026

14962353-0003